Afghanistan and the Troubled Future of Unconventional Warfare

Afghanistan and the Troubled Future of Unconventional Warfare

Ily S. Rothstein

NAVAL INSTITUTE PRESS
Annapolis, Maryland

Naval Institute Press
291 Wood Road
Annapolis, MD 21402

Library of Congress Cataloging-in-Publication Data
Rothstein, Hy S.
  Afghanistan and the troubled future of unconventional warfare /
    by Hy S. Rothstein.
      p. cm.
  Includes bibliographical references and index.
  ISBN 1-59114-745-X (alk. paper)
  1. United States—Military policy. 2. United States—Armed Forces. 3. Special operations
(Military science)—United States. 4. Counterinsurgency—United States. 5. Afghan War,
2001– I. Title.
  UA23.R7658 2006
  355.02'18—dc22

                                    2005031132

Printed in the United States of America on acid-free paper ∞
13 12 11 10 09 08 07 06   9 8 7 6 5 4 3 2
First printing

To the few special warriors who, against all odds, keep unconventional warfare alive.

The smaller the unit the better its performance.

——T. E. Lawrence

⣿Contents

ⲈForeword

THESE ARE DIFFICULT TIMES FOR AMERICA'S SPECIAL FORCES. Our most skilled and elite military units have been in the forefront of what has evolved into a brutal war of terror and counterterror in Afghanistan and Iraq. The U.S. Navy's SEALs and the U.S. Army's Delta Force (along with other commando units whose existence is not officially recognized) have suffered grievous casualties in combat, and are suffering today the inevitable result of steadily increasing rotation and deployment—resignations and retirements are up and morale is down. The inside stories are sometimes shocking.

There was a SEAL team on a hunter-killer assignment in 2005 against a high-value Taliban operative that ran across a sheepherder in the rugged Hindu Kush separating Afghanistan and Pakistan. The herder was taken into custody. A call went to a tactical operations center for guidance—should the mission be aborted? No officer was on duty at the time. The SEAL team leader chose not to kill the herder—one of the unstated options, of course—but instead turned him loose. The Taliban were alerted, and seized the SEAL team. There was a call for help, but the quick reaction force—helicopters and two companies of army Rangers—that had been on twenty-four-hour standby at the nearest American base had been disbanded. Their services were needed elsewhere. The rescue effort was slow in getting organized. Three SEALs died.

There are the Delta Force troops assigned to various task forces whose main mission has become nothing more or less than the capture or, if necessary, the assassination of known and suspected insurgents inside Iraq and Syria. Those who are captured are to be treated very brutally—and they often are—to get immediate and actionable intelligence about future operations. Such assignments may be thrilling to some, but not to all. There is talk—only to trusted friends and former colleagues—of disillusionment over the missions and shame over some of the accepted interrogation techniques.

There were the many SEALs who were reassigned from combat duty in the field to security and protection for senior Americans inside Iraq, including senior U.S. Army officers. One disgusted senior team leader resigned and remained in Iraq to start up a security company. He, like many other SEALs, was willing to risk his life for his country but not to serve as a security guard. A contract was negotiated with an agency of the Iraqi government for nine million dollars—more than enough to get the job done and provide for a goodly profit. When the negotiated documents arrived, the money allotted was not nine million, but twenty-seven million, with the added eighteen million assigned to Iraqis now living in the United States. What to do? Should the corruption be reported? The question bounced around the SEAL community and the advice was cynical—sign the contract, and look the other way. He did.

Of course, the ability to get very tough, and being superbly trained in how to do so, is part of the ethos of the U.S. Special Forces community. But it is far from the whole package and, as Hy Rothstein explains so carefully and persuasively in this book, it has been counterproductive thus far in the post–September 11 world. Rothstein is not a dove—his career and current job tells us otherwise—but he understands a lesson that has been lost to the current political and military leadership. His message is simply this: Let's remember the true definition of unconventional warfare, and put that discipline to work against our guerrilla enemies in the War on Terror—rather than rely on direct strike missions and wars of attrition. Kicking down doors does not do it. "Simply put," Rothstein explains, in one of this book's more important passages, "even the best precision-guided munitions are ineffective against an insignificantly disposed and untargetable enemy. The pursuit of attrition efficiencies against an irregular enemy can only be damaging to one's own cause… by producing collateral damage, antagonizing the population, increasing the ranks of the enemy, and eventually demoralizing one's own forces as a result of increasingly well-coordinated attacks generated by an increasingly hostile population."

Rothstein's solution is uncomplicated—the real mission of unconventional warfare is all about the building of personal relationships and trust that "are critical to operational success in the non-Western world." Once we have that trust, which can only be developed by face-to-face contact, "we will find it easier to gather the intelligence we need to fight terrorism because we will have entered the human world where the terrorists live and operate." Our special force troops, Rothstein insists, "must be diplomats, doctors, spies, cultural anthropologists, and good friends—all before their primary works comes into play."

He warns us that using our special operations forces as "elite shock troops" will be unproductive, unsuccessful, and result in the spread of terrorism.

That last sentence pretty much sums up what has taken place since the fall of 2001, as the men in charge in the Bush administration have focused on killing and capturing—what Rothstein calls the warrior virtues of the Special Forces. Changing the way America's leadership looks at war, and chooses to fight it, may be impossible, but Rothstein has given all Americans who worry about the future—and the increasing spread of terrorism—a book full of talking points for future debates, and future political campaigns, perhaps. The colonel demonstrated courage and his love for America while on active duty, and he continues to honor America—and exemplify courage—in this important and instructive book.

Rothstein ends his extended argument with a prescient line from another failed American war—in Vietnam. At the end of combat a North Vietnamese colonel was told by an American that his armies had never defeated American combat forces on the battlefield. His answer: "That may be so, but it is also irrelevant."

Seymour Hersh
December 2005

ᴵˡⁱ Introduction

WHAT DOES THE PERFORMANCE OF U.S. FORCES in Afghanistan say about the ability of the United States to wage warfare against enemies who may not engage us on a conventional battlefield or in an orthodox manner? A discerning observer of the events in Afghanistan cannot help but question the inconsistency between the rhetoric describing an unconventional war effort and the actual fight. While the Taliban was soundly defeated using orthodox methods, the United States proved far less capable in defeating the insurgent-like targets that were a product of the successful orthodox campaign. This study will show that the U.S. military is not able to wage unconventional war despite significant investment in special operations capabilities. This hypothesis will be examined through imperatives taken from the literature on organizational theory and military innovation that are relevant to unconventional warfare as illuminated by U.S. military operations in Afghanistan.

AFGHANISTAN—A TALE OF TWO WARS
Operation Enduring Freedom, the U.S. response to the terrorist attacks on the World Trade Center and the Pentagon on September 11, 2001, appears to have been a masterpiece of military creativity and finesse. The plan capitalized on using U.S. air power and U.S. Special Forces, working with the Afghan opposition to crush the Taliban and cripple the al Qaeda network inside Afghanistan. Though impressive, early successes were not exploited, and as a result, achieving the endgame has been more difficult than necessary.

The Taliban had been crushed by an impressive display of power. The initial phase of the war was appropriately conventional. Attrition warfare, capitalizing on superior firepower, was used against an enemy that presented a lucrative array of targets. Certainly, the importance of special operations forces (SOF) cannot be overstated. They tied the air campaign to a ground campaign and directed precision fires against Taliban and al Qaeda positions. However, their use does not make the fighting that led to the disintegration of the Taliban an unconventional war. SOF were used, but the war strategy remained quite conventional. Furthermore, there was no reason why the fight should have been unconventional, considering the conventional disposition of the enemy. Simply put, it appears that the United States achieved the correct result but failed to recognize the strategy that had led to success.

However, the disintegration of the Taliban made the conceptual distinction between unconventional and conventional a serious matter. This is because the luxury of facing a conventional enemy disappeared when the Taliban fell. Consequently, the relevance of conventional warfare also declined as the nature of the war changed. After being confronted with a drastically altered operational setting, the orientation of the U.S. military did not change. In fact, as the war became increasingly unconventional, the U.S. response became more conventional. The command arrangement evolved into a large and complex structure that could not (or would not) respond to the new unconventional setting.

Why does the U.S. military have great difficulty in developing strategies to defeat irregular threats? More important, why have special operations forces turned on their unconventional roots and embraced what can be described as "the hyperconventional?" There are no simple answers. Nevertheless, unconventional warfare (UW) represents an indirect and ultimately local approach to waging war. It is protracted, and success is often difficult to measure. That this happens to be the antithesis of the Pentagon's long-standing preoccupation with rapidly achieved, measurable effects should help explain the lack of enthusiasm for UW in senior Department of Defense (DoD) circles.

The result has been a campaign in Afghanistan that effectively destroyed the Taliban structure but that has been significantly less successful at being able to achieve the primary policy goal of ensuring that al Qaeda could no longer operate in Afghanistan. Stability in Afghanistan remains illusive. Adjustments at the margin to revitalize UW will fail. Only significant structural and cultural changes to the SOF community can restore a UW capability.

THE STRUCTURE OF MILITARY RESPONSE

Even powerful states can face disaster if their military does not appropriately respond to a changing security environment. This study will show that the U.S. military has not been able to change to meet and overcome the challenge of irregular threats. The U.S. Army in Vietnam is an example of this problem. If military doctrine is to enhance the security of a state, it must adapt to both the grand strategy of the state and the threats faced by the state. A country rarely faces a single security threat. Therefore, a state has to make choices and accept risk as it develops its security strategy. Military establishments can have organizational goals that do not fully contribute to enhanced security for the state. For example, development and implementation of technological innovations that enhance the overall capacity of a particular military service, but are tangentially related to a state's most likely security threats, may drain economic resources away from more appropriate defense investments and consequently undermine security. Similarly, and directly significant to this study, a focus on the acquisition of high technology for deployment against a sophisticated enemy may significantly limit a state's ability to deal with lesser threats from an unsophisticated foe.[1]

Organizational theory is a powerful tool for explaining why organizations may not adequately respond to changing environments. According to this theory, leaders of military organizations are likely to be concerned with the resources and prestige of their organization as currently positioned and to stress adherence to standardized procedures for accomplishing routine tasks. These conditions often prevent military organizations from effectively responding to their country's changing security needs. Conversely, military organizations are not always unresponsive to a country's security needs. Therefore, identifying the internal conditions that facilitate organizational change is perhaps more useful than simply understanding why organizations resist change.[2]

Dependency relationships also affect how the organization responds to changing security needs. Every organization has dependency relationships with other units in the system. To the extent that an organization needs external organizations less than external organizations need it, the organization has power. That is, power is a function of asymmetric mutual dependence. Organizations that have power over others are able to impose elements of structure on them. This structure can be viewed as a method of oversight that can inhibit necessary change in organizations that have a high level of dependence on other units.[3]

Similarly, organizational change can be paralyzed as a result of how individual members expect leaders to behave based on previous experience. These expectations will affect the way members of an organization respond to new requirements. This study will examine how institutionally conditioned choices have marginalized the capability of the United States to conduct unconventional warfare.[4]

The structure of civilian institutions also influences change in military organizations. In the United States, civilian leaders with management responsibility for military institutions have difficulty agreeing on how to design and monitor these institutions. The division of power built into the structure of the U.S. government often results in the military hearing contradictory messages. Division of power is less of a controlling factor in military organizations than it is in civilian institutions. Consequently, parochial interests that ensure or enhance military institutional power can have a greater effect on change than grand strategy promulgated by civilian leaders. Conversely, when civilians within divided institutions agree on a change, the solution is very often a compromise that still does not adequately address the security needs of the state. Moreover, this agreement or compromise solution makes further change more difficult.[5]

The original selection criteria of personnel and the institution's incentive structure are powerful forces in shaping policies and exercising control over military institutions. Civilian leaders can best tie grand strategy to needed military change when they can intervene in the selection and promotion process. The preferences of military organizations will be conditioned by civilian leaders' choices. Said another way, military leaders will respond in a manner that has been rewarded in the past. Military organizations will develop their own biases that will determine the institution's standard set of responses absent strong civilian oversight.[6]

Civilian leaders can exercise control passively as well as by actively intervening in the promotion process. For example, the mere fact that civilian leaders have intervened in the past will most likely cause military institutions to act in anticipation of civilian leaders' concerns. Therefore, civilian leaders may exercise a subtle form of control. Whether intervention in the incentive structure is passive or active, civilian leader preferences can determine which issues the military pays attention to.[7]

Strong policy disagreements within institutions tend to encourage distrust among the units within a bureaucracy. We see this between the CIA and the Defense Department as well as between conventional and special operations forces. This distrust can limit the way civilian leaders choose personnel to lead military organizations. For example, noncontroversial appointments are more likely to take place in environments where distrust exists. This has important ramifications for the ability of civilian leaders to select innovative military leaders capable of generating needed change.[8]

There can be little doubt that the structure of civilian institutions and how civilian leaders choose to set up and oversee military organizations are crucial variables in determining an organization's preferences. This study will examine the Defense Department's ability to innovate during the planning and execution of the war in Afghanistan.

The following questions will be addressed in this study:
- How should we characterize the Afghanistan campaign?
- How has the nature of the war changed?
- Has the United States made necessary adjustments to changing conditions?
- Are command and control arrangements adaptive to the nature of the environment?

- Do long-standing administrative and organizational dependencies affect organizing for combat employment?
- Do external players and stakeholders influence operational designs?
- Do institutional norms constrain military operational art?
- Is the United States prosecuting a war in a manner that is likely to result in victory?
- Is the United States capable of waging unconventional warfare?

ORGANIZATION OF THE STUDY

Chapter 1 assesses the current capacity of the United States to conduct unconventional warfare by reviewing operations in Afghanistan that resulted from the attacks on the World Trade Center and the Pentagon on September 11, 2001. Chapter 2 first addresses the issue of what constitutes a special operation as well as what constitutes a special operations force. Next, the historical development of SOF capabilities is traced to provide the necessary context for the current problem. This historical journey shows how SOF has developed into a hyperconventional force at the expense of maintaining a sophisticated unconventional warfare capability. Chapter 3 develops the theoretical framework for this study, in which organizational theory, in general, and contingency theory, in particular, are examined. These theories are used to show how the current Defense Department structure, effective in conducting orthodox military operations, is incompatible with the nature of unconventional warfare. This chapter also examines concepts of innovation. Though militaries obviously change, studies in innovation suggest that change in military organizations will be difficult. This follows from the basic purpose of an organization, to build stylized templates to overcome uncertainty. The process that eventually results in change is inconsistent with the requirement of unconventional warfare and the almost-daily need to be innovative.

Chapters 4 and 5 will draw on the implications of contingency theory and processes of innovation developed in chapter 3 and use the case of the current war in Afghanistan to assess the Defense Department's capacity to conduct unconventional warfare. U.S. military operations will be assessed, with special attention placed on the two distinct phases of the war—before and after the disintegration of the Taliban. Chapter 6 draws implications from the case study and makes recommendations about what needs to be done to reap the benefit of the substantial capability that exists in U.S. SOF.

Afghanistan and
the Troubled Future
of Unconventional Warfare

Chapter 1

The Challenge of Unconventional Warfare

ON SEPTEMBER 11, 2001, two hijacked commercial airplanes crashed into the World Trade Center towers in New York City. The crashes set the buildings ablaze, and within two hours, both towers collapsed under their own weight. Almost simultaneously, another hijacked airliner crashed into the Pentagon, quickly collapsing a significant portion of that building. At about the same time, a fourth hijacked airliner, now believed to be headed for a target in Washington, D.C., crashed in a Pennsylvania field when passengers attempted to take back the airplane from the hijackers. In a period of less that three hours, about three thousand people had been killed in a sophisticated series of coordinated terrorist attacks. The United States found itself thrust into war. This war was, and remains, very different from the wars the United States had previously fought. The nature of the war was sufficiently challenging that the Pentagon was unable to produce a timely and acceptable response. Though the military would provide the majority of the tools, the CIA provided the initial blueprint. Of significance was the fact that this devastating surprise attack was carried out by a nonstate actor fighting the United States asymmetrically. This was an act of war unfathomable for a nation accustomed to thinking about war in terms of interstate conflict. This new kind of war challenged civilian and military decision makers with a complex series of questions. How should the United States prosecute a war against an amorphous enemy who chooses not to fight in the symmetrical, conventional manner to which we have become accustomed? Can old ways of thinking and previously successful strategies using precision weapons systems be adapted to fit the new situation? Conversely, is a new strategy required? What type of organizational structure is necessary to facilitate operations against this amorphous foe? How do we regain the initiative and shape the strategic battle arena to end the war in a manner of our own choosing?

These types of questions are not new. Leaders have faced a common dilemma throughout history when faced with new forms of war—how does one counter such new forms and prevail? The answer has varied with time and changing conditions. For the United States, superior strength and technology have, in the recent past, provided the decisive advantage. During the last hundred years, the U.S. military has been viewed as a force with an overpowering capability, able to win wars through brute strength. The need for daring, cleverness, or finesse simply did not exist. This power to overwhelm an opponent was central to a strategy that brought victory in two world wars and in the Persian Gulf War. This same strategy failed in Vietnam and produced marginally adequate results in Korea. The focus of this study is to illuminate the dynamics that keep the United States from planning and executing successful unconventional warfare.

ATTRITION

Operation Enduring Freedom appears to have been a masterpiece of military creativity and finesse. The military plan capitalized on using well-chosen U.S. air power and U.S. Special Forces, working with the Afghan opposition, to crush the Taliban and cripple the al Qaeda network inside Afghanistan. But the U.S.-led military campaign has hardly been small in scale. Those who describe the war as an asymmetric application of America's military power are correct—the United States overwhelmed the Taliban with a correlation of force ratio not previously seen in modern warfare. Though impressive, has Operation Enduring Freedom been a tough test? More important, have the impressive results achieved thus far preordained a successful final outcome in the war?

Military theoretician Edward Luttwak has noted that all armed forces combine elements of attrition warfare with maneuver warfare in their overall approach to war. The closer a military is to the extreme of pure attrition, the more inward the focus. Internal administration and operations receive the most attention, and the organization is much less responsive to the external environment comprising the enemy, terrain, and the specific phenomena of any one particular conflict. Therefore, a well-managed, attrition oriented force cannot be adaptive to the external environment.[1]

By contrast, the closer an armed force is to the maneuver end of the attrition-relational maneuver spectrum, the more it will be externally focused. Studying the enemy, identifying his weaknesses, and configuring one's own capabilities to exploit those weaknesses achieves victory. Accordingly, success is a product of the ability to interpret the external environment, with all its complexities, and then to adapt one's internal machinery to suit the requirements of the particular situation. Consequently, a military with a high maneuver content cannot maximize internal efficiencies or set optimal organizational structure and methods. It must continually reconfigure for changing situations.[2]

Militaries develop their position on the attrition-maneuver spectrum according to the societies they serve. The high cost of the attrition model is balanced by the high risk of the maneuver model. Generally, rich nations opt for attrition, whereas poor nations with military ambitions must learn to use maneuver, which offers a high payoff for lower costs, but correspondingly higher risks.

There is no inherent virtue in either attrition or maneuver warfare. However, any equality between the two approaches ends in the case of fighting an unconventional war. This is because, as targets become less and less defined and better dispersed, the relevance of attrition also declines. Accordingly, the closer a military organization is to the maneuver end of the spectrum, the greater will be its effectiveness in unconventional warfare. Moreover, the pursuit of attrition efficiencies in the form of generating firepower is likely to be counterproductive in the long term by antagonizing the local population.[3]

THE EXISTING REALITY

One would think that well-trained, competently led armed forces should be able to adapt to a particular set of circumstances regardless of their original position on the attrition-maneuver spectrum. The reality is different. As previously noted, an attrition-based military force is inward regarding. This quality, in a country with large armed forces, cannot help but produce a complex internal structure that is overregulated, bureaucratic, and rigid to a point that inhibits innovation. Additionally, internal operations in large, inward-regarding organizations have a tendency to absorb a great deal of the energy of staff and commanders, thereby reducing the amount of effort available to tackle the intricacies of external issues.

The American way of war is solidly anchored to the attrition side of the attrition-maneuver spectrum. This is why in Vietnam, for example, the U.S. Military Assistance Command, Vietnam (USMACV), evolved into a large and complex headquarters that could not adequately respond to an unconventional external setting. Similarly, when the United States goes to war, any war, we see the air force bombing away. It seems these developments can't be helped. Bureaucratized services can only reproduce their own image. If the enemy chooses not to cooperate by playing his assigned role in attrition warfare, this trivial matter will simply be ignored.

AFGHANISTAN

At the beginning of the Afghan campaign, President George W. Bush told reporters that it would be "a different kind of war." Defense Secretary Donald Rumsfeld told reporters, "You don't fight terrorists with conventional capabilities. You do it with unconventional capabilities." What did the president and the defense secretary mean by "different" and "unconventional?" Was it an attempt to break the anchor chain and move the U.S. military toward the maneuver end of the attrition-maneuver spectrum? The war is certainly different. But it has been largely executed in a conventional manner. Also, the U.S. military has remained firmly anchored to the attrition end of the attrition-maneuver spectrum. Evidence to the contrary simply does not exist despite the defense secretary's claim of "unconventionality."[4]

The conventional nature of U.S. military thinking was demonstrated throughout the planning and prosecution of the war in Afghanistan. The military, which seemed to have contingency plans for the most inconceivable scenarios, had no plans for Afghanistan, the sanctuary of Osama bin Laden and his network. There was nothing on the shelf that could have provided even an outline for dealing with an unconventional enemy.[5]

On September 12, President Bush asked Secretary Rumsfeld what the military could do immediately in response to al Qaeda's attacks. "Very little, effectively," the secretary replied.[6] Rumsfeld had already pressed General Tommy Franks, the commander of the U.S. Central Command (CENTCOM), who was responsible for South Asia and the Middle East, for a war plan. Franks responded that it would take months to draw up plans and deploy enough forces to the area for a major military assault in Afghanistan.[7] Franks's conception of warfare was conventional, based on a career of training, education, and experience. Attriting the enemy would require a buildup of forces and logistics.

Rumsfeld wanted Franks to think in terms of days or weeks. After all, al Qaeda was a guerrilla organization whose members lived in caves, rode mules, and drove sports utility vehicles. The secretary of defense didn't quite know what he wanted, but he did know that it would have to be creative and he wanted it fast. The secretary also seemed to understand that his order for creative thinking and quick response would severely challenge the military establishment.[8]

At the 4 PM National Security Council (NSC) meeting of September 12, President Bush made it clear that he wanted a military plan that would inflict pain and destruction on the terrorists. While the military was struggling with how to develop a response that satisfied the president's and defense secretary's demands, the CIA had already developed a proposal. On September 13, George Tenet, the director of central intelligence (DCI), brought his counterterrorism chief, Cofer Black, to the NSC to present the details of the CIA proposal.[9]

The Agency's plan involved bringing together expanded intelligence-gathering resources, sophisticated technology, CIA paramilitary teams, and opposition forces in Afghanistan in a classic unconventional warfare campaign. These assets would quickly be combined, with U.S. military air power and special forces completing the lethal package designed to destroy the terrorist network.[10]

The Agency's paramilitary teams had been in contact with Northern Alliance leaders for several years. Tenet was confident that he could insert teams inside Afghanistan with each opposition faction warlord. These Agency teams, along with special forces teams to direct the U.S. Air Force bombing effort, would give the Northern Alliance the edge needed to defeat the Taliban. Cofer Black was so confident in the plan that he told the president it would result in "an unfair fight for the U.S. military." Black also told the president that Americans were going to die. Risk was inherent in this type of operation. "That's war," Bush said. The president and Black understood what seemed to be obvious—death and accepting risk were part of warfare.[11]

The CIA's proposal had a powerful effect on the president. For the first time, he was being told without reservation that there was a way to track down and destroy the terrorists. The Agency had an unconventional plan. Perhaps even more appealing, Black told the president that CIA teams could be rapidly inserted into Afghanistan and that the Taliban would crumble in a matter of weeks.[12] That afternoon at the NSC meeting the president would announce that he was going to approve the CIA proposal.[13]

President Bush was excited about the CIA's plan. However, he wanted to be sure that he was not being rash. Consequently, he asked his national security team to assemble for the weekend at Camp David to review the bidding. Tenet had further developed the Agency's earlier proposal. The plan now included a full-scale covert attack on the financial base of the terrorist network and a comprehensive attack matrix designed to thwart terrorist activities in eighty countries. The CIA would also "buy" key intelligence services worldwide in an attempt to obtain all the intelligence that was available. The president was pleased with the Agency's proposal.[14]

General Henry H. Shelton, who would complete his tour as chairman of the Joint Chiefs of Staff in two weeks, made the final presentation at Camp David. Shelton had three options for Afghanistan. The first option was a cruise missile strike against al Qaeda targets. This option could be rapidly executed with little risk. No one in the room, including Shelton, was enamored with this option.[15]

The second option simply added manned bomber attacks to the cruise missile option. The combination of cruise missiles and bombers would be more lethal but would take longer to execute.[16]

Shelton's final option included all the elements of the second option along with elite special forces elements deployed inside Afghanistan. This option would take a minimum of ten to twelve days to execute, because time would be needed to position combat search and rescue (CSAR) teams in the region to recover any downed pilots. During a break, Bush commented to Vice President Dick Cheney and Deputy Secretary of Defense Paul Wolfowitz that he found Shelton's military options "unimaginative."[17]

The lack of good targets presented the Defense Department with a problem.[18] The U.S. military possesses a lethal and sophisticated array of weapons systems, all designed to destroy an opponent's ability to wage war. But what if the enemy does not have high-value targets to attack. This was the situation in Afghanistan. There was little infrastructure to destroy and few high-value military targets to attack. To a large extent, U.S. military capabilities were neutralized by the absence of lucrative targets to engage.

Immediately after the World Trade Center and Pentagon attacks, the president made it clear that he intended to go after states that supported or harbored terrorists. Perhaps the president's message and the lack of good targets in Afghanistan encouraged both Rumsfeld and Wolfowitz to raise the issue of Iraq. Wolfowitz had long been an advocate of destroying Iraqi president Saddam Hussein and his regime. He strongly believed that there was no greater menace in the world. Although unsubstantiated, Wolfowitz also believed there was a good chance that Iraq was involved in the September 11 attacks.[19]

Iraq posed a serious issue for the president and his national security team. The United States could not risk getting bogged down in Afghanistan. The history of the British in the nineteenth century and the Soviets in the twentieth century caused Condoleezza Rice, the president's national security adviser, to wonder whether history would repeat itself for the United States in the twenty-first century. Perhaps Rice fueled Wolfowitz's aggressive stance on Iraq when she put on the table the notion of possibly launching military action elsewhere as an insurance policy in case things went bad in Afghanistan.[20]

For the U.S. military, combat operations in Iraq were straightforward. The Gulf War demonstrated the capability of the U.S. military to destroy high-value military targets with extraordinary precision. Iraq offered the U.S. military an opportunity to wage the type of war it was comfortable with by attacking a state known to support terrorism. It also offered the Department of Defense an opportunity to spearhead a complementary effort in Iraq to what was shaping up to be an unconventional war in Afghanistan led by the CIA.

Secretary of State Colin Powell objected to expanding the war to Iraq unless there was clear evidence linking Iraq to the September 11 terrorist attacks. He was concerned about creating and maintaining a coalition. Iraq would significantly complicate the current situation. Besides, Iraq could be dealt with later, if necessary. The window of opportunity, and perhaps hope, for the Defense Department to extend the war into Iraq closed quickly. President Bush informed the group that he had heard enough debate over Iraq. Future discussions were to focus only on Afghanistan. Consequently, the military still needed to find targets for its sophisticated weapons systems.[21]

The targeting dilemma was simplified by the relationship between the Taliban and the al Qaeda terrorist organization. Not only did the Taliban openly support al Qaeda, but it also was impossible to clearly separate Taliban military forces from al Qaeda fighters. President Bush offered the Taliban a means of preserving their regime when he directed the secretary of state to issue an ultimatum to the Taliban to turn over Bin Laden and other al Qaeda leaders or suffer the consequences. The Taliban would not turn Bin Laden over. As a result, the very conventional, though inept, Taliban military presented the United States with a target array to work against. Rumsfeld would later comment that the United States had to hit Taliban military targets, limited as they were, because there were not a lot of al Qaeda targets to hit.[22]

The Pentagon was still having difficulty putting together an executable war plan. Military planners attempt to minimize risk and increase available options by requesting everything and anything that might be useful in a war. These types of requests include overflight and basing rights from foreign countries, which may want to know more about our intentions than we are willing to divulge. Consequently, these broad military requests require the State Department to engage in prolonged negotiations that ultimately delay military operations.[23]

While the Pentagon was trying to figure out how to prosecute the war, the Agency had infiltrated its first team into Afghanistan. A seasoned CIA Directorate of Operations officer, identified only as Gary, and nine other members of his team touched down in the heart of Northern Alliance territory on September 26, 2001. They flew in on a Russian-made, CIA-owned Mi-17 helicopter that had upgraded avionics, night-vision capability, and a paint job to match the Northern Alliance fleet. Two Northern Alliance officers and a small security team met the Agency team on the ground. The team's gear was loaded onto a truck, and everyone quickly moved to a house in a secure village to discuss business.[24]

Cofer Black had given Gary his mission immediately after the September 15 Camp David planning session. Black told Gary to go convince the Northern Alliance to work with him and to prepare the ground to receive U.S. military forces to conduct operations to destroy the Taliban and al Qaeda. Black made it very clear that killing Bin Laden and other al Qaeda members was the ultimate objective. U.S. and Northern Alliance objectives overlapped nicely with regard to eliminating al Qaeda forces and going through the Taliban to do so. After all, the same people who attacked New York and the Pentagon had recently assassinated Ahmad Shah Massoud, the charismatic leader of the Northern Alliance. The Alliance was quick to welcome

Gary and his Agency team. They would soon be on the move against their enemy, the Taliban.[25]

The president could not help compare the responsiveness of the CIA with the caution and risk-adverse philosophy of the military. In fact, this philosophy had been codified in both the Weinberger and Powell doctrines during the 1980s and 1990s. Still, there needed to be a better balance between preserving people's lives and showing action. It was becoming clear to the president and his national security team that a full military operation, combining air activities and boots on the ground, would be essential to demonstrate the seriousness to the world of America's intentions to root out terrorism. The president wanted to commence military operations by early October.

The Pentagon was still waiting for basing rights for CSAR teams in order to pick up any pilots who were forced down during the bombing campaign. Rumsfeld was also still not satisfied with the target lists. The CIA team that was with the Northern Alliance wasn't providing enough intelligence. Rice saw the problem as a circular one. Without intelligence, targets could not be effectively identified. Getting intelligence was a problem, because they had not been able to get enough people on the ground. To make things worse, General Franks said it would take ten days for special forces to get ready to go, but that without basing rights, the teams could not get into Afghanistan.[26]

Eighteen days after September 11, the Pentagon was developing a response, but not a strategy. For Secretary of State Colin Powell, it was a nightmare, visions of Vietnam—bomb and hope. The United States could not figure out how to win a guerrilla war. This explains why the U.S. military response focused on aerial bombing. One CIA team of ten men had easily made it into Afghanistan. Soon more would follow. Unfortunately, there were no prospects of getting special forces in anytime soon. Positioning CSAR teams and the bombing campaign had a higher priority. The situation was bleak. Rice summarized the situation at the September 30 principals' meeting. The military needed bases from which to launch bombers and CSAR aircraft. That was understood. When it came to employing special forces, much less was understood. The U.S. military knew how to bomb. Running elite special operations units against an unconventional enemy was a different matter.[27]

Bush was anxious to take the war to the enemy. The CIA team in the North believed that massive bombing of the Taliban front lines would cause them to break. Neither the Agency nor the U.S. military had anyone in the South. Identifying an opposition group to work with in that region was a problem. Ironically, CSAR capability in the South was falling into place. Aircraft carriers would provide the platforms for CSAR operations.[28]

October 1 was General Richard B. Myers's first day as chairman of the Joint Chiefs. At the morning NSC meeting, he announced that it was likely that Uzbekistan would provide basing for CSAR to cover the North. However, it would take sixty-seven C-17 flights to carry in enough equipment, personnel, and helicopters to have the necessary recovery capability. It would also take about twelve days before CSAR was up and running. The president was concerned about the extended time line for the infiltration of special forces teams. Myers had stated that all activities in the North would be delayed. In the South, Myers was ready to launch bombers and cruise missiles, but special operations in the South would have to wait until opposition groups were identified.[29]

Rumsfeld offered a solution to the bombing dilemma at the October 2 NSC meeting. The secretary was willing to accept risk in the North. B-2 bombers and cruise missiles could hit targets in the North without CSAR support. The B-2s were stealth bombers that could not be picked up by Taliban radar. The unmanned cruise missiles did not present any risk at all. The B-2 crews would only be in jeopardy if their planes had an accident or serious mechanical failure. In the South, all systems would be available to drop bombs, because CSAR support was in place.[30]

Rumsfeld's solution was safe, less than optimal, and a compromise. It fit what Powell called "bomb and hope." In the North, the high-flying B-2s would be at a disadvantage without special forces units on the ground to identify targets with laser designators. In the South, there was no opposition group ready to take advantage of bombing strikes. Rumsfeld offered action but not a strategy or war plan.

Although Rumsfeld did not present a war strategy, his aggressiveness and constant pressure on Myers and Franks yielded some results. At the NSC meeting on October 4, General Myers announced that CSAR units should be ready to operate out of Uzbekistan by October 8. Additionally, special forces units were flowing into Oman, and the carrier, *Kitty Hawk,* would be in place by October 13 to support operations in the South. Myers indicated that special forces units should be able to enter the northern areas after the initial bombing of that area.[31]

On October 5, the CIA dispatched a message to key agency personnel who were running operations in and around Afghanistan that outlined the military strategy. The message listed the following points:

1. Instruct all tribal allies to ground and identify all their aircraft immediately.
2. Instruct the tribals to cease all significant military movement—stand down and hold in place.
3. The future plan is to have the opposition forces drive to isolate enemy forces, but wait before moving.
4. Instruct all assets through Afghanistan to begin sabotage operations immediately everywhere. This includes tossing hand grenades into Taliban offices,

disrupting Taliban convoys, and pinning down Taliban supply convoys.

5. Paramilitary insertions will go on in the South and be combined with air strikes.
6. Define no-strike zones—hospitals, schools, and so forth.
7. All tribal faction leaders should identify and locate primary targets.
8. Identify possible escape routes out of Afghanistan for Bin Laden and his al Qaeda leadership and set up reconnaissance of the routes for interdiction.
9. Be prepared to interrogate and exploit prisoners.
10. Assess humanitarian needs.

The Agency leadership made a point to share the full text of this message with General Franks to ensure that CIA and DoD efforts in the global war on terrorism were fully integrated. However, the CIA message, which outlined a war strategy, was strong indication of who was leading the charge. The Agency was preparing the battlefield for the war.[32]

On the afternoon of October 7, President Bush announced through the major networks that the U.S. military had begun strikes against al Qaeda targets and Taliban military facilities in Afghanistan. The Taliban had not turned over Bin Laden, and the al Qaeda leadership and was now paying the price. Secretary Rumsfeld and General Myers appeared at a press conference in the Pentagon shortly after the president's remarks. The secretary outlined the following six goals for the military operation:

1. Send a message to the Taliban.
2. Acquire intelligence.
3. Develop relations with anti-Taliban groups.
4. Make life increasingly difficult for terrorists.
5. Alter the military balance in Afghanistan.
6. Provide humanitarian relief.[33]

General Myers presented some details about the ongoing strikes. He simply described the numbers and types of aircraft and the number of cruise missiles involved in the initial strike. Myers presented data but little useful information. Perhaps Myers was trying to safeguard sensitive operational information.[34]

The target problem resurfaced the day after the initial strikes. General Myers said that the bombers did not know what to hit. Aircraft would loiter, waiting for targets to emerge. This was an incredible situation. After a day of strikes, the vast military capability of the United States was helpless in the absence of clearly identified military targets. The inability to strike at targets was the result of a lack of actionable intelligence, and this type of intelligence could best be acquired with boots on the ground.[35]

On October 10, General Franks said he had a special forces A-team waiting to deploy into Afghanistan. The Agency team had already been on the ground for two weeks. Secretary Rumsfeld was hot about the Defense Department's inability to get teams in. The president expected boots on the ground and DoD wasn't delivering. It would be almost impossible to control, or at least coordinate, combat operations against the Taliban and al Qaeda without special forces teams on the ground. Furthermore, generating target lists that could make a difference for U.S. bombers required the type of intelligence that could only be obtained from people located on the front lines.[36]

To make things worse, based on multiple sources, the CIA had determined that the bombing had little effect on the Taliban. If anything, the bombing had a unifying effect. In fact, intelligence indicated that about a hundred people a day were traveling from Pakistan to Afghanistan to join the Taliban. Mohammed Fahim, the Northern Alliance commander, told Gary, the Agency's team leader on the ground, that bombing all around the country wasn't accomplishing anything. Fahim pointed to the Taliban front lines and said that if they were bombed, the Alliance would take Kabul in a day. The bombing campaign was simply not doing much to change the balance in Afghanistan.[37]

The Agency had people on the ground since September 26. The Agency and the Defense Department were joined at the hip as far as anyone in Washington was concerned. The reality was a bit different. Though the spirit of cooperation was very high, the military needed their own people on the ground who would respond directly to a military chain of command. On October 19, twenty-three days after the first Agency team entered Afghanistan, U.S. Special Forces Operational Detachment 555 infiltrated into Afghanistan on two MH-53J Pave Low helicopters. Gary, the Agency's team leader, met them on a remote landing zone. Don Rumsfeld was finally able to report that a special forces team was on the front lines.[38]

October 23 was the fourteenth day of bombing. The special forces detachment was with the Northern Alliance located within five hundred meters of the Taliban front lines. The team was in a position to relay target information for the ongoing air campaign. However, nothing was happening. There are three possible explanations for the lack of movement.

First, the air campaign had not yet dropped bombs on frontline Taliban positions. This emboldened the Taliban and demoralized the Northern Alliance forces. Second, many Northern Alliance units were still waiting the delivery of arms and ammunition. Last, Fahim was visiting Tajikistan, and without him, nothing was going to happen. In discussing Afghan culture, the war cabinet had concluded that Afghan loyalty could not be bought, only rented. Though only one special forces team had been on the ground less than four days, Rumsfeld was developing a contingency plan to Americanize the ground operation by putting 50,000 troops into Afghanistan.[39]

Additional Agency and special forces teams were slowly getting into Afghanistan. Still, the pattern of bombing did little to support a Northern Alliance offensive. The Agency team leader reported that the Alliance was losing confidence. The Taliban front lines were intact, and reinforcements from Pakistan were flowing in daily. The cable went on to say that the Taliban front lines would crumble after three or four days of concentrated bombing. However, without this effort, the fight could be lost. George Tenet carried this cable to the White House.[40]

By late October, the focus of the air campaign finally shifted from fixed assets to targeting Taliban and al Qaeda forces in the field.[41] It is very important to note that at this time, these forces were as conventional as an opponent could be. They consisted of units—with typical military organizations, tanks, and artillery—that were all occupying traditional fighting positions. In addition, the Taliban forces were disposed along front lines facing a determined, but undermanned and poorly equipped opposition in the Northern Alliance. Consequently, the late October bombing effort significantly attrited the conventionally disposed Taliban and al Qaeda forces.[42]

It is important to note that the first month of the war produced limited results. The Taliban hung on to power. Many experts said a ground invasion would be necessary; others claimed that intensifying the air campaign would lead to toppling the Taliban. The number of U.S. special operations forces and CIA teams in Afghanistan had been increasing. In the North, U.S. Special Forces teams assisted Northern Alliance elements with communications, coordinating air strikes, and bringing in ammunition, food, medical supplies, and winter gear. In the South, other Special Forces teams did the same with tribes from that region led by Hamid Karzai.[43]

By late November, Mazar-i-Sharif, Kabul, and Kunduz had fallen. In addition, more than a thousand U.S. marines established a base of operations south of Kandahar, which was still under Taliban control. Special forces teams were working closely with anti-Taliban Pashtun tribes to tighten the noose around Kandahar. On December 8, 2001, Taliban and al Qaeda elements fled the city, moving to the relative safety of the mountains. The Taliban no longer held power, cities, or transportation routes. They had been crushed by an impressive display of power.[44]

Up to this point for the U.S. military, the war was appropriately conventional. Attrition warfare, capitalizing on superior firepower, was used against an enemy that presented a lucrative array of targets. The Taliban unwisely allowed the United

States to apply an asymmetric advantage against its inferior army. Certainly, the importance of special operations forces cannot be overstated. They tied the air campaign to a ground campaign and directed precision fires against Taliban and al Qaeda positions. However, their use does not make the fighting that led to the disintegration of the Taliban an unconventional war. Special operations forces were used, but the military war plan remained firmly planted at the attrition end of the spectrum. Furthermore, there was no reason why the fight should have been unconventional, considering the conventional disposition of the enemy. Simply put, it appears that the United States achieved the correct result but failed to recognize the strategy that had led to success.

SNATCHING DEFEAT FROM THE JAWS OF VICTORY

Up until the disintegration of the Taliban in mid-December, the United States faced a relatively target-rich environment that facilitated an attrition campaign. Also, up until this point, the conceptual distinction between unconventional and conventional was trivial, considering the execution of the war was appropriate to the disposition of the enemy. However, the disintegration of the Taliban made the conceptual distinction between unconventional and conventional a serious matter. This is because the luxury of facing a conventional enemy disappeared when the Taliban fell. Targets became less defined and better dispersed. Consequently, the relevance of attrition also declined. Unfortunately, the orientation of the U.S. military did not change as the nature of the war changed.

After being confronted with a drastically altered operational setting, the present military response was exacerbated by the evolving command and control arrangements. In the early stages of the campaign, the joint special operations task force (JSOTF) headquarters that was tasked with integrating anti-Taliban ground operations with the U.S. air campaign effectively communicated directly with General Franks through a daily video teleconference link. This unorthodox arrangement gave a relatively low-level commander a direct link to the theater commander. This unorthodox command arrangement proved effective in the conventional fight that led to the collapse of the Taliban.[45]

To their credit, military planners in Washington and Tampa never eliminated the possibility that a U.S. conventional ground force would be needed to finish the job. There were already some conventional forces in the region guarding airfields that were supporting the air campaign. In late November, the 10th Mountain Division headquarters was alerted and deployed to Bagram, Afghanistan, to take charge of all military operations in the country. The 10th Mountain would report to the theater land component headquarters now operating in Uzbekistan, and the theater land component would report to General Franks in Tampa. The JSOTF, which had been reporting directly to Franks, would now be subordinate to the 10th Mountain Division. In other words, the special operations headquarters would now have to work through two cumbersome conventional headquarters, located in separate countries, to get approval to conduct operations in Afghanistan.[46]

As the war became increasingly unconventional, the command and control arrangements became more conventional.[47] The command arrangement evolved into a large and complex structure that could not adequately respond to the new unconventional setting. The bureaucratized military reproduced their own image.

Chapter 2

☰ Historical Background—
☰ Context

THE FUTURE CAN CLEARLY AND WISELY BE APPROACHED if the path leading to the present is known. In assessing strategic choices, decision makers often do not have available the clarifying perspective provided by history. The reasons the U.S. military has difficulty waging unconventional war become clear when viewed through an historical lens. Recognizing this problem, this chapter traces the history of special operations forces (SOF) in the U.S. military.

The U.S. military has undergone many organizational and doctrinal changes since its inception as a small militia force in 1775. But the year 1945 marked the beginning of an era of dramatic change. The new global realities of the post–World War II period suggested the need for a force able to respond to a spectrum of conflicts. This led to the building of a special warfare capability as a response to military challenges for which conventional forces were not suited.

A few conventionally minded military leaders hesitantly accepted special warfare as a legitimate tool in the military arsenal; most, however, questioned the validity and appropriateness of adopting unconventional operations as a legitimate form of warfare. The tensions of the Cold War somewhat resolved the ambivalence in favor of coordinating in a single operation the techniques of both types of warfare. This Faustian bargain preserved the existence of special warfare units for a while, though at a price. The intended characteristics of special warfare were in conflict with the values, goals, and missions of the larger military. Accordingly, special warfare had to conform to the conceptions of warfare valued by leaders who dominated the organization and controlled its future. This survival instinct altered the nature and perhaps the definition of unconventional warfare. More important, it limited the uniformed military's ability to offer the president and defense secretary an alternative to conventional warfare. This was the case in Afghanistan.

Doubts about the value of unconventional warfare still exist. Former secretary of defense Les Aspin originally planned to have the assistant secretary of defense for special operations and low intensity conflict (ASD/SOLIC) report to another assistant secretary of defense rather than to the under secretary for policy. Most remarkably, in the aftermath of the initial success in Afghanistan, Defense Secretary Donald Rumsfeld intended to eliminate ASD/SOLIC. Negative and neutral views of SOF are still common at lower levels throughout the U.S. military. Critics complain that SOF not only require different command and control arrangements, weapons, equipment, training, intelligence support, and funding than conventional forces they displace, complement, or supplement, but they also divert many first-rate officers and noncommissioned officers from army, navy, and air force units. They doubt that SOF are worth the effort. It is dangerous to discount history, especially when lives and the security of a nation are at stake.

WHAT ARE SPECIAL OPERATIONS?

The U.S. military, like all modern major powers, is trained, structured, and equipped for World War II-like clashes—massive tank battles advancing across the countryside, accompanied by devastating doses of artillery and air power. This is called conventional warfare, because it follows the established conventions for the conduct of warfare. U.S. military forces have engaged in this kind of bruising conventional combat twice in the past fifty years. These were in Iraqi in 1991 and in 2003. Both wars were of short duration. The rest of the time, the armed forces have been doing something else.

U.S. military personnel have fought not only in the large-scale conventional combat, but also in a variety of ambiguous, smaller-scale conflicts. During the last fifty years, a special capability was developed to deal with these kinds of lesser, but messy, politically charged situations that often straddled the tenuous boundary between an uneasy peace and something that was not quite war. Places like Somalia, Haiti, Rwanda, El Salvador, and Nicaragua, to name a few, are illustrative of situations that straddle this boundary. Generically, these ill-defined, constantly shifting forms of conflict can be termed unconventional warfare (UW), because they do not follow the conventions of military conflict. They are not usually waged by the professional armed forces of a state, forces do not usually attempt to seize and hold terrain, and sometimes they are not even waged for a specific reason.[1]

The Department of Defense (DoD) defines unconventional warfare as:

A broad spectrum of military and paramilitary operations, normally of long duration, predominantly conducted by indigenous or surrogate forces who are organized, trained, equipped, supported, and directed in varying degrees by an external source. It includes guerrilla warfare and other direct offensive, low visibility, covert, or clandestine operations, as well as the indirect activities of subversion, sabotage, intelligence activities, and evasion and escape.[2]

The DoD has conveniently categorized much of the unconventional threats under the heading of military operations other than war, or MOOTW. More recently, these types of operations have been referred to as stability and support operations, or SASO. These include, but are not limited to, humanitarian assistance, insurgency and counterinsurgency, noncombatant evacuation, counterdrug operations, shows of force, nation assistance, disaster assistance, recovery operations, strikes and raids, and more.[3]

Conventional forces can easily conduct many of these tasks—for example, shows of force or strikes and raids. However, some situations involve complex combinations of missions such as humanitarian or disaster assistance, nation assistance, and perhaps even counterinsurgency, all occurring at once and in the same area. The Haiti intervention of 1994 is an example of such a mission.

This study argues that, for the most part, conventional forces are not the best military forces for such missions. These situations are characterized by a lack of a defined enemy; the need for influence, negotiation, and even community leadership and by the ability to resort to deadly force if necessary. The component of the U.S. military best prepared for these environments is the SOF.

What Are Special Operations Forces?

The term special operations forces has come to include a wide variety of military organizations, often with very different missions. This study posits that a number of these organizations perform essentially the same missions as conventional forces. The army Ranger battalions, army special operations aviation forces, and nearly all air force SOF fall into this category. Others, such as the army's Special Forces Operational Detachment Delta, perform very narrow, specialized functions. Still others, notably U.S. Army Special Forces, actually perform functions that make them well suited for unconventional warfare of the kind described here.

The best known of the special operations units is the U.S. Army Special Forces (SF), better known as the Green Berets. First brought to prominence during the Vietnam War, army SF acquired an image as deadly, commando-style, jungle fighters that has not diminished over the years. In addition, the U.S. Navy and Air Force have created their own special operations units on a smaller scale than the army. The air force units, in particular, function chiefly to support army SOF by providing transportation, medical evacuation, and fire support.

SOF Missions

The question of exactly what special operations forces do is less straightforward than one might expect. Special operations are not well defined. The U.S. Special Operations Command (USSOCOM) defines special operations as follows:

Special operations encompass the use of small units in direct or indirect military actions that are focused on strategic or operational objectives. They require units with combinations of specialized personnel, equipment, training or tactics that exceed the routine capabilities of conventional military forces."[4]

The Army Special Forces Command (USASOC) manual on special operations forces states that these forces are "specially organized, trained and equipped military and paramilitary forces that conduct special operations to achieve military, political, economic or informational objectives by generally unconventional means in hostile, denied or politically sensitive areas."[5]

These two definitions differ in an important way. Though both combine some of the same elements, the USSOCOM version emphasizes one view of SOF, while the USASOC version stresses another. USSOCOM's definition indicates that SOF are special because they have unique equipment and perform tasks that "exceed the routine capabilities of conventional forces." The tasks and methods themselves are, by implication, conventional.[6] The stress in the USASOC definition is on the use of these forces for "political, economic or informational objectives," beyond ordinary military ones and employing something called "unconventional means." This reflects an important difference about what is special about special operations. Are these essentially conventional soldiers with a very high level of proficiency? Or are they something else, dedicated to purposes and functions that are different and using methods that are outside the conventional mold of most military forces, that is, unconventional?

This disagreement is reflected in a division of opinion within the special operations community as to whether they ought to be "shooters or social workers." The result is an uneasy division of labor between the two extremes, with SOF units dedicated to both sorts of missions. The argument is perhaps most pointed when applied to the numbered army special forces groups that conduct unconventional warfare. Most other SOF are doing the same as their conventional counterparts and are "special" only because of their high degree of proficiency and because they have some equipment and training not available to conventional forces.[7]

This tension between the definitions is a consistent theme running through the history of special operations forces at least since World War II. It is not mere semantics, but reflects a real divergence of opinion among military leaders, planners, and ordinary soldiers about the nature, purpose, functions, and methods of special operations forces.

The focus of this study is on army special operations forces, principally U.S. Army Special Forces, civil affairs, and psychological operations, because these constitute the original, largest, most active group of special operators and are arguably the core for unconventional warfare.

It Is Not Easy Being Special

Despite a distinguished history, Army Special Forces has not had an easy time. The U.S. military and American culture, in general, have long distrusted the whole idea of elites on the principle that such organizations have no place in a democracy. The specific arguments against elite units are well known—that they have limited utility; require a disproportionate amount of support; take the best personnel from other units; gain undeserved public attention, thus damaging the morale of other units; have a tendency toward individualism; exhibit barbaric behavior; and resist traditional discipline. None of these arguments is completely correct, but over the years there has been an uncomfortable amount of truth in them. In the wake of the Vietnam War, these and other accusations nearly resulted in the disappearance of special operators in all the services. By the time the Iran hostage rescue became a spectacular failure, in 1980, these forces were at their lowest ebb ever.[8]

Beginning in the 1980s, those most concerned in the army special operations community deliberately set out to preserve the special forces (SF) concept by attacking these arguments at their roots and by making special operations forces a part of the conventional army. A major effort was launched to give special forces the image of "the quiet professionals." To a large degree, this has been accomplished.

By the mid-1990s, even the much-loved Green Beret headgear had often been relegated to photo opportunities and ceremonial occasions. One special operations general said with pride that SF liaison elements were becoming a permanent part of every conventional army corps headquarters, where they would wear the corps insignia and the corps headgear.[9]

In 1992 Army Magazine published an interview with Lt. Gen. Wayne J. Downing, then commander of the U.S. Army Special Operations Command. As illustrated in the excerpt below, this article revealed the triumph of the conventional model.

> In past decades, special operations forces were cast in the light of unconventional warfare which often carried with it the view that they were outside the mainstream Army. It is true that special operations forces have unconventional capabilities in the sense that they possess specialties, equipment and mission areas not allocated to other units; however, as special operations forces have become doctrinally established, their roles have become conventional in the sense that this is the way the Army fights today. Drawing from the lessons of Desert Storm, special operations forces in the near future will become firmly linked to each of the Army's corps with coordination teams assigned to that level of command.[10]

In the same article, the general declared: "I guess the message I have for the rest of the Army and for the rest of the armed forces is that we have very capable special operations forces that are partners—work together—with other elements of the armed forces to accomplish the mission." [11]

Joining the conventional armed forces was seen by special operations leaders as the way to preserve and enhance an important military capability. However, something vital may have been lost in doing so. While the SOF were becoming more conventional, conflict was becoming less so. There was a rise in insurgency and irredentist movements, often wrongly characterized as terrorists. Unstable governments in Haiti, Liberia, Somalia, and Cambodia collapsed and required foreign intervention. Even large-scale drug trafficking became a threat, and state-to-state conflict had new competition as nonstate actors became more important sponsors of violent conflict. [12]

LOOKING BACK

Army SOF became, almost by accident, a unique politico-military instrument, capable of operating in the vague gray area between political conflict and open war. First organized to raise and train partisans in the event of Soviet invasion of western Europe, the special forces had, from the outset, a very close relationship with the field of psychological operations. During the Vietnam War, the long-neglected field of civil affairs enjoyed a resurrection and eventually became a part of army SOF. In the past, the most notable arena of this gray area conflict has been insurgency and counterinsurgency. But after the demise of the Soviet Union and the coming of the new world security environment, there has been an increase in the number of unconventional conflicts in which there is no clear dominance of the military but in which military forces are still significantly involved. The recent phenomenon of failed states offers a venue for politico-military involvement that cannot be ignored. This suggests a greater need than ever for military-political competency in these unconventional conflicts. [13]

Largely because of benign neglect, the civil affairs and psychological operations units became organizationally associated with the Green Berets in a single command—the U.S. Army Special Operations Command. Collectively, they combine the types of skills that are key in "gray area," or unconventional warfare. At the same time, the U.S. forces most likely to conduct these operations successfully have shown a tendency to neglect this field in favor of purely military competencies. Indeed, for many years the special forces attempted to distance themselves from the civil affairs and psychological operations components, because these units were thought to detract from the commando image preferred by many SF soldiers and leaders. This is a strange and troubling outcome and the process by which it came may have handicapped the ability of the United States to successfully confront the most likely threats of the twenty-first century. [14]

What Do SOF Do and How?

There is another dimension worth considering that may have contributed to this benign neglect. Developing a new military capability within the U.S. military requires a complex bureaucratic process. Creating a force for some vague class of conflicts called unconventional warfare compounds the standard difficulties. The bureaucrats demand a clear statement of what the purpose of any new capability is and how this capability is to be employed before such a force can be organized and trained. For the conventional army, these questions are relatively easy to answer. Conventional forces exist to render the military force of an enemy state incapable of preventing the United States from working its will. This is usually accomplished by force and violence. This simple concept leads to the answers to a host of questions. What skills should such a military force include? What types of equipment should it possess? How large should it be? Should it expect to operate in all geographic areas?[15]

Unfortunately, the purpose of an unconventional warfare force is not so easily defined. Certainly, it must serve the national interests of the United States. However, there is no clear task so easily defined as the "destruction of the enemy army" and no method so easily specified as "the direct application of violent force." Combat is not the only way to apply military power, but it is certainly simple, direct, and easily understood. Consequently, the basic questions about unconventional war have never been adequately answered. As a result, the UW capability that grew up did so largely by accident and improvisation.[16]

Doctrine: Figuring Out What to Do and How to Do It

Doctrine is a set of principles or techniques accepted as correct by practitioners in a field of endeavor, in this case the military. For the Defense Department, doctrine consists of "fundamental principles by which the military forces or elements thereof guide their actions in support of national objectives. It is authoritative but requires judgment in application."[17] Army doctrine is a set of principles for the conduct of ground combat. Unconventional warfare, which often includes ground combat, is not principally about violent conflict, and this creates difficulty in devising military doctrine.[18]

The U.S. military has long struggled with the problem of violent conflict that seems to fall short of war in the usual sense. In the past, the response has been to embrace the conventional model of war and label all violent conflict that fell short of real war as aberrations, special cases that are not the proper business of soldiers. It is no surprise that doctrine and concrete solutions for dealing with these types of conflicts have not arisen. Given the well-known military attachment to the tried and proven, and the skepticism for vague, esoteric ideas, it is surprising that any official attention has been paid to the subject of UW.[19]

Military strategists tried to give form to these lesser conflicts by adopting at least three successive ways to characterize this environment: low-intensity conflict, military operations other than war, and, most recently, stability and support operations. None of these descriptions proved satisfactory. All this seems a bit vague and did little to help guide the planner or young soldier in Mogadishu when the streets were filled with Somali gunmen.[20] The frustration with these forms of conflict arises because they are, indeed, complex and difficult to deal with using a conventional template. There is no shortage of thoughts on the subject in both academic and military circles. At the same time, there seems to be very little coherence and very limited agreement.

SOF MISSIONS

As a result of all that is discussed above, the missions assigned to SOF tend to be something of an incoherent collection of mismatched activities stemming from a variety of sources, including congressional legislation, the desires of the services, initiatives by the special-operations community, and historical precedents. Some of these, notably civil affairs and psychological operations, are actually capabilities rather than missions.

As defined by USSOCOM, SOF accomplish the following missions and collateral activities:

Missions

Direct Action (DA): Rapid, small-scale strikes and raids to seize or destroy enemy personnel or materiel

Special Reconnaissance (SR): Reconnaissance of especially difficult objectives, often in denied areas

Foreign Internal Defense (FID): Assistance to foreign governments threatened by lawlessness, subversion, or insurgency

Unconventional Warfare (UW): Support to long-duration military or paramilitary operations by indigenous or surrogate forces. Includes guerrilla warfare and other forms of low-visibility military activities

Combating Terrorism (CT): Offensive measures to prevent, deter, or respond to terrorism

Counterproliferation (CP): Actions taken to seize, destroy, capture, or recover weapons of mass destruction (i.e., nuclear, biological, radiological, or chemical weapons)

Civil Affairs (CA): Activities concerning the relations between military forces and civil authorities and civilian populations to facilitate military operations

Psychological Operations (psyops): Operations to convey information to foreign audiences to induce or reinforce attitudes favorable to the originator's objectives

Information Operations (IO): Actions taken to achieve information superiority by affecting adversary information systems while protecting friendly information and information systems

Collateral Activities

Coalition Support: Communication, coordination, training, and liaison to integrate foreign forces into coalition command and intelligence structures

Combat Search and Rescue (CSAR): Recovery of distressed personnel during wartime or contingency operations

Counterdrug Activities (CD): Detection, monitoring, and countering the production, trafficking, and use of illegal drugs

Countermine Activities (CM): Activities to reduce or eliminate the threat of mines, booby traps, and other explosive devices, including the threat to noncombatants

Humanitarian Assistance (HA): Programs to relieve suffering from natural or man-made disasters or endemic conditions such as hunger or disease

Security Assistance (SA): Programs that provide defense articles, military training, or other defense-related services to foreign governments in furtherance of U.S. national policies

Special Activities: Actions abroad in support of U.S. policies that are planned and executed so that the role of the U.S. government is not apparent or acknowledged publicly. A presidential finding and congressional oversight is required for such.[21]

THE NATURE OF WAR

At a very general level, all conflict is a struggle between opposing forces, each seeking to gain or maintain power. Power, in turn, can be defined as the ability to compel action. Violent, organized struggle between competing political entities is commonly referred to as war. Primarily, this means open war, but it can also include a wide variety of less-violent disagreements or confrontations. The U.S. military, however, has historically focused on one form of violent, organized, conflict—conventional war.

The army's manual for operations defines war as "A state of open and declared armed hostile conflict between political units such as states or nations; may be limited or general in nature."[22] The manual is presumably referring to conventional war, although it does not make this distinction. Also, by this definition, the United States has had few wars. Yet, it has been involved in a wide variety of hostile conflicts that were neither open, nor declared, nor involved fighting states or nations.

The army's notion of war aligns well with the influential realpolitik formulation of Hans J. Morgenthau, that politics in general is a struggle for power. In this formulation, the threat of physical violence is "an intrinsic element of politics." But, the actual exercise of violence is seen as nonpolitical, "the abdication of political power in favor of military or pseudo-military power." The Morgenthau formula reflects a basic belief that politics and military operations are separate, largely autonomous and ought to be that way, as if they connected only at the very highest levels of strategy. But even a cursory examination of ill-defined conflict suggests that there is little autonomy between the military and political spheres. This is the arena of unconventional warfare.[23]

Furthermore, there are troublesome indications that the nature of power may have changed. After all, Vietnam, a low-technology, agricultural nation, managed to defeat the United States without fielding comparable armed forces or developing anything like comparable national economies. Student revolutionaries were able to seize and hold the U.S. embassy in Iran and hold it for more than a year. A mob in Mogadishu was able to force a change in U.S. policy. Political power seems to have become more diffuse as actors other than states become more influential. The result has been the emergence of what Seyom Brown called a polyarchy, meaning that nonstate actors such as corporations, terrorist groups, and special-interest communities would begin competing for advantage in the international arena. At the same time, the spread of modern technology, including weapons, has strengthened weak states and nonstate actors, further confusing the issue of power and its application. In short, conventional military power may not always be the currency of international relations; instead, a variety of other, less well-defined, conflict forms have gained importance.[24]

Unconventional warfare occurs in precisely this area, the gray area, where violence has entered the practice of politics but the struggle has not yet reached the level of conventional warfare. In fact, the protagonists may work diligently to prevent conventional war from occurring, because if it does take place, they lose their advantage. It is also in this gray area that the unique capabilities of SOF have their greatest strategic utility.

THE ROLE OF THE SOLDIERS

In conventional war, the role of soldiers is straightforward—they are an instrument for the application of force and violence. This application is different from other forms of force and violence, such as criminal activity, because it is sanctioned by the state. This particular application of force also differs from police work in that the purpose of the police is not to apply violence but to apprehend criminals. Soldiers do not traditionally seek to apprehend the enemy. However, unconventional warfare may find them doing exactly that.

Unlike soldiers, police do not carry weapons for the express purpose of killing those who defy their will. This is precisely what soldiers do in conventional war, and they do so by acting as an agent of a state, carrying out their work under the authority of that state, and recognizing the state's monopoly on the legal use of force and violence. Police use of force and violence is not about killing people and destroying the infrastructure of another state; military violence is.[25]

These are the central characteristics of the conventional model of warfare—it is armed violence on a large scale executed by specialized agents of a state. Carl von Clausewitz's notion that war is a political phenomenon is understood but exists largely in the background. Politics is not considered to be the business of soldiers. In fact, the conventional model assumes that once competent political authority declares a state of war, it becomes the business of the military until such time as the enemy state has lost its ability to resist.[26]

It should be understood that "unconventional" has taken on a broader meaning than the accepted DoD definition. Its common use includes any poorly defined conflict that does not follow the conventional model. This includes violence where either the belligerents are not the agents of a legitimate state or that they do not use military force as their principal method. Even the U.S. military does not use the term unconventional war as one might expect. Instead, the term is used as General Downing used it, to indicate techniques or unorthodox methods that include guerrilla warfare and other direct offensive, low visibility, covert or clandestine operations as well as intelligence activities. These techniques are only unconventional in the sense that they are not the common practice of the army or the central focus of its efforts. This last point is important in understanding the full meaning of General Downing's remarks. The fact that UW is not central to the army's view of the world is key in understanding the conventionalizing of special operations forces. As long as UW was identified as the main function of SOF, and as long as UW was seen as a peripheral function, SOF were doomed to secondary status, the first choice to lose valuable resources. To survive, SOF would have to be accepted as valuable players on the conventional team. SOF had to be part of the conventional armed forces.[27]

A STERILE BATTLEFIELD

The army's notion of warfare is unduly restrictive. The army also marginalizes the people who live in the areas where fighting occurs. This is reflected in the descriptions of combat in military field manuals. The fighting seems to take place in an empty world. Illustrations usually show tanks and troops maneuvering across an open, partially wooded landscape, broken only by the occasional lonely farmhouse. Newer manuals depict forces deployed across a desert. These forces maneuver to defeat another army and seize terrain. The occupants of that terrain are not a consideration. This is not to say that military doctrine completely ignores the fact that civilians on the battlefield are common in warfare. Civilians will simply be dealt with by military units that are peripheral to the main effort.

The USASOC official history of army special operations makes the point that civil affairs and psychological operations (psyops) units were excluded from the planning for the Gulf War until very late in the process. The reason for this, the history notes, was "the Army's unfounded belief that it would operate in an environment virtually free of civilians."[28] This is in marked contrast to a realistic view of the world and is one of the problems with the application of the conventional model of war. The massive firepower favored by conventional planners will affect the population to some degree. Civilians cannot be expected to vacate their homes. This has been demonstrated in places like Beirut, Port-au-Prince, Mogadishu, and Afghanistan, where U.S. service members found themselves surrounded by thousands of people and occasionally fighting in the midst of them.[29] This problem affects army doctrine most strongly, because unlike the navy and air force, the army's domain is the ground, the place where people live.[30]

UNCONVENTIONAL WAR

Unconventional warfare, by contrast, not only recognizes the presence of a civil population, it also occurs in the midst of the population. In most cases, physical terrain is not important. In most forms of unconventional warfare, the objective is the allegiance of the people around whom, and presumably on whose behalf, the conflict is taking place. This is where the often-neglected, but terribly important, capabilities of the civil affairs and psyop components of SOF become critical. They are key in the struggle for people's minds and for their allegiance.[31]

Civil affairs units contain the expertise for working with the civilian population and restoring, or sometimes creating, the civic infrastructure of society. psyops units have the ability to perform an information function that allows a society to operate beyond the bounds of the village. They can help provide newspapers, radio and television broadcasts, and even loudspeaker teams to advise and inform the population. Most important, these units can help create a stable environment by increasing a government's legitimacy in the eyes of its constituents. Both civil affairs and psyops units are important capabilities for unconventional warfare.

People who do not understand the dynamics of UW are likely to give the wrong advice at crucial times, miss opportunities, and jump when they should have stood still. Unconventional warfare is primarily about politics but most often has a significant violent component. In theory, it is possible to adapt the conventional U.S. military structure to UW, but the reality is different. This was clearly demonstrated in the Vietnam War, where a conventional structure proved incapable of defeating an unconventional opponent. Massive firepower may win battles if the enemy is willing to fight in a manner that exposes his forces. Massive firepower will not be decisive if the enemy is unwilling to expose himself as a target.

THE U.S. MILITARY EXPERIENCE WITH UNCONVENTIONAL WARFARE

The U.S. Army's history of unconventional warfare began with continental militia in the American Revolution, which first fought its better-armed and better-trained opponents with a combination of political organization and guerrilla tactics. But when George Washington took command of the immature Continental Army, his first order of business was to create an army that could fight in the properly accepted European manner. Washington wanted a proper army; he wanted a conventional army. This was the only way, it was believed, to defeat the British.[32]

For the most part, Washington's emphasis marked the beginning of the end of serious thought within U.S. military circles about unconventional warfare methods until the twentieth century.[33] Even during the Civil War, when the famous Southern guerrillas, John S. Mosby and William Clarke Quantrill, developed colorful reputations with their daring raids and ambushes, the U.S. Army viewed them as nothing more than bandits with Southern sympathies who could expect to hang if captured.[34]

The army had considerable early experience with civil affairs, especially as they pertained to military government, beginning with Andrew Jackson's administration of New Orleans after the War of 1812. Army officers also worked closely with civil government in the California Territory during the 1840s and in Arizona and New Mexico following the Mexican War of 1846–48. By the close of the nineteenth century, U.S. soldiers had acquired further civil affairs experience in Cuba, Puerto Rico, and the Philippines. Unfortunately, this rich experience in unconventional warfare, counterinsurgency, and civil affairs was never adequately captured as doctrine.[35]

The frontier campaigns of the late nineteenth century are clear examples of the army's passion to be a proper, conventional force, on par with her European counterparts, despite an unsuitable environment to do so. Often criticized, the standard offensive mode of warfare involved heavy columns, tethered to slow-moving supply trains, moving ponderously through vast Western lands in search of an enemy who could easily observe the army's movements and vanish instantly. It is odd that the best army leaders of the period faithfully refused to face up to the realities of the frontier mission. It appears that because the army considered these campaigns to be aberrations, formal doctrine for Indian fighting was never developed.[36]

Likewise, the Boxer Rebellion of 1900 cost soldiers' lives but caused scarcely a ripple in Army Field Service Regulations. Similarly, the counterguerrilla campaign in the Philippines at the beginning of the twentieth century had no noticeable effect on U.S. military doctrine. It did, however, mark the army's first use of pacification techniques for counterinsurgency—measures intended to win the loyalty of the population from the guerrillas to the government. This early experiment in pacification was notably successful, but was never formalized, and army methods and practices continued to be rigidly conventional. Though numerous, experiences outside the conventional model were treated as abnormalities.[37]

WORLD WAR I

World War I saw no special operations in the modern sense. The U.S. Expeditionary Force did make use of psychological operations late in the war by producing propaganda leaflets. The propaganda section produced twenty surrender leaflets. Millions of copies were distributed over German lines by aircraft. The leaflets were simply comparing meager German field rations with the relatively plentiful food given Allied prisoners of war. These straightforward appeals were effective against German war-weary soldiers and were credited with numerous individual surrenders. Civil affairs functions were simply handled by the tactical units of the U.S. Third Army assigned to occupation duties.[38]

WORLD WAR II

World War II was the beginning of modern special operations and unconventional warfare for the U.S. military. For the first time, the U.S. government organized what would now be called special operations units. This included a collection of conventional organizations ranging from the commandos of the U.S.-Canadian First Special Service Force to navy combat and reconnaissance units, Marine raiders, the Alamo Scouts, and the 5307 Composite Unit. The army's original Ranger battalions were conceived during the war, and after repeated activation and inactivation, continue to exist today.[39]

THE ORIGINS OF MODERN SOF—RANGERS AND OSS

Of all the World War II special operations organizations, the Rangers and the paramilitary Office of Strategic Services (OSS) were the clearest forerunners of today's U.S. Special Operations Forces. They may also be the source of the confusion that surrounded the exact nature of the activities included in current special operations.

The mix of Ranger, psyop and civil affairs units, army special operations aviation units, and special forces all under the heading of special operations confuses and misleads. Ranger operations with supporting special operations aviation units fit neatly with the definition of conventional warfare. The others fit more logically under the label unconventional warfare.[40]

Rangers

The army's Rangers are regarded as the elite infantry of the U.S. military. They are a product of World War II that began as an experiment whose purpose was to benefit from the success of the British Commandos. Army Ranger units were formed to provide combat experience for U.S. soldiers by allowing them to accompany British Commando units on combat missions inside occupied western Europe.[41]

These men would then return to regular army units, where their experience would be of benefit. The men of the first Ranger battalion were recruited from U.S. forces then stationed in England. The unit was activated on June 19, 1942. The men received commando training in Northern Ireland before accompanying British troops into combat. However, with the allied invasion of Africa looming, the first complete battalion of Rangers to graduate from British commando training was assigned to the U.S. 1st Infantry Division for the landings.[42]

Today the Rangers are part of U.S. Special Operations Forces. What is special about them, however, is not so much what they do, but the proficiency with which they do it. Essentially, Rangers perform ordinary infantry functions, although they do so to a very high standard. Unfortunately, these highly trained and highly moti vated battalions were misused and quickly lost the special capabilities they originally held.[43] Though the Ranger battalions were dissolved after World War II, the concept of Rangers as highly trained conventional infantry remained firmly embedded in the Army's institutional memory, to be revived again and again.

Office of Strategic Services

The OSS, more than any other organization, can be identified as the direct ancestor of U.S. unconventional forces, especially the U.S. Army Special Forces. The influence of the OSS was profound. Much of what is really special about special operations has been passed down from the OSS.

The OSS was a civilian, or more accurately, a paramilitary agency that conducted a variety of wartime missions. U.S. Army Special Forces was designed based on the OSS concept. During World War II, small OSS teams would aid anti-German partisans in occupied territories by providing advice, liaison, and logistics assistance. OSS operators helped raise and train antifascist guerrillas in Yugoslavia, Burma, France, Norway, and China. Generally, the OSS enjoyed cordial relations with conventional commanders, who grew to appreciate the timely and accurate intelligence provided on the enemy.[44]

The OSS also gained a reputation for independence and daring that did not sit well with conventional commanders. To make matters worse, the organization began as a personal project of President Franklin Roosevelt. Roosevelt personally selected William O. Donovan, a well-connected Wall Street lawyer and World War I hero, to direct the newly formed Office of Coordinator of Information (OCI). OCI's mission was psychological warfare.[45]

Donovan had an expanded view of the proper role and function of the OCI. He recognized the strategic function of OCI as primarily psychological warfare (psywar). However, he saw psywar incorporating not only the overt information and persuasion functions traditionally associated with psychological warfare, but also a variety of secret intelligence, sabotage, subversion, and guerrilla activities. Donovan's idea of psychological war included the use of all means by which the goal is obtained other than those used by conventional military organizations. In other words, anything that was not conventional operations belonged to OCI. Donovan's close relationship with Roosevelt helped to sell this concept.[46]

This broad definition of psychological warfare was not welcomed in the Pentagon, because it would give Donovan potential control over almost any operation that was not clearly conventional. A strong lobbying effort was mounted, and in 1942 OCI's strategic psychological warfare function was transferred to the Office of War Information (OWI). The army also created a Psychological Warfare Branch in 1942, but dissolved it later that year when the OSS regained responsibility for military tactical psywar.[47]

All this bureaucratic maneuvering created a certain amount of confusion, and largely by default, conventional commanders in the various theaters performed psychological warfare in the traditional vein, tactical, short-range, short-term attempts to undermine enemy morale and induce surrender through the use of loudspeaker messages, leaflets, and radio broadcasts.[48]

Donovan's focus, however, was on special operations. OSS assumed responsibility for the missions historically ignored and scorned by many diplomats and military professionals. These missions included espionage, sabotage, "black" propaganda, guerrilla warfare, and other activities that were considered incongruous with traditional military activities. In December 1942, the Joint Chiefs finally agreed to give the OSS responsibility for guerrilla warfare. Donovan got what he wanted. This was also the initial mission given to U.S. Army Special Forces units when they were formed ten years later.[49]

The War Department never viewed the OSS favorably. The Joint Chiefs initially refused to provide personnel and supplies to the OSS and didn't give the new organization operating authority. Only after President Roosevelt personally intervened was the OSS was finally given an operational responsibility. Despite, or because of, their high-level sponsor, Donovan and the OSS were viewed with contempt.[50]

The OSS was strongly opposed by the army staff in general, and particularly by the intelligence chief, Maj. Gen. George Strong. Strong viewed guerrilla warfare as essentially unsound and unproductive. If guerrilla warfare were to be carried out at all, Strong felt it should be conducted by conventional army units and take the form of raids. The JCS was also concerned that OSS personnel would be conducting operations in U.S. theaters of war outside the control of the conventional theater commander. Accordingly, in 1942 JCS placed OSS-deployed elements under the control of the theater commanders in whose areas they were operating. OSS teams would no longer report directly to their own Washington headquarters. Only the personal relationship between Donovan and the president kept OSS operations alive.[51]

The Critics Gather

For all their accomplishments, the Rangers and the OSS both continued to have their critics. Their operations were accepted as important by the military only insofar as they supported the conventional battle. But even this was insufficient to gain acceptance. The arguments marshaled against them were very similar to those that would be heard again and again throughout the history of special operations forces. Little credit was given for their successes.

Both during and after World War II, senior military leaders generally felt that special operations units contributed little to the overall success of the allies. Critics charged that these elite units did nothing that could not be done equally well by conventional infantry. In the Pacific, Gen. Douglas MacArthur would not even permit the OSS to operate. MacArthur rejected OSS assistance in organizing the Philippine resistance. In evaluating OSS performance to the French Resistance, the War Department General Staff summary refers to the "so-called resistance activities in France," and grudgingly, credits "local French . . . for the end results accomplished."[52]

To be sure, many OSS activities were haphazard, poorly organized, and uncoordinated with overall operations. However, it is also true that the small-scale OSS unconventional warfare operations in Burma, Yugoslavia, China, Norway, and France tied down several German and Japanese divisions while maintaining the spirit of resistance in the occupied nations and providing tangible evidence of Allied support.[53]

Some critics not only felt that specialized units did not add much to the war effort but they also claimed that they were actually detrimental. These critics believed that these units were undeservedly glamorized, detracting from the record of conventional units. Another criticism was that such special organizations were counterproductive, because they monopolized needed resources and the most talented personnel for what were considered secondary operations. Additionally, the perceived arrogance and general boldness exhibited by these elites further aggravated an already-hostile environment.[54]

Toward the end of World War II, Donovan proposed that the OSS capability be maintained in the form of a central intelligence authority that would benefit by retaining many of the wartime OSS operatives. The notion of a peacetime organization conducting the same type of activities conducted by the OSS during the war generated critical headlines and public outrage that convinced Roosevelt to wait for a more opportune time. After the president's death in April 1945, it seemed unlikely that Donovan's proposal would receive serious attention.[55]

Under pressure from the military, the State Department, the FBI, and his personal convictions, Roosevelt's successor, Harry S. Truman, saw a spying and sabotage agency in peacetime as both unnecessary and politically unwise. The OSS was quickly disbanded on October 1, 1945, less than sixty days after the Japanese surrender. OSS research and analysis functions were assigned to the State Department and its remaining operational elements to the War Department. Once under the War Department control, OSS unconventional capabilities vanished almost immediately in the postwar drawdown.[56]

Some OSS personnel were given the option of joining the regular military, where they became influential in developing U.S. special operations capabilities during the 1950s. OSS veterans such as Aaron Bank, Herbert Bruckner, Jack Shannon, and Caesar Sivitella would revitalize the unconventional warfare concept in doctrine and practice and go on to become the founders of U.S. Army Special Forces. William Colby, another distinguished OSS veteran, would go to the newly formed Central Intelligence Agency (CIA), where he would conduct paramilitary operations in Southeast Asia and eventually become director of the Agency. Edward Lansdale was assigned to both military intelligence and the CIA after the war, a special arrangement that continues today.[57]

It is important to note that the special operations conducted during World War II were almost exclusively in support of conventional operations. The Rangers provided support by conducting special purpose raids and by acting as elite infantry. The OSS teams tied down large numbers of enemy forces by conducting sabotage in the enemy's rear area. They also kept resistance movements alive in occupied areas and helped direct their efforts against a common enemy.

Military planners never recognized the efforts of the OSS and the partisans they supported as anything other than simply an extension of conventional operations.

There was also a strong tendency for strategic-level planners to see these partisans only in the context of the allied struggle against the Axis powers and not in the context of their own domestic political environment. The fact that men like Josip Broz Tito in Yugoslavia and Ho Chi Minh in Indochina were outright revolutionaries with serious long-term interests was unimportant to U.S. senior planners.[58]

Conversely, OSS operators found issues such as socioeconomic and political factors to be of great importance in planning and conducting operations. In fact, these issues were crucial in determining whether an operation would ever be executed. Bank offers a clear example of this when he explains that an OSS plan to infiltrate members of the French army into Indochina for a raid against the Japanese was canceled because Ho Chi Minh's OSS-assisted Vietminh would be hostile toward the French operatives. The relationship between OSS and War Department staffs were often strained because of the different variables that were considered in the planning and conduct of operations. This friction contributed to anti-OSS feelings in the upper levels of the uniformed services.[59]

In the end, there was no serious attempt to capture the World War II special operations experiences in the form of military doctrine. Little attention was paid to unconventional warfare until hostilities in Vietnam; and then, counterguerrilla techniques were emphasized rather than the more complex considerations of counterinsurgency.

THE EARLY POSTWAR ERA

Shortly after World War II, U.S. defense policy became centered on containing Soviet expansion, and from the late 1940s to the early 1990s, containment was the central element of U.S. national security policy. This policy focused on nuclear war to the detriment of other forms of engagement, including unconventional warfare.

Shortly after dissolving the OSS, President Truman established the Central Intelligence Group (CIG) to reconcile conflicting intelligence assessments produced by various elements within the U.S. government. As a result of the 1947 National Security Act, the CIG was replaced with a permanent national intelligence structure, a Central Intelligence Agency (CIA), directly responsible to the president, and an advisory National Security Council (NSC). During this period, the newly established CIA began to experiment with intelligence gathering and supporting foreign resistance movements.[60]

It didn't take long before the newly created NSC issued directive NSC 4, "Coordination of Foreign Intelligence Measures." This directive ordered the secretary of state to coordinate anticommunist propaganda. A classified annex, NSC 4A, directed the CIA to support the State Department with covert operations. There was an overlap, which still exists, between CIA covert action and military special operations and unconventional warfare. Consequently, NSC 4A also called for the agency to coordinate with the Joint Chiefs of Staff for the planning and conduct of operations during wartime. This directives assumed a clear distinction between peacetime and wartime, a condition that is anything but clear.[61]

It wasn't long until the first postwar involvement in counterinsurgency was under way. After communist guerrilla activity began in Greece in 1946, President Truman presented what became known as the Truman Doctrine. This doctrine held that in order to protect its own national security, the United States must "support free peoples who are resisting attempted subjugation by armed minorities or by outside pressures."[62]

The Truman Doctrine program for security assistance to Greece established the prototype for such assistance efforts. Congress authorized funding for relief assistance and also for the employment of U.S. civilian and military personnel. A U.S. military mission was dispatched to Greece, where it assisted in rebuilding the Greek army along conventional lines. The insurgency gradually died out for various reasons, most of them unconnected with the new U.S.-model Greek army. However, the training given to the Greek military was erroneously considered a primary factor in the defeat of the insurgents. The awkward fact that the Greek problem had been a communist insurgency rather than a partisan resistance was not allowed to cloud the issue. The vital distinction between insurgency and guerrilla war was obscured and largely lost. This presumed comparison between guerrilla war, a military technique, and insurgency, a political condition, became a root cause of much subsequent difficulty. The army was content to learn the wrong lessons from its involvement in this counterinsurgency effort.[63]

THE EMERGENCE OF DOCTRINE

The army's first attempt to write a doctrine for dealing with guerrillas and conducting unconventional warfare was based on the experience in Greece and the partisan support operations of World War II. FM 31-20, Operations Against Guerrilla Forces, published in 1951, stated that guerrilla war was war conducted by irregular forces in conjunction with regular forces as a phase of a normal war. The manual stated that guerrilla operations were usually of short duration and executed by employing regular forces in the enemy's rear areas.[64]

The subsequent versions of the manual continued to characterize counterguerrilla operations as purely a tactical military issue. While political factors were recognized, they remained in the background. More important, the doctrine reflected an unambiguous theme—that guerrilla operations required little special expertise and were simply incidental to, and supportive of conventional operations. General Maxwell Taylor reinforced this thinking by stating, "If the armed forces were prepared to cope with nuclear war, they could take care of lesser contingencies."[65] This became the central concept to the U.S. approach to insurgency and the preferred model of unconventional warfare for the U.S. military.

THE ERA OF MASSIVE RETALIATION

During the Dwight D. Eisenhower administration, U.S. national security policy had become fixed on the Soviet threat. This meant that U.S. forces needed to be able to meet and defeat the heavy-armored formations of the Soviet Union on the plains of Western Europe. The need to counter Warsaw Pact forces in Western Europe served as both the justification for a large standing armed force and the principal mission requirement driving military force structure and doctrine.[66]

Despite this situation, this fixation on the Soviet conventional threat led the U.S. military into the arena of unconventional war. It soon became clear that the United States was unlikely to pay for the kind of standing peacetime armies that could defeat the awesome conventional Soviet armored threat. Unlike the Soviet autocracy, with its command economy, the United States had to look for a more cost-effective solution.

Eisenhower wanted maximum security at minimal cost, which led to a policy of nuclear deterrence. He referred to his concept of security as "massive retaliation." The president also expressed his preference for the conventional model of military operations, disdaining the messy business of small, unconventional wars. "I saw no sense in wasting manpower in costly small wars that could not achieve decisive results under the political and military circumstances then existing."[67] The idea that anything other than large-scale conventional combat could ultimately be decisive never seemed to have crossed Ike's thoroughly conventional mind.[68]

Two army chiefs of staff who served in the Eisenhower administration, Generals Matthew B. Ridgeway and Maxwell D. Taylor, opposed Eisenhower's defense policies. For Ridgeway and Taylor, unless national survival was at stake, the United States would not use nuclear weapons. Nuclear deterrence was largely a bluff. Secondly, if the use of nuclear weapons had limited applicability, they believed that strong conventional forces would best serve the U.S. national interest.[69]

Ridgeway and Taylor both arguably had a parochial agenda. A national defense based largely on nuclear retaliation was not agreeable to army planners. Still, there was logic in their criticism. Accordingly, General Taylor proposed a national military program based on his belief that U.S. interests would be threatened by a series of limited wars and Soviet-backed insurgencies in third world nations. The intent of Taylor's program was to improve the army's capability to fight small wars in non-European environments. Although Taylor and Ridgeway seemed to grasp the limitations of a strategy of massive retaliation, their concept of limited war meant small-scale conventional war below the nuclear threshold. For the army, it also represented a means of survival in a policy environment oriented toward nuclear war.[70]

After retiring from the army in 1959, Taylor wrote *The Uncertain Trumpet,* in which he reiterated his belief that Soviet nuclear arms, the rise of mutual deterrence, and Soviet aggressiveness made armed conflict short of nuclear war likely, demanding flexible "limited war" forces. However, this was not an endorsement of an unconventional warfare concept or a recommendation for the enhancement of a special operations capability within the armed forces. General Taylor's intention was simply to enhance U.S. conventional abilities so U.S. policy makers would not be forced to use nuclear weapons for any issue short of national survival. It is ironic that Taylor's book came to the attention of Sen. John F. Kennedy, the Democratic nominee for president. Kennedy was impressed and used the general's arguments in criticizing Eisenhower's defense policies during the 1960 presidential campaign.[71]

SPECIAL FORCES PERSEVERE
In spite of what appeared to be an overt bias against unconventional warfare, special forces (SF) continued to exist in small units overseas and in an obscure corner of Fort Bragg. The army's feeling about the role of SF is illustrated by the 1960 decision to assign an official lineage, a sort of military pedigree, to these forces. This official lineage consisted entirely of various elite, special-purpose conventional units, including Rogers's Rangers of French and Indian War fame and extending through the World War II Ranger battalions and the Canadian–U.S. 1st Special Service Force. The OSS, not being an army organization, was not initially included. Even the very successful irregular warfare exploits during the American Revolution of Francis Marion and Nathaniel Greene were unclaimed. It certainly seemed that the army did not want to claim any heritage to unconventional warfare.[72]

The election of John F. Kennedy as president in 1960 marked a sea change in military thinking in the White House. Kennedy had long been concerned about the threat of communist-supported insurgencies. He was especially concerned by Soviet premier Nikita Khrushchev's pledge to support wars of national liberation, with the clear implication that this was an important step in the collapse of the West. Kennedy directed Robert McNamara, his secretary of defense, to begin developing a counterinsurgency capability.[73]

McNamara soon told an army audience, "To deal with the Communist guerrilla threat requires some shift in our military thinking. We have been used to developing big weapons and mounting large forces. Here we must work with companies and individual soldiers."[74] It is important to note that McNamara's emphasis was on scale rather than on fundamental changes in the way of dealing with this new threat. It is also interesting that McNamara would be a key player in sending massive amounts of weapons and large conventional forces to fight in Vietnam.

SOUTHEAST ASIA

By the late 1950s, the United States found itself drawn into operations against communist revolutionary movements around the world, especially in Southeast Asia. Initially, unconventional warfare activities in Laos and Vietnam had been the responsibility of the CIA, although a small number of special forces soldiers were assigned to the U.S. Military Advisory Group in Vietnam during the 1950s. In Laos, special forces personnel had participated in Project White Star since 1959. By 1961 three hundred of them were part of a joint DoD-CIA project to enable the Lao army to counter insurgent activity by Pathet Lao guerrillas operating with assistance from the North Vietnamese army. Since the departure of the French, the SF soldiers had become active combat advisers as well as trainers.[75]

From the viewpoint of the Special Warfare Center,[76] the Laos mission provided a chance to test their methods, weapons, and communications in combat. It gave them their first large-scale success, new credibility, and a wealth of experience plus visibility in the White House. It also affirmed a SF-CIA connection that made U.S. military leadership nervous and that continues today.

In addition to their popularity with the White House and the CIA, the special forces were attracting attention both publicly and inside the army, but in a manner that would later prove problematic. Kennedy was concerned about communist encroachment in the third world. The continuing insurgency in Laos and later in Vietnam worried him greatly, and he was convinced that the struggle in Southeast Asia was an example of Soviet-sponsored insurgency. President Kennedy soon realized that the special forces provided the only available tool that would allow him to quickly influence events in Laos and Vietnam.

In 1961 the president visited Fort Bragg to see the SF soldiers in action. Although what he saw was partly show, Kennedy witnessed a display of combat skills from bows to exotic rifles, hand-to-hand combat abilities, and multilingual fluency that was impressive. Kennedy was struck by the dash and daring of the elite soldiers and equally struck by the fact that they had been trained to fight as guerrillas. Their individual and collective excellence appealed to him. The president saw the special forces as a remedy for Soviet-supported insurgency.[77]

The special forces now had a high-level sponsor just as had been the case with the OSS and Roosevelt. Kennedy's relationship with the SF grew so close that he insisted on personal contact with the commander of the Special Warfare Center, BG William P. Yarborough. Still, the concept of unconventional warfare met with considerable resistance from within the military establishment. The president also tended to treat the special forces as a separate service. He would occasionally ask why the SF did not have a representative at meetings involving the four military services. This special relationship that provided access, visibility, and influence for the SF was not welcomed at the JCS level.

Friction between the Joint Staff and the SF was made worse by National Security Action Memorandum (NSAM) 162, published in 1962. This memorandum assigned additional SF personnel to support CIA covert paramilitary operations. To make matters worse, the same memorandum directed the DoD to increase overall support to covert operations both in cooperation with the CIA and unilaterally. The Pentagon was not only losing control of a unique military capability; it was also being directed to pay the CIA's bills.[78]

The army leadership felt that the special forces should be treated as a subcomponent of the conventional army and not as if it was a unique force in its own right. The SF's high-level sponsorship constrained the response from the senior levels of the army. Accordingly, a clever plan to put the special forces back in their box was implemented. The plan called for superficial compliance coupled with long-term diminishment. Funding needs were usually approved quickly, material requests were approved more slowly, and personnel requests were often not met at all. Fixing this situation would eventually require legislation mandating change.[79] Legislation would eventually modify behavior, but it would not change attitudes about SOF.

The selection of the U.S. Army Special Forces as the instrument of Kennedy's policy of anticommunist engagement in Southeast Asia is generally portrayed as the result of their military skills and self-proclaimed elite status, all of which appealed to the president's own values. But at least as important in the choice of SF was the type of flexible soldier they produced and attracted and the unit's emphasis on foreign language ability. Little attention was paid to the organization's intensive area orientation, an OSS technique formalized in SF doctrine as the "area study." This technique amounted to an in-depth study of the geographic area in which the SF unit was to be employed. This was not simply a weather and terrain analysis of the type made by conventional units, but also a thorough demographic analysis of the area of operations. More important, it was an attempt to understand the political context and motivations of the struggle. These elements quickly became obscured and lost in favor of the image of the special forces soldier as a deadly and resourceful fighter on the mythical model of the American frontiersman.

Regardless of the army leadership's apparent lack of enthusiasm, the men of the special forces, along with their psyops and civil affairs brethren, were soon deeply embroiled in the Vietnam conflict, a long, costly, and frustrating struggle that would shape the future not only of special operations forces but of the entire U.S. military as well.

LEGISLATIVE CHANGE

"I think we have an abort situation," Defense Secretary Harold Brown informed President Jimmy Carter on April 24, 1980. Carter simply responded, "Let's go with his [the ground commander's] recommendation." The mission to rescue fifty American hostages had to be aborted. At a desolate site in Iran known as "Desert One," tragedy occurred minutes later, when two aircraft collided on the ground and eight men died. The failed mission struck a blow to American prestige and further eroded the public's confidence in the U.S. government.[80]

The event culminated a period of Special Operations Forces (SOF) decline in the 1970s. SOF capabilities had deteriorated throughout the post-Vietnam era, a time marked by significant friction between the SOF and the conventional military and by significant budget cuts for special operations. The Desert One disaster led the Defense Department to appoint an investigative panel, chaired by the former chief of naval operations, Adm. James L. Holloway. The Holloway Commission's findings caused the Defense Department to create the Counterterrorist Joint Task Force and the Special Operations Advisory Panel.

Desert One did serve to strengthen the resolve of some within the Department of Defense to reform the SOF. Army chief of staff General Edward C. "Shy" Meyer called for a further restructuring of special operations capabilities. Although unsuccessful at the joint level, Meyer consolidated army SOF units under the new 1st Special Operations Command in 1982, a significant step to improve the army SOF.

Yet, there was a small but growing sense in Congress of the need for military reforms. In June 1983, the Senate Armed Services Committee, under the chairmanship of Sen. Barry Goldwater, began a two-year-long study of the Defense Department that included an examination of SOF. Two events in October 1983 further demonstrated the need for change—the terrorist bombing attack in Lebanon and the invasion of Grenada. The loss of 237 Marines to terrorism, combined with the command and control problems that occurred during the Grenada invasion, refocused congressional attention on the growing threat of low-intensity conflict and on the issue of joint interoperability.[81]

With concern mounting on Capitol Hill, the Department of Defense created the Joint Special Operations Agency on January 1, 1984. Unfortunately, this agency had neither operational nor command authority over any of the special operation forces. Consequently, the agency did little to improve SOF readiness, capabilities, or policies. This is hardly what Congress had in mind as a systemic fix for the SOF's problems. Within the Defense Department, there were a few staunch SOF supporters. Noel Koch, principal deputy assistant secretary of defense for international security affairs, and his deputy, Lynn Rylander, both advocated SOF reforms.[82]

At the same time, a few visionaries on Capitol Hill were determined to overhaul SOF. They included Senators Sam Nunn (D-Ga.) and William Cohen (R-Maine), both members of the Armed Services Committee, and Representative Dan Daniel (D-Va.), the chairman of the Readiness Subcommittee. Congressman Daniel had become convinced that the U.S. military establishment was not interested in special operations, that the country's capability in this area was second rate, and that SOF command and control was an endemic problem. Senators Nunn and Cohen also felt strongly that the Department of Defense was not preparing adequately for future threats. Senator Nunn expressed a growing frustration with the service's practice of reallocating monies appropriated for SOF modernization to non-SOF programs. Senator Cohen agreed that the United States needed a clearer organizational focus and chain of command for special operations to deal with low-intensity conflicts.[83]

In October 1985, the Senate Armed Services Committee published the results of its two-year review of the U.S. military structure, entitled "Defense Organization: The Need For Change." Mr. James R. Locher III, the principal author of this study, also examined past special operations and speculated on the most likely future threats. This influential document led to the Goldwater-Nichols Defense Reorganization Act of 1986.[84]

By spring 1986, SOF advocates had introduced reform bills in both houses of Congress. On May 15, Senator Cohen introduced the Senate bill, cosponsored by Senator Nunn and others, which called for a joint military organization for the SOF and the establishment of an office in the Defense Department to ensure adequate funding and policy emphasis for low-intensity conflict and special operations. Representative Daniel's proposal went even further—he wanted a national special operations agency headed by a civilian who would bypass the Joint Chiefs and report directly to the secretary of defense. This would keep the Joint Chiefs and the services out of the SOF budget process.[85]

Congress held hearings on the two bills in the summer of 1986. Adm. William J. Crowe Jr., chairman of the Joint Chiefs of Staff, led the Pentagon's opposition to the bills. He proposed, as an alternative, a new special operations forces command led by a three-star general. This proposal was not well received on Capitol Hill. Congress wanted a four-star general in charge to give SOF more clout.[86]

Retired Army Maj. Gen. Richard Scholtes gave the most compelling reasons for change. Scholtes, who commanded the joint special operations task force in Grenada, explained how conventional force leaders misused SOF during the operation by not allowing them to use their unique capabilities. The result was high SOF casualties. After his formal testimony, Scholtes met privately with a small number of senators to elaborate on the problems that he had encountered in Grenada.[87]

Both the House and Senate passed SOF reform bills, which then went to a conference committee for reconciliation. Senate and House conferees forged a compromise. The bill called for a unified combatant command headed by a four-star general for all SOF, an assistant secretary of defense for special operations and low-intensity conflict (SOLIC), a coordinating board for low-intensity conflict within the National Security Council, and a new Major Force Program-11 (MFP-11) for SOF (the so-called "SOF checkbook"). The House had conceded on the issue of a new civilian-led agency but insisted on including a separate budget line to protect SOF funding. The final bill was attached as a rider to the 1987 Defense Authorization Act and was signed into law in October 1986. Congress had mandated that the president create a unified combatant command. Congress clearly intended to force the Department of Defense to face up to the realities of past failures and emerging threats. The Department of Defense was responsible for implementing the law.[88]

The legislation promised to improve SOF in several respects. Once implemented, MFP-11 provided SOF with control over its own resources, better enabling it to modernize the force. Additionally, the law fostered interservice cooperation. A single commander for all SOF activities promoted interoperability among the forces assigned to the command. The establishment of a four-star commander and an assistant secretary of defense for special operations and low-intensity conflict would give SOF a voice at the highest levels of the Defense Department.

MALICIOUS IMPLEMENTATION

Implementing the provisions and mandates of the Nunn-Cohen Act, however, was neither rapid nor smooth. One of the first issues to surface was appointing an assistant secretary of defense, whose principal duties included examining special operations activities and low-intensity conflict activities of the Department of Defense. The DoD was moving slowly toward establishing the SOLIC office. Many of the Pentagon's steps signaled to SOF supporters that the implementation of the legislation was unfortunately malicious. Assistant Secretary of Defense Richard Armitage, who actively fought against the passage of the legislation, was attempting to gain control of the new organization. One of Armitage's first steps was to appoint his deputy, Lawrence Ropka Jr., as the interim head of the new office. Once in charge, Ropka held a staff meeting and said, "If you favor implementing this legislation, you're being disloyal to the Pentagon."[89] This was just the kind of attitude that Congress feared.

There were other examples of malicious avoidance of implementation of the legislation. Armitage and Ropka limited the size of the initial SOLIC staff to thirty-nine. Offices headed by assistant secretaries normally have hundreds of staff personnel. Even more telling, Office of the Secretary of Defense leadership had decided to move the SOLIC staff outside the Pentagon into an unsecured building. It should not have been a surprise that the handling of the new SOLIC organization infuriated Capitol Hill. SOF supporters in the Senate were angry enough to delay all confirmations of Reagan administration high-level appointees until a suitable nominee for the new assistant secretary was received by the Senate.[90]

Still, the administration would not submit an acceptable nomination for the new assistant secretary of defense (ASD) post. Congress had lost all patience. In November 1987, the House and Senate conference committee on the National Defense Authorization Act acted on the recommendation of Senate Armed Services Committee staffer, Jim Locher, to solve the impasse over the ASD nomination. In December 1987, the Congress directed Secretary of the Army John O. Marsh to carry out the ASD (SOLIC) duties until a suitable replacement was approved by the Senate. Not until eighteen months after the legislation passed did Amb. Charles Whitehouse assume the duties of ASD (SOLIC).[91]

Meanwhile, the establishment of USSOCOM provided its own measure of excitement. A quick solution to manning and basing a brand new unified command seemed to be to abolish an existing command, United States Readiness Command (USREDCOM), a command that did not appear to have a viable mission in the post Goldwater-Nichols era, and redesignate it as USSOCOM. USREDCOM's commander, Gen. James Lindsay, had had some special operations experience. On January 23, 1987, the Joint Chiefs of Staff recommended to the secretary of defense that USREDCOM be disestablished to provide billets and facilities for USSOCOM. President Ronald Reagan approved the establishment of the new command on April 13, 1987. The Department of Defense activated USSOCOM on April 16, 1987 and nominated General Lindsay to be the first commander in chief (USCINCSOC). The Senate accepted him without debate.[92]

USSOCOM had its activation ceremony on June 1, 1987. Guest speakers included William H. Taft IV, deputy secretary of defense, and Adm. William J. Crowe Jr., two men who had opposed the Nunn-Cohen amendment. Admiral Crowe's speech at the ceremony advised General Lindsay to integrate the new command into the mainstream military. Crowe said:

> First, break down the wall that has more or less come between special operations forces and the other parts of our military, the wall that some people will try to build higher. Second, educate the rest of the military—spread a recognition and understanding of what you do, why you do it, and how important it is that you do it. Last, integrate your efforts into the full spectrum of our military capabilities.[93]

Putting this advice into action would pose significant challenges, considering the opposition the Defense Department had shown.

THE STRATEGIC UTILITY OF SPECIAL OPERATIONS

The fundamental purpose of a military organization is its role in implementing national policy. Accordingly, it is important to identify what is distinct and what is distinctly valuable about special operations forces. Colin Gray uses and defines the term "strategic utility" to mean "the contribution of a particular kind of military activity to the course and outcome of an entire conflict."[94] In contrast, tactical utility refers to the impact of a military activity on a particular engagement.

There are a few general points about the concept of strategic utility that will help in understanding why the SOF are particularly strategically useful. First, accomplishing maximum results with minimum effort is a military virtue. In military terms, this is called economy of force. Yet, this principle must be balanced with the need for reliable action. There are cases where brute force is not applicable. Special operations, when properly applied, are expressions of agility, maneuver, and finesse. There are missions that only SOF can properly perform. Conversely, special operations are not always an alternative approach to war. In fact, a special operation can have utility as a precision door opener for a conventional force.[95]

Second, special operations often have strategic value even if there are no immediate effects on a battlefield, on a campaign, or on a war as a whole. This means that special operations can have strategic value when conducted independently or when conducted in coordination with conventional forces. A strategic perspective is needed to be able to understand the concept of strategic utility. Very often the strategic significance of a special operation is not contained within that operation. The strategic significance of a special operation lies in its contribution to the outcome of the war or the achievement of some other policy goal.[96]

Finally, tactical success has a way of dominating serious debate over strategic utility. Tactical success may be self-validating, but it may also result in self-deception. Special operations must never become ends in themselves. These operations should be approached as a component of a broad strategic plan. Explanatory cover such as assertions about the value of the operation on morale, or for testing new techniques, equipment, ideas, and men cover nothing more than an example of tactics driving strategy. Political decision makers and military planners must be aware of the need to integrate special operations into the strategic blueprint.[97]

There are numerous examples of special operations that demonstrate strategic utility. However, there are three categories of operations that are exceptionally significant—economy of force, expansion of choice, and shaping of the future.

Economy of force refers to the claim that special operations can achieve significant results with limited forces. Special operations have historically acted as force multipliers for conventional forces by preparing the battlefield for conventional operations. Partisan operations during World War II by the OSS fit this claim. Missions such as intelligence gathering, deception, and sabotage can open the door and facilitate successful conventional operations. Additionally, amphibious raiding during World War II demonstrated the low cost of special operations compared to the results achieved.[98] Accelerating the pace of military success can also be achieved by special operations. The Brandenburgers and the Luftwaffe's paratroopers served this purpose.[99] They were accelerators of success for conventional operations. In conflicts of all kinds, special operations forces can conduct operations at a fraction of the cost of conventional forces and deliver an asymmetric return on investment.[100]

Expansion of choice means that special operations can expand the options available to political and military leaders. Policy requires a means of implementation. In peacetime, special operations provide policy makers with a unique tool to support political goals. In wartime, special operations increase the choices available to military commanders. Arguably, after the terrorist attacks in the United States on September 11, 2001, the initial U.S. response in Afghanistan was an option made available by a special operations capability.[101]

Many claim that there are always alternatives to the use of force. There are, of course, four traditional instruments of statecraft—diplomatic, economic, military, and informational. However, there are some situations that cannot be resolved without resort to force or coercion. A special operations force provides decision makers with a means to use force flexibly, minimally, and precisely. Simply possessing a proven capability can affect the calculus of an opponent. In December 1996, the Tupac Amaru stormed the Japanese ambassador's residence in Lima, Peru. The ambassador was hosting a party and hundreds of diplomats were in attendance. Diplomatic negotiations were going nowhere, but the discovery, by the press, that the United States had positioned a special operations force within striking distance of Lima and was conducting rehearsals to rescue the Americans held hostage, resulted in the release of the Americans, British, and German hostages. All others remained in the ambassador's residence for several months until the Peruvians mounted a successful rescue operation. Intelligence reports indicated that the Tupac Amaru released only the Americans, British, and German hostages because of the proven special operations capability of their home governments. In times of both war and peace, whether operating independently or in support of a larger operation, special operations enhance the flexibility with which force can be applied. Special operations can offer a low-cost solution to precisely targeted problems.

Finally, shaping the future refers to special operations as a major contributor to unconventional warfare and the unique way this activity can shape the future course of political events. The previous two claims apply mostly to special operations as part of a larger conventional operation. But unconventional warfare can prepare the political ground for power struggles to be resolved in a way that supports U.S. interests without the introduction of large numbers of conventional forces. In fact, conventional forces rarely offer a viable alternative. For example, the United States special operations community has long been engaged in Latin America. Although the degree of influence this contact produced is difficult to judge, the fact that over a forty-year period almost every country in Latin America adopted a democratic form of government with the support of the military elite in those countries cannot be ignored.[102]

During conflict, special operations can shape people's views of their occupier. OSS operations encouraged people to resist, which obliged the occupier to wage war against a civilian population. This not only tied up enemy forces in rear area missions but it also led to stronger resistance movements. Special operations can demonstrate continuing political interest and commitment in an area. The commitment of special operations forces to a country can be a more important gesture than other forms of action. Special operations can be designed to achieve military or political-psychological objectives that ultimately lead to achieving strategic effects. These specially designed operations can shape the future in conflicts of all kinds. However, it is important to note that political conditions must be favorable for such operations to succeed.[103]

Chapter 3

Organizational Theory and Processes of Innovation

A COMMON REMARK WITH RESPECT TO ORGANIZATIONS is that it is not the organization that's important, it is the people in it. There is a great deal of truth in the view that people make a difference. But there are two errors in the "only people matter" view. The first is that people are the products, not only of their biology, family, and schooling, but also of their organizational position or role. As Herbert Simon said many years ago, a person

> does not live for months or years in a particular position in an organization, exposed to some streams of communication, shielded from others, without the most profound effects upon what he knows, believes, attends to, hopes, wishes, emphasizes, fears, and proposes.[1]

Most great military leaders were not simply gifted people who happened to be generals; they were people whose views and skills had been shaped by the organizations in which they spent their lives.[2] Moreover, what they were able to accomplish depended on having the authority and resources with which to act. This is the second difficulty with the view that only people matter. Herbert Simon comments:

> If organization is inessential, if all we need is the man, why do we insist on creating a position for the man? Why not let each create his own position, appropriate to his personal abilities and qualities? Why does the boss have to be called the boss before his creative energies can be amplified by the organization? And finally, if we have to give a man some measure of authority before his personal qualities can be transformed into effective influence, in what ways may his effectiveness depend on the manner in which others are organized around him?[3]

An organization is not simply, or even principally, a set of boxes, lines, and titles on an organizational chart. An organization, in the words of Chester Barnard, is a

46

"system of consciously coordinated personal activities or forces."[4] The most important thing to know is how that coordination is accomplished.

GERMAN MILITARY ORGANIZATION

The development of German military doctrine in the interwar years presents an interesting case of why organization matters. The German system of coordination was designed to enhance the capacity for independent action toward a general goal and within an overall system of discipline. The key difference between the German army in 1940 and its French opponents was not in grand strategy, but in tactics and organizational arrangements well suited to implementing those tactics. Both sides drew lessons from the disastrous trench warfare of World War I. The Germans drew the right ones.[5]

By the end of that war, it was evident to all that large frontal assaults by infantry against well-entrenched soldiers manning machine guns and supported by artillery would not be successful. A rifleman who must cross three hundred yards of no man's land, staggering through shell holes made by artillery bombardment and desperately trying to get over or around barbed-wire barricades had no chance against the fire of dug-in machine guns. The French decided that, under these circumstances, the advantage belonged to the defense. Consequently, they organized their armies around a squad of twelve men whose task it was to fire and support a machine gun. The rifle was regarded as a secondary weapon. These soldiers, dedicated to the support of the machine gun, were ideally suited to defend a trench but hopelessly ill suited to a war of maneuver.[6]

The Germans drew a different lesson. Trench warfare led to stalemate, and Germany, surrounded on all sides by potential enemies with larger manpower reserves, could not afford a stalemate. Therefore, the defensive advantage of entrenched machine gunners had to be overcome. There were two ways to accomplish this—to make the attacking soldiers bulletproof by putting them in armored vehicles, or to make them hard to shoot by deploying them as infiltrators who could slip through weak points in the enemy's line and attack the machine guns from the rear. When we think about the Panzer divisions with their hundreds of tanks, we may suppose that the Germans chose the first way. They did not. The Panzers were chiefly designed to exploit a breakthrough, not to create one. To create it, the Germans emphasized infiltration warfare.[7]

This type of warfare not only fit the lessons of World War I; it also fit the realities of Germany's geopolitical position. Under the Treaty of Versailles, Germany was limited to a small professional army that would have to contend with enemies in both the east and the west. It could not match the combined manpower of all of these rivals, and it could not afford a war of attrition. Thus, a quick and decisive offensive waged by numerically inferior forces was essential to success.[8]

Such tactics required a certain kind of organization, and the Germans set about creating it. An army that could probe enemy defenses, infiltrate points, and rapidly exploit breakthroughs could not be an army that was centrally directed or dependent on detailed plans worked out in advance. It had to be an army equipped and organized in such a way as to permit independent action by its smallest units.

Designing and equipping such a unit were the easiest tasks. The difficult and crucial job was to staff and lead it in such a way that it was capable of intelligent, aggressive, and independent action. This meant that the best soldiers would have to be placed in the squads and not assigned to headquarters or other rear elements. The officers and noncommissioned officers commanding these small units would have to be given substantial freedom of action. Officers and men alike would have to be given incentives that rewarded fighting prowess and risk taking. Following each battle, there would be a rigorous evaluation of the efforts and results. For two decades, the German army devoted itself to solving these organizational problems.[9]

What resulted was a system wholly at odds with the stereotypical view of the German army as composed of fanatical soldiers blindly obeying the dictates of a Prussian general staff. The central concept was *Auftragstatik,* translated by Martin van Creveld in his analysis of German fighting power as a "mission-oriented command system." Commanders were to tell their subordinates precisely what was to be accomplished but not how to accomplish it. The mission must "express the will of the commander in an unmistakable way," but the methods of execution should be limited "only where essential for coordination with other commands." The German army had remarkably little paperwork. Orders were clear but brief.[10]

Soldiers and officers were indoctrinated with the primacy of combat and the central importance of initiative. The 1936 command manual put it this way:

> The emptiness of the battlefield demands independently thinking and acting fighters who exploit each situation in a considered, determined, and bold way. They must be thoroughly conscious of the fact only results matter. . . . Thus decisive action remains the first prerequisite for success in war.[11]

To maintain fighting spirit among the squads, platoons, and companies on which combat success so heavily depended, the German army was recruited and organized on a local basis. Military units up to the size of a division were formed out of men with the same regional backgrounds—Prussians, Saxons, Bavarians, and so on. When replacements were necessary, they were drawn, so long as wartime exigencies permitted, from the same regions and organized into groups that were then given their final training by a division's field replacement battalion to ensure that the new troops would be organized and trained by the men alongside whom they would fight.[12]

The result was an organization well adapted to the task of getting men to fight against heavy odds in a confused, fluid setting far from army headquarters and without detailed instructions. As Creveld summarizes it, the German soldier "fought for the reasons men have always fought: because he felt himself a member of a well-integrated, well-led team whose structure, administration, and functioning were perceived to be . . . equitable and just."[13]

CREATING ORGANIZATION—BUREAUCRACY

Leaders who wish to improve an organization often begin by trying to clarify its goals. Sometimes this is useful. But government agencies, much more than business firms, are likely to have general, vague, or inconsistent goals about which clarity and agreement can only occasionally be obtained. Often, any effort to clarify them will result either in the output of meaningless verbiage or the exposure of deep disagreements. The German, French, and British armies all had the same goal—to defeat the enemy. Thinking harder about that goal would not necessarily have led to any deeper understanding of how one defeats an enemy.[14]

There are two ways to look at government agencies: from the top down and from the bottom up. Most books, and almost all elected officials, tend to take the first view. The academic perspective, much influenced by Max Weber, typically centers on the structure, purposes, and resources of the organization. The political perspective draws attention to the identity, beliefs, and decisions of the top officials of the agency. These are important matters, but arguably the emphasis given to them has caused us to lose sight of what government agencies do and how the doing of it is related to attaining goals.[15]

By looking at bureaucracies from the bottom up, we can assess the extent to which their management systems and administrative arrangements are well or poorly suited to the tasks the agencies actually perform. By taking this perspective we can explain behavior that otherwise seems puzzling. This approach is more likely under the contingency theory model that will be discussed later.[16]

RULES AND DISCRETION

Max Weber was the first to observe and write about bureaucracies that developed in Germany during the nineteenth century. He considered them to be efficient, rational, and honest and a big improvement over the haphazard administration they replaced. Weber said that the great virtue of bureaucracy, indeed defining characteristic, was that it was an institutional method for applying general rules to specific cases, thereby making the actions of government fair and predictable.[17]

Bureaucratic coordination of activities, he argued, is the distinctive mark of the modern era. Bureaucracies are organized according to rational principles. Offices are ranked in a hierarchical order, and their operations are characterized by impersonal rules. Incumbents are governed by well-defined responsibilities and delimited spheres of duty. Appointments are made according to specialized qualifications.[18]

This bureaucratic coordination of the actions of large numbers of people has become the dominant feature of modern organizations. Only through this organizational device has large-scale planning, both for the modern state and the modern economy, become possible. Only through it could heads of state mobilize and centralize resources of political power, which in feudal times had been dispersed in a variety of centers. Only with its aid could economic resources be mobilized, which lay fallow in premodern times. Bureaucratic organization is to Weber the privileged instrumentality that has shaped the modern polity and the modern economy. Bureaucratic types of organization are technically superior to all other forms of administration.[19]

According to Max Weber, modern organizations functioned according to six principles:

1. Fixed and official jurisdictional areas that are governed by rules, that is laws and administrative regulations
2. Hierarchy and levels of graded authority, where the lower offices are supervised by the higher ones
3. Management based on official documents ("the files")
4. Officials with thorough and expert training
5. Requirement that the officials work full time
6. Management following of rules

While these principles seem obvious today, German government agencies were pioneering modern administration to replace practices dating back to the Middle Ages owing loyalty to the king, dukes, and the church.[20]

Today we speak of a "Weberian bureaucracy," meaning one that fits his ideal type closely. Conversely, there are obvious negative features about bureaucracy. Its major advantage, the calculability of results, also makes it unwieldy and even paralyzing in dealing with individual cases. Modern bureaucratized systems have become incapable of dealing with individual particularities. It can over-conform to its rules and procedures, treating an individual like a number and generating red tape. It can ignore the wishes of elected leaders. It can displace goals, perhaps advancing the interests of the employees rather than the people it is supposed to serve. Yet, according to Weber, there is a single best way for an organization to be structured.

A by-product of Weberian bureaucracy is what has come to be known as standard operating procedures (SOPs). In recent decades, the U.S. Army has devoted much of its peacetime efforts to elevating SOPs to the level of grand tactics. However, when war breaks out, SOPs break down. The reason is obvious; outcomes suddenly become visible. Staying alive, taking real estate, and killing the enemy are such important outcomes that the only SOPs that continue to have much force are those that contribute directly to producing those outcomes. At least that is almost true. Some SOPs, such as those that seem central to the mission of the organization, continue to exert influence even though they are actually getting in the way of producing good outcomes. The U.S. Army in Vietnam tried to apply doctrines and SOPs designed for large conventional wars in central Europe to the unconventional war of the Vietnamese villages. Because they were facing the enemy at close range, the smallest organizational units—the squads, platoons, and companies—were the first to see the error in this. Some managed to change operating procedures even when larger units—divisions and corps—led by men far from the scene of battle adhered to the old view.[21]

A New Look at the Organization

In 1971 Graham Allison published *Essence of Decision*. The book promised to take readers behind the scenes of the Cuban missile crisis and, in doing so, to present models for interpreting and explaining U.S. foreign policy. Allison presented three, now-familiar models for analyzing decision making: Model I (the rational actor); Model II (organizational behavior); and Model III (governmental politics, better known as bureaucratic politics). According to Allison, many analysts miscalculate by relying too heavily on Model I—in short, by assuming that foreign policy decisions reflect the priorities of a rational state and failing to recognize the importance of organizational constraints and bureaucratic influences. *Essence* explained foreign policy, and more broadly, decision making, as the result of a process, not of values or ideology. Some claim that Allison's book turned the analysis of policy largely into the study of organizations and bureaucracies.

Model I (the rational actor) explains government action as rational choice that will maximize strategic goals and objectives. The actor (government) is a rational, unitary decision maker. The actor has one set of specified goals, one set of perceived options, and a single estimate of the consequences that follow from each alternative. This model presumes that action is in response to a specific problem rather than a large number of partial choices in a dynamic setting. Governmental action selects the alternative whose consequences rank highest in terms of goals and consequences. The job of the rational agent is to maximize the value of the action.[22]

Model II (organizational behavior) posits that governmental behavior can be understood less as deliberate choices and more as outputs of large organizations functioning according to standard patterns of behavior. In this model the actor (government) is not a monolithic government but rather a constellation of loosely allied organizations. Consequently, problems are broken down and parceled out to various organizations. These organizations have their own parochial priorities and perceptions that are enhanced by: selective information available, recruitment of personnel, tenure of individuals, small group pressures inside organization and distribution of rewards. Accordingly, organizations develop stable propensities concerning operational priorities, perceptions and issues.[23]

In addition, organizational activity is characterized by: goals that are defined by constraints (e.g., budget) that define acceptable performance, sequential attention to goals, standard operating procedures (SOPs)—programs for producing specific actions. While standardized procedures are useful to deal with the routine by reducing uncertainty, they are much less useful when situations cannot be construed as standard.[24]

Model III (governmental politics, better known as bureaucratic politics) explains government action as result of politics. The decisions and actions of governments are not chosen but are the result of compromise, conflict and confusion of officials with diverse interests and unequal influence. The actor (government) is not a unitary agent nor a conglomeration of organizations, but rather a number of individual players (people in jobs). Each player's position is determined by the factors that encourage organizational parochialism as well as the factors that exert pressure upon the leaders of these organizations. Organizational goals and interests are also intermingled with personal interests.[25]

Events raise issues and force players to take stands. Power determines each player's impact. Power (effective influence on government decisions and actions) is an elusive blend of bargaining advantages and skill in using bargaining advantages. Bargaining advantages include formal authority and responsibility, actual control over resources, expertise, control of information, the ability to affect other players' objectives and access to players who have bargaining advantages.[26]

The players influence decisions and actions through action channels and knowing the rules of the game. An action channel is regulated means of taking governmental action (federal budget process). These structure the game by pre-selecting the players. The rules of the game come from various statutes, court interpretations, executive orders, conventions, and even culture. Rules establish the positions and limit the range of government decisions and actions. Each player uses power at his discretion for outcomes that will advance his conception of national, organizational, group, and personal interests.[27]

Allison's model and study of the Cuban missile crisis offers some general propositions. These include:

- Organizational activity according to SOPs and programs does not constitute far-sighted, flexible adaptation
- Actions are often determined by organizational routines, not governmental leaders
- Alternative options defined by organizations are most likely severely limited in both number and character.
- Long range planning tends to become institutionalized and then disregarded.
- Tradeoffs are neglected—hard choices among goals are seldom made
- Most organizations define "health" in terms of growth in budget, manpower, and territory.
- A considerable gap separates what leaders choose and what organizations implement.
- Existing organizational orientations and routines are not impervious to directed change.
- There is a need to target personnel, rewards, information, and budgets over time.
- Leadership tenure is short—directed change is uncommon.

CONTINGENCY THEORY

Isolated from Allison's model and in contrast to the classical scholars, most organizational theorists today believe that there is no one best way to organize. What is important is that there be a fit between the organization's structure, its size, its technology, and the requirements of its environment. This perspective is known as "contingency theory."[28]

Features of Contingency Theory

If we look around, we will notice that we live in a world in which change is the only certainty. Change in technology, social environment, economic and political environment, globalization, and ecological well-being is making us rethink the way we adapt to change. This applies to organizations, because organizations are part of our environment. Managing this change requires a different approach both by the individual and by the organization itself.

In a stable competitive environment, a relatively simple and mechanical organization is enough for success. But in a rapidly changing and unpredictable environment, success requires organizations to be flexible and dynamic and to have the ability to renew themselves and to innovate. This introduces us to contingency theory. Contingency theory accepts social and environment change in people and their business.

Origin and Development of Contingency Theory

The contingency approach is the outcome of research studies conducted by Tom Burns, G. M. Stalker, Joan Woodward, Paul Lawrence, Jay Lorsch, and others in the 1950s and 1960s. These organizational experts analyzed the environments and structures of several British and Scottish firms. Their goal was to determine what organizational attributes are related to certain external characteristics of the environment or the nature of the organization's primary task. The following two studies are representative of the many conducted by this group of researchers.

Burns and Stalker Study

One of the best studies conducted on how organizations must vary if they are to cope effectively with different environmental circumstances was conducted by Tom Burns and G. M. Stalker. Burns and Stalker examined some twenty British firms from a variety of industries. This provided an unusually good comparative sample. Their work examined how management practices in these companies were related to certain elements of their external environment. Next they explored the relationship between internal management practices and these external conditions to discover its effect on economic performance. Early in the fieldwork the authors were struck with the distinctly different sets of management methods and procedures they found in the different industries. Two divergent systems of management practice emerged. One system, to which we gave the name "mechanistic," appeared to be appropriate to an enterprise operating under relatively stable conditions. The other, "organic," appeared to be required for conditions of change or uncertainty. Their principal characteristics are summarized below.[29]

In mechanistic systems, the problems as a whole are broken down into specific tasks. Each individual pursues his task as something distinct from the whole as if it were the subject of a subcontract. Somebody at the top of the organization is responsible for seeing to its relevance. In line with Weberian bureaucracy, the technical methods, duties, and powers attached to each functional role are precisely defined. Interaction within the organization tends to be vertical, between superior and subordinate. Internal operations and relationships are governed by instructions and decisions issued by superiors. This command hierarchy is maintained by the implicit assumption that all knowledge about the situation is, or should be, available only to the head of the firm. Management operates a simple control system, with information flowing up through a succession of filters, and decisions and instructions flowing downward through a succession of amplifiers.[30]

In contrast, organic systems are suited to unstable environments where problems and requirements for action arise that cannot be easily broken down into specific tasks and distributed within a clearly defined hierarchy. Individuals have to perform their tasks in the light of their knowledge of the tasks of the organization as a whole. Jobs lose much of their formal definition in terms of methods, duties, and powers, which have to be redefined continually by interaction with others participating in a task. Interaction runs laterally and vertically. Communication among people of different ranks tends to resemble lateral consultation rather than vertical command. Omniscience can no longer be ascribed to the head of the concern.[31] These findings suggest that effective organizational units operating in stable parts of the environment are more highly structured, while those in more dynamic parts of the environment are less formal.

Woodward Study

Another study conducted in 1953 by Joan Woodward, one of England's leading industrial sociologists, started with the question of whether the principles of organization detailed in the expanding body of management literature correlate with business success when put into practice. To address this broad question, the researchers selected the geographical area of South Essex and studied virtually all the firms in the area that employed at least 100 people. This sample of 100 firms included a diverse line of businesses. The study made a detailed examination of the firms' characteristics, with particular attention to management practices. Early in the study the researchers began to realize that there was no significant direct association between the management practices of these firms and their business efficiency or their size. Woodward commented: "The widely accepted assumption that there are principles of management valid for all types of production systems seemed very doubtful—a conclusion with wide implications for the teaching of the subject."[32]

The researchers then sought some other basis of accounting for the variations in management practices. They found that when the firms were grouped according to their techniques of production and the complexity of their production systems, the more successful companies in each of these groupings followed similar management practices. The three broad groupings were:

1. Small-batch and unit production (special-purpose electronic equipment, custom-tailored clothing)
2. Large-batch and mass production (standard electronic components, standard gasoline engines)
3. Process or continuous production (chemicals, oil refining)

When further broken down and arranged, these three broad classifications formed a rough scale of the predictability of results and the corresponding degree of control over the production process. This ranged from low predictability for small-batch and unit production to high predictability for process production. As an example of predictability, Woodward points out: "Targets can be set more easily in a chemical plant than in even the most up-to-date mass-production engineering shops, and the factors limiting production are known more definitely."[33]

The general conclusion of this study was that the pattern of management varied according to these technical differences. This was especially true of the more successful firms. In other words, economic success was associated with using management practices that suited the various techniques of production.

ADDITIONAL FINDINGS THAT CONTRIBUTE TO CONTINGENCY THEORY

In their own study conducted in 1967, Lawrence and Lorsch determined that organizations functioning in a complex environment adopted a much higher degree of differentiation and integration than those operating in simple environments did. For these two management thinkers, the key issue is environmental uncertainty and information flow. They advocated exploring and improving the organization's relationship with the environment, which was characterized with respect to a certainty-uncertainty continuum.[34]

Since there is no "one best way" to structure an organization, an organization will face a range of choices when determining how it should be structured. Successful organizations adopt structures that are an appropriate response to a number of variables, or contingencies, which influence both the needs of the organization and how it works. Overall contingency theorists have found that three variables are particularly important in influencing an organization's structure. These are:

1. Size—This refers to capacity, number of personnel, and outputs.
2. Technology/task—Consider check processing at a bank. This activity is usually performed by a business unit that is highly formalized, has a great deal of specialization and division of labor, and high centralization of decision making. In contrast, the creative section of an ad agency is usually not formalized at all, the division of labor is often blurry, and it is highly decentralized.
3. Operating environment—It appears that certain activities naturally go with certain structures. Joan Woodward found that by knowing an organization's primary system of production, you could predict its structure.[35]

There are some additional aspects of the operating environment that must be mentioned.

Adaptation. Organizations facing complex, highly uncertain environments typically differentiate so that each organizational unit is facing a smaller, more certain problem. For example, if Japanese tastes in cars are quite different from American tastes, it is really hard to make a single car that appeals to both markets. It is easier to create two separate business units, one that makes cars for the Japanese market and the other that makes cars for the U.S. market.[36]

Natural selection. Organizations whose structures are not fitted to the environment will not perform well and will fail.[37]

Dependence. The world can be viewed as a giant network of organizations linked by buying and selling relationships. Every unit has suppliers (inputs) and customers (outputs). Every unit is dependent on both their suppliers and their customers for resources and money. To the extent that a company needs its suppliers less than they need it, the unit has power. That is, power is a function of asymmetric mutual dependence. Dependence is itself a function of the availability of alternative supply. Organizations that have power over others are able to impose elements of structure on them. For example, General Motors is famous for imposing accounting systems, cost controls, and manufacturing techniques on their suppliers.[38]

Stakeholders. The sets of entities in an organization's environment that play a role in the organization's health and performance, or that are affected by the organization, are called stakeholders. Stakeholders have interests in what the organization does and may or may not have the power to influence the organization to protect their interests. Stakeholders are varied, and their interests may coincide on some issues and not others. Therefore, you find stakeholders both cooperating with each other in alliances and competing with each other. Furthermore, if the bonds among the stakeholders are closer than the bonds with the organization, the stakeholders may side with each other against the organization and won't act in ways that negatively affect other stakeholders.[39]

Institutionalization. Under conditions of uncertainty, organizations imitate others that appear to be successful. In other words, if nobody really knows what makes a movie successful, and then somebody has a blockbuster hit, everybody else copies both the movie and the organizational structure that produced the movie, hoping that they will get the same results. This can cause whole industries to adopt similar structural features.[40]

Implications

There are two significant implications of contingency theory. If there is no "one best way," then even apparently quite similar organizations may choose significantly different structures and still be reasonably successful in accomplishing their missions. Second, if different parts of the same organization are influenced in different ways by the variables bearing upon them, then it may be appropriate for them to be structured differently.

In brief, contingency theory involves a comprehensive view of the organization with inherent diagnosis of people, task, technology, and environment and then suggests solutions. The alternative to anticipating events, planning, and being prepared is firefighting—being surprised by random events threatening the organization's position. Firefighting frequently diverts management's attention from day-to-day maintenance tasks that keep the organization whole and functioning smoothly.

The main features of the contingency theory are as follows:

1. Organizations have to deal with different situations in different ways.
2. There is no single best way of management applicable to all situations.
3. To be effective, the managers must regulate the organization to be in harmony with the needs of the members from within as well as with the external environment.
4. The external environment is not static, but flexible and fast changing.
5. Organization should design its structure, leadership style, and control systems in order to be adaptive to the prevailing situation.
6. Since management effectiveness and success are directly related to its ability to cope with the changing environment, it should sharpen its diagnostic skills to be proactive to anticipate and understand environmental changes.
7. No single rule or law will solve management problems at all times, all places, and for all individuals or institutions. The manager has to study the external environment and define the course of his strategies and action process.[41]

Management is essentially situational. Consequently, the techniques of management are contingent on the situation. In other words, the diversity and complexity of the external situation with which the organization interacts should determine the management technique. Management should therefore adopt its approach and strategy in tune to the requirements of each particular situation. Management policies and practices that spontaneously are responsive to environmental changes are more effective. Accordingly, the organization should design its structure, leadership style, and control systems to be adaptive to the situation prevailing.

Since management effectiveness and success are directly related to the ability to cope with a changing environment, organizations should sharpen their diagnostic skills to be proactive and to anticipate and comprehend environmental changes. In short, the successful manager should recognize that there is no one best way to manage. They must not consider particular management principles and techniques as applicable to all time and all needs. There is no solution of universal applicability, because two situations may not be identical.

How Is Contingency Theory Useful?
Contingency theory's approach is pragmatic and open-minded. It discounts preconceived notions. It advocates that the problems faced in each situation be analyzed and suitable options be identified to effectively and efficiently solve the problem. It thus avoids preconceived value judgments and widens the horizons of leaders.

It guides them to be alert and adaptive to environmental variables while choosing their styles and techniques. It provides freedom of choice by liberating leaders from dogmas and preconceived principles. Therefore, leaders get the opportunity to become innovative and creative.

Leading is not a pure science. It is a practicing art. Contingency theory focuses attention on situational analysis to help leaders to be pragmatic and develop competence for all situations. It combines the mechanistic and organic approaches to fit the particular situation. It is an improvement over Weberian bureaucracy. Contingency theory advances further and stresses the need to additionally examine the relationship between the organization and its environment. The process to identify the best leadership or management style might now conclude that the best style depends on the situation. If one is leading troops in the Persian Gulf, an autocratic style is probably best (many might disagree here, too). If one is trying to convince an Afghan resistance group to attack a mountain stronghold, a more participatory and facilitative leadership style is probably best.

To sum up, contingency theory represent the following attributes:
- It treats each organization as a unique entity.
- It identifies the exact nature of interdependencies and their impact on organizational design and managerial style.
- It is more pragmatic, down to earth, and action oriented.
- It firmly rejects blind application of principles regardless of realities of individual situations.
- It relates organizational structure and design to the environment.
- It is neither vague nor complex, but pragmatic and action oriented.

Some Closing Thoughts on the Organization
Classical bureaucracy compared with contingency theory can be viewed as a thrust in one of two directions—either toward greater order, systematization, routinization, and predictability, or toward greater openness, sharing, creativity, and individual initiative. One thrust is to tighten the organization; the other to loosen it up. Are opposite forces building up in modern organizations with the manager caught between them?

I do not want our brief discussion to leave the reader with the impression that classical organizational theory has no current value. Instead, classical organizational theory presents a special case that can now be subsumed within a more general theoretical framework. The principles of the classicists can be treated as one end of a continuum, with the principles of contingency theory at the other. However, choosing where on the continuum to be is a strategic choice that must come after answering the fundamental question—what business are we in? Once that decision is made, whether explicitly or implicitly, the attributes of the chosen environment can be analyzed. Internal attributes of the organization, in terms of structure and orientation, can be tested for goodness of fit with the various environmental variables and the predispositions of members. Unit performance emerges as a function of this fit.[42]

PROCESSES OF INNOVATION

The U.S. military is going through a transformational process during wartime and in the face of rapid strategic and technological change and uncertainty. An extensive body of literature exists that attempts to make some sense of and guide this effort. Exploring this scholarship gives us a sense of how difficult and complex innovation and, more so, transformation is and how it might be brought to happen through deliberate effort.[43]

Barry Posen's *The Sources of Military Doctrine: France, Britain and Germany between the World Wars* is a superb example of contemporary scholarship of military innovation. Posen's investigation is penetrating. He examined how doctrine changes or fails to change as policy and the security environment change. For his analysis, Posen used two of the most popular and powerful models in contemporary political science, the organizational theory or bureaucratic model and the balance of power or realist model.[44]

Organizational Theory and Innovation

Posen starts by developing hypotheses on innovation from organizational and balance-of-power theories. For Posen, organization theory suggests that innovation in military organizations will be infrequent and only occasionally will be advocated by the military. This follows from the basic purpose of an organization, to overcome uncertainty. Organizations seek to achieve certainty by establishing SOPs and by distributing power and authority to enforce these procedures. Collectively, these SOPs become programs or, in military terms, doctrine.[45]

Interestingly, by adopting an offensive doctrine, a military organization can maximize its ability to overcome uncertainty. An offensive doctrine overcomes uncertainty, because it allows a military force to take the initiative and plan what it wants to do rather than respond to what someone else does. Furthermore, offensive doctrines, which are more costly than defensive warfare, serve the self-interest of military organizations because they allow a military to increase its size and resources.[46]

Regardless of the particular doctrine an organization adopts, those who hold power and authority in the organization have a vested interest in holding on to that power and authority and in the doctrine associated with their status. This helps explain why they are reluctant to change and even more reluctant to innovate. Furthermore, opposition to change is strengthened by the organization's desire to avoid uncertainty, which change increases and innovation increases even more. Still, change does usually occur after an organizational failure (when a military suffers defeat), when feeling external pressure from outside (in the case of the military, when it is pressured by civilians), and when it wishes to expand. Posen notes also that military organizations appear to learn from their own experience in war.[47]

Innovation and Balance-of-Power Theory
When Posen contemplates military innovation in light of balance-of-power theory, his investigation starts with the bureaucratic point of view. Specifically, innovation is difficult and tends to require external intervention. However, as Posen continues his investigation, he concludes that unlike the bureaucratic model, balance-of-power theory is superior to organization theory as an explanation of innovation, because it predicts when intervention is likely to occur. Balance-of-power theory assumes that in an anarchic world, violence and power politics are a constant feature of the international milieu. Civilians become concerned about military matters as external threats increase. This situation often results in the political leadership encouraging or directing the military to meet the threat. At the same time, the increased uncertainty that results from a rising threat pushes military officers to be more concerned with meeting the threat than with enforcing SOPs. New and different threats cause military leaders to become more open to civilian intervention. Therefore, balance-of-power theory predicts that an increased external threat will lead to innovation through civilian intervention. Also, bureaucratic politics and balance-of-power theories are both part of the explanation of innovation or of its absence, with balance-of-power theory a marginally slightly more powerful tool, because civilian intervention is critical for innovation.[48]

Posen's proposition that civilian intervention is usually necessary to bring about military innovation is not universally accepted. Stephen Peter Rosen, for example, points out that civilians, to include the president of the United States, have a hard time getting bureaucracies to do what they want them to do. To begin with, directions from the top are usually general in nature and therefore lack specificity. This lack of precise direction is even more evident when innovation is required. By their very nature, orders to innovate are inherently ambiguous and therefore difficult to specify in advance. Furthermore, Rosen does not see validity in the claim that civilians work through military "mavericks" to bring about innovation, an explanation offered by Posen.[49] The reality is that mavericks tend to generate resentment and thus resistance to change among their colleagues than interest in it. Finally Rosen considers the case of antiaircraft defense by the Royal Air Force before

World War II to assess the claim that civilian intervention is necessary to bring about innovation. Rosen's study of the case convinces him that steady doctrinal development within the military, not intervention by civilians or military mavericks, explains peacetime innovation.[50]

Like Rosen, Emily Goldman believes that Posen's mistake was to place too much emphasis on the bureaucratic politics model.[51] Goldman views Posen as too pessimistic about the likelihood of innovation within military organizations. Goldman notes that this is not the only way to think about the military. Citing the work of Samuel Huntington, Goldman argues that the military can be thought of as a professional organization.

> The military is a profession that strives to achieve efficiency in attaining its goals. For the military, this means maximizing its ability to secure the state. Military organizations respond to the dictates of strategic geography, technological developments, and enemy behavior in rational pursuit of their goals.[52]

Goldman sees military personnel not simply as interested in preserving their authority and increasing their resources. They also want to make their nation more secure, and they act rationally with this end in mind. This is in contrast to Posen's account of military innovation.

With an appreciation of the military, Goldman makes use of organizational learning theory instead of the bureaucratic politics model used by Posen. Goldman claims that organizational learning theory begins with the assumption that all organizations pay attention to their external environment in addition to their internal politics. They want to achieve an optimal result. This means that military organizations really want optimal national security, not just bigger budgets. Therefore, in seeking optimal national security, the military pays attention to the external world. According to Goldman's model, to achieve an optimal outcome, organizations evaluate their tasks, skills, and procedures and do so by observing and interpreting their experience. Evaluation through observation and interpretation is how organizations learn. Learning occurs when organizations are prompted from the outside in three ways: "when domestic political incentives encourage learning, when knowledge and experience make learning possible, and when threats make learning urgent."[53] For a military organization, learning can become appealing because of incentives or pressure to learn from civilians, or from other military organizations that are successfully responding to a threat.[54]

Several propositions flow from Goldman's framework that are succinctly stated by David Tucker.

> If learning is advantageous, possible, and vital from the viewpoint of an organization, then it will learn. The greater the connection of desirability, possibility,

and urgency, the greater the likelihood that learning will occur. Furthermore, military organizations will adopt new missions and tasks in order to be more effective in the future and give up missions and tasks that decrease their effectiveness. They will do so, contrary to the organizational politics model, even if this means sacrificing autonomy and resources because organizations want to achieve an optimal result in the world and not just increase their autonomy and resources.[55]

Goldman examines three cases of military innovation from the interwar period through the lens of organizational learning theory: mechanization in the army, amphibious warfare in the Marine Corps, and carrier aviation in the navy. Her examination suggests that the learning model provides a better explanation for the behavior of organizations than the bureaucratic politics model. Goldman concludes that innovation occurs in these cases when desirability, possibility, and urgency are present, even if this change diminishes the relative status quo of an organization. To illustrate, the Marines adopted amphibious assault as their core mission even though it increased their dependence on, and relative standing of, the navy. Conversely, in the case of mechanization in the army, when desirability, possibility, and urgency were low, only incremental change occurred. Goldman explains the navy's partial acceptance of the aircraft carrier as the replacement for the battleship as an instance in which the desirability and possibility of learning were moderate and urgency high, an explanation she takes as further confirming the learning model. When possibility, urgency, and desirability are present and moderately high, innovation is likely.[56]

Kimberly Zisk is optimistic about military innovation. She sees military officers as professionals concerned with national security and therefore responsive to external threats. Furthermore, she considers that even bureaucratic interests might encourage a military to innovate.[57] If the innovation promises more resources, then the organization has an incentive to innovate. Still, Zisk concedes, like Posen, that a military organization's bureaucratic interests also impede innovation. Zisk claims that military officers can be both professional and bureaucratic, because they "tend to see the health of their institution [their bureaucratic concern] as a determining condition of the health of national security [their professional concern]."[58]

This convenient merging of professionalism and self-interest offers the possibility of overcoming the separate but related problems that limited Posen's and Goldman's accounts of innovation. Accounting for the military's sensitivity to external threats, Zisk is not pressed to rely on civilian intervention to explain military innovation. This helps more to explain when militaries do innovate on their own than does Posen's account. Still, by acknowledging the bureaucratic interests of the military, Zisk explains why the military may not always innovate, even when it is aware of changing external threats, thereby avoiding Goldman's problem of not being able to explain failure to innovate.[59]

Zisk constructs a framework on the understanding that the military is both professional and bureaucratic. Military officers will respond to changes in the external security environment because they are professional. However, they will also both respond to internal threats to their autonomy and resources and prefer innovations that enhance their bureaucratic position because they are bureaucrats. Faced with both external and internal threats, military officers will respond first to the internal threat. Zisk argues that the bureaucratic nature of military organizations means that when change occurs, it occurs slowly, as part of a political process that follows policy debates and the building of coalitions to support the change. This process is affected by both the idiosyncratic preferences of leaders and changes in personnel. Additionally, Zisk argues that broadened policy communities can also influence change. Coalitions for change, built in this community, can provide a civilian push to innovate that does not strain civil-military relations because it is not a direct bureaucratic battle between civilians and the military.[60]

Zisk's conception of innovation has three main points. First, organizational interests may impose constraints, but they do not determine behavior. Second, organizational and strategic motives coexist in individuals and organizations and influence each other. Third, extended policy communities can influence and sustain innovation by mitigating competition between interest groups.[61]

Zisk tests her propositions with three cases of Soviet reaction to changes in U.S. or NATO doctrine: flexible response in the 1960s, the Schlesinger Doctrine in 1974, and AirLand Battle and Follow-on Forces Attack in the 1980s. Zisk concludes that the tests validate her conception of when innovation occurs. Having been validated, the propositions amount in Zisk's view to a new theory about the question of doctrinal innovation and international competition.[62] Tucker summarizes this new approach with precision:

> First, organizational interests may impose constraints but they do not determine behavior. "Individuals and their ideas matter." Second, organizational and strategic motives co-exist in individuals and organizations and influence each other. "Institutional perspectives color reactions to foreign threats; foreign influences change institutional perspectives." Third, policy communities, "extending through and beyond interest groups" can influence and sustain innovation by mitigating competition between interest groups.[63]

The political nature of innovation within organizations in acknowledged by Zisk's careful discussion about coalition building throughout policy communities. Stephen Rosen also makes this point when explaining peacetime innovation. After

considering and rejecting the views that innovation always follows defeat and innovation must be instigated by civilians, Rosen argued that, in peacetime, military
organizations were political communities in which ideology and values and who is
promoted affect the distribution of power. The ideology and values are new ways of
fighting—amphibious assault or carrier aviation—developed in response to changes
in the international security environment. Senior officers decide who is promoted.
If innovation is to occur and take hold, they must back the new ideas and support
them by promoting into positions of power those who hold them. In its emphasis
on ideas, politics, and the importance of personnel changes, Zisk's work supports
Rosen's view of peacetime innovation. Zisk and Rosen both agree that direct civilian efforts to push the military to innovate are unlikely to succeed. Rosen argued
that military organizations, if they are professional, are separate from and, at least to
some degree, closed to civilians. He contended, therefore, that civilians would have
the greatest effect on military innovation if they "devise a strategy that reinforces the
actions of senior officers who already have legitimate power in the military."[64]

Zisk distinguishes her approach from Posen's when she presents the profes-
sional/bureaucrat relationship in her conclusions. There she says that internal and
external perspectives influence each other. This is different from saying that internal
concerns will tend to override external and, if true, would indeed be a new, appealing approach to military innovation, explaining both when militaries innovate, they
are professional, and when they do not, they are bureaucrats.[65]

Figure 3.1 depicts the relationship between external and internal threats that
we have just sketched.[66]

		External Threats	
		High	Low
Internal Threats	High	1 Indeterminate	2 Determinate (Least likely)
	Low	3 Determinate (Most likely)	4 Indeterminate

Figure 3.1 External and internal threats

In boxes one and four, the importance of the external and internal threats
is about the same. As a result, they cancel each other out. This would mean that
other factors such as organizational culture and individual idiosyncrasies would have
greater influence on whether innovation occurred than in the situations represented
in the other two boxes. In boxes two and three, one threat dominates. In box two,

in which the internal threat is high and the external threat is low, we should expect internal or bureaucratic considerations to prevail. Since such considerations tend to lean against change, innovation should be less likely under these circumstances. Civilian intervention to initiate change might not work in this case, especially if the internal threat includes bad civil-military relations. In this case, civilian intervention in favor of some change is likely to make the military resist rather than adopt that change. If innovation did occur, it would occur because it served the interests of the military organization. In box three, in which the internal threat is low and the external threat high, internal bureaucratic issues should have less importance. In these circumstances, innovation should be more likely to occur and civilian intervention more acceptable.[67]

In sum, figure 3.1 suggests that there are three different configurations that affect the likelihood of innovation. One in which external threats play the greatest role (box three) and innovation is most likely; a second in which internal threats play the most important role (box two) and innovation is least likely; and a third in which a number of different factors might play a role (boxes one and four) and the outcome is unpredictable. In all of these cases, an additional consideration is that various actors involved may well estimate differently the importance of various internal and external threats.[68]

The view of innovation presented in figure 3.1 appears to be complete enough to provide some understanding of how innovation occurs yet flexible enough to respect the complex nature of military innovation. An alternative interpretation of technological innovation by Matthew Evangelista challenges this assessment, because it denies that either external or internal factors, alone or together, account sufficiently for technological innovation. Internal factors, as represented in the bureaucratic politics model, explain continuity and stagnation better than they explain change and innovation. After examining U.S.-Soviet innovation in nuclear weapons, Evangelista concludes that the relative strength of state and society is critical, at least in understanding the different processes of weapons development in the United States and the Soviet Union. In other words, variables other than the international system and bureaucratic interests are more important in explaining innovation. He suggests that the strong state and weak society of the Soviet Union lead to a top-down approach, while the weak state and strong society of the United States led to a bottom-up approach.[69]

Evangelista challenges the relationship presented in figure 3.1. He does not see the interplay of external and internal threats as setting up different environments in which other variables have degrees of influence on innovation. Instead, Evangelista sees other factors, particularly scientific entrepreneurship, as creating an environment in which actors use external and internal threats to build a case for favored technologies.[70]

Other accounts of technological innovation generally support the analysis implied in figure 3.1. For example, Stephen Rosen considers several explanations of how technological innovation occurs. There is evidence that scientists and technologists develop new technologies and push them onto a reluctant, tradition-bound military. Rosen cites the case in which scientists pushed the atom bomb on the military, but he argues that the military did not always act as a reluctant recipient of technology in the face of such pushing. Rosen also cites evidence that the military has often demanded that the technologists labor to meet an operational need with innovative hardware. Evidence that the military must be pushed and yet also pulled is what we should expect if military men are both bureaucrats, devoted to personal and organizational self-interest, and professionals, sensitive to external threats. Because of this dual character, external and internal threats will be important in determining when military innovation occurs. This means, however, that the "push and pull" understanding of technology would fit into the model of figure 3.1.[71]

A good case can be made that the relationship between internal and external factors is of countervailing value. If this is true, other factors involved in innovation have greater significance. Even in those cases in which either the external or internal threat is determinate, other factors will still influence the outcome. Indeed, several analysts have noted that the perception of threats is subjective, subject to personal and institutional prejudices, for example. This means that the factors that determine an organization's openness to change are themselves determined by other factors, several of which may well be peculiar to a given organization or situation.[72]

Many scholars see innovation as a phenomenon that defies rigorous analysis. Williamson Murray emphasizes the role of chance. Reviewing the interwar years, he concludes that innovation does not "reduce to simple, linear processes" and "is more of an art than a science."[73] In a concluding essay to a collection of studies of how several different countries innovated between the wars, Dennis Showalter argues that general rules or formulas are less important for understanding innovation than the particular circumstances of each case.[74] The stunning German thrust through the Ardennes that destroyed the Third Republic at the beginning of World War II was the result, we are inclined to think, of twenty years of carefully planned change. Yet, it also resulted from a set of happy (for the Germans) accidents such as Seeckt's ascent to power, Manstein's meeting with Hitler, and Rommel's leadership at the crossing of the Meuse.[75] In other words, successful innovation can be an accident or two from failure. The presence of the accidental or random implies as well that there may be more than one way to innovate in a given situation. In hindsight, we see what was progressive and what was not, but this perspective—the Whig perspective, as Showalter calls it—is not, of course, the vantage point of those who must actually change a military.

In both his own examination of innovation in bureaucracies and his review of the literature on the subject, for example, James Q. Wilson found that executives played a critical role. The leadership of an organization decides which threats it will respond to and whether to protect subordinates who have new ideas. Wilson argues that the importance of executives explains why little progress has been made in developing theories of innovation. Not only, as others have noted, are individual innovations so different as to defy general theories, but they are also "so heavily dependent on executive interests and beliefs as to make the chance appearance of a change-oriented personality enormously important in explaining change."[76]

Other Factors Influencing Innovation

No account of innovation is complete if it does not go beyond internal politics and external threats to take other factors into account. Innovation is an intensely political business. Organizational culture and the prevailing assumptions, ideas, and norms that guide action, must be accounted for.[77] Zisk, for example, declares that individuals and their ideas matter. Rosen makes this point by describing peacetime innovation as a political process that revolves around whose conception of future warfare will prevail. Zisk explicitly connects these "ideas that matter" to the organizations that individuals inhabit. Individuals view events through a lens, "a social construction of reality," provided by their organization. Zisk asserts that "response to particular environmental stimuli depend[s] on the organizational culture of the individual military institution."[78] Such organizational cultures are particularly important in the discussion of innovation, because external and internal threats figure prominently in innovation, and the assessment of these are very much informed by the norms of the organization in which they act. This is especially true of organizations such as the military services that take in their members when they are young and subject them throughout their careers to training, indoctrination, and incentives that shape their views and actions.

The importance of organizational culture in understanding military innovation is obvious, though little is written to explain how it develops or changes. Deborah Avant offers what appears to be a simple explanation. She suggests that ideas are only as strong as the incentives that support them. Said another way, culture results from the incentives that operate on and in an organization. Avant's thinking might appear to take us back to the bureaucratic or political view of innovation, in which the interests of an organization determine what it thinks about any given issue. This view is part of Avant's discussion. Her account of incentives and of military change is more complicated than that. However, Avant uses principal-agent theory and thinking about the economics of institutions to explain why military organizations change or fail to change. It looks beyond the dynamics internal to an organization to its institutional setting and the influence this setting has on both civilian and military actors. Although not interested in culture or using that concept as an analytical tool, Avant shows how the culture or preferences of a military organization result from the historical interaction between civilian and military institutions. She pays attention to formative experiences during state building that shapes institutional perspectives, which in turn shape civil-military relations and the prospects for innovation in military organizations.[79]

A virtue of Avant's analysis is that it explains why innovating to meet unconventional threats is more difficult for some organizations than for others. Avant does not argue that the army is incapable of innovation. On the contrary, she argues that during the Cold War, even as it refused to change to meet the threat from insurgency, the army innovated in response to the changing threat in Europe.[80] In adapting to one threat but not the other, the army was repeating the performance it first gave during the Indian Wars in the 1870s and 1880s. As in that case, following success in a great war, success that confirmed the army's focus on materiel superiority, firepower, and attrition, the army refused to adapt to a different kind of threat. One officer who did innovate to fight the Indians, George Crook, was eventually removed by General Philip H. Sheridan, who along with General William T. Sherman did so much to shape the professional attitudes of the army following the Civil War.[81] In the case of counterinsurgency, the budgetary incentives provided by the focus on major conventional war, Avant reminds us, are only part of the explanation for the army's preference.[82] Increased funds were available for counterinsurgency, but the army did not accept this mission. It responded to political pressure and budgetary incentives by renaming various aspects of its traditional activities "counterinsurgency," but it did not change its traditional approach. It innovated within the bounds of that traditional approach, but that approach set limits to its adaptability. According to Avant, the service that best adapted to the conditions in Vietnam was the Marine Corps, a service that came of age and largely remains in search of a mission and thus has seen, in changing conditions, not threats to a traditional way of doing things, but opportunities to make itself useful.[83] As in its adoption of the amphibious assault mission before World War II, the Corps' adaptability results from the desire to stay alive. More important, over time, this ongoing concern has made adaptability a major part of the Corps' professional ethos. Accordingly, the Marine Corps is more likely to adapt to unconventional missions than is the army, not because it is by nature more suited to unconventional threats but because over time it has developed an organizational culture that emphasizes the need to adapt to new and unmet threats. The Corps' famously effective congressional liaison and public relations are the result of this need to stay attuned to changing perceptions of unmet threats and to sell its ability to meet them. Because the other services have traditionally focused on conventional threats, the Marines have often found themselves with only the unconventional to focus on. As Avant says, when speaking of the Cold War era, "only the players without a chance in the main game (the most unimportant players, by definition) had the incentive to focus on, or remain flexible to, any other threats."[84]

Avant argues that the process she traces with the army applies to the navy and the air force as well.[85] For each of these services, internal and external threats, that is bureaucratic concerns over budget and turf and operational concerns about the kinds of enemies we face, do not by themselves explain how the services respond. They confront these threats with certain ideas of what they are and what war is, ideas that have been forged through a complex organizational, institutional, and historical process. The result of this process is an institutional culture, the conceptions or ideas that guide action. These services innovate or fail to innovate as a result of this interplay between external and internal threats and culture, the interplay itself regulated by how salient the threats appear to be, an issue that is itself subject to the influence of prevailing ideas. The Cold War played to the strengths of these three services, particularly the army, because conventional warfare fit the problem in Europe, the theater of central concern. The army innovated to meet the changing requirements of this kind of fight. Since the end of the Cold War, the army has had more difficulty adapting to the changes in our strategic requirements because, despite the example of the Gulf Wars, these changes have tended to demote the significance of conventional warfare. The Marine Corps, almost irrelevant in the first Gulf War, has since come into its own, adapting more easily than the other services to the changed security environment, because in this environment, unconventional threats are more significant and because the Marine Corps has had to be more adaptive. The Corps, like the other services, has been shaped by the interplay of internal and external threats with institutional and historical factors. However, in its case, the result has been a service culture that encourages adaptation and does not shun unconventional threats.

THE GLOBAL SECURITY ENVIRONMENT—IMPLICATIONS FOR UW

The nature of U.S. national security has undergone fundamental changes since the disintegration of the Soviet Union and more recently since the terrorist attacks on the U.S. homeland. Cold War concepts of security and deterrence are no longer completely relevant. Globalization has produced economic integration, new technologies, and prosperity for much of the world's population. On the negative side of globalization, we find ourselves in a security environment characterized by instability, uncertainty, and chaos. In fact, some people seem to reject modernity altogether and prefer returning to the questionable glories of past centuries.

In other words, global political violence is clashing with global economic integration. The causes and consequences of the resultant instabilities tend to be exploited by rogue states, substate and transnational political actors, insurgents, illegal drug traffickers, organized criminals, warlords, militant fundamentalists, and ethnic cleansers with the will to conduct terrorism and other forms of asymmetric warfare. Their intent is to impose self-determined desires for change on a society, state, and other perceived symbols of power in the global community.[86] Conventional warfare is poorly suited to deal with these threats.

The solution to the problem goes beyond simply destroying small bands of terrorist fanatics and the governments that support them. History strongly indicates that it is important to take additional measures. Once one of these threats to global security is brought under control or neutralized, development or reconstruction efforts must be taken to preclude the seeds that created that organization in the first place from germinating again.

The complex new global security environment contains several types of ambiguous and uncomfortable wars and their aftermath.[87] A deeper look into that picture would provide several snapshots that show a global insurgency that uses terrorism as the tool of war. This picture would also show unspeakable human destruction and misery, and related refugee flows, accumulating over the past ten years. During the period since the first Gulf War, anywhere from 00 to 210 million people have lost their hopes, their property, and their lives. The resultant political alienation, sufficiently reinforced by economic and social deprivation, tends to direct the survivors and their advocates toward conflict and the tactics of despair, the most visible being terrorism.[88]

The primary implication of the complex and ambiguous situations described above is straightforward. That is, winning the military struggle against Osama bin Laden and his Taliban protectors will not end the threat of terrorism against the United States, or anyone else in the global community. This is because the Taliban and Osama bin Laden are not isolated cases. They are only one component of the entire global security problem that is a manifestation of a complex and potentially durable human motivation and weak governance phenomena. This condition required an unconventional application of military strategy and resources.

Contemporary terrorism is a descendent of the type of low-intensity conflict seen in the third world over the past fifty years. It is popular, in part, because the sorts of rural and urban insurgencies that proved effective during the Cold War are no longer as expedient as they once were. More important, as the means of causing mass destruction become less expensive and more available, the angry, the frustrated, and the weak rely on more asymmetric forms of violence to impose their own vision of justice on peoples, countries, and the global community.[89]

CONTINGENCY THEORY AND PROCESS FOR INNOVATION— IMPLICATIONS FOR UW

The discussions about organizational theory and processes of innovation overlap in many areas. For both, however, there is inertia that affects organizational change and innovation. That said, the diverse nature of the threat discussed above requires innovative thinking and nonstandard organizational solutions.

What does the study of organizational theory in general and contingency theory, in particular, tell us about how to organize military power to prevent or reduce the effects of current and future threats? Organizational scholars have concluded that Weberian-type bureaucracy found in many large, modern organizations is ineffective in coping with the demands of a dynamic and uncertain environment. Additionally, standardized procedures, a fundamental tenet of bureaucracy, inhibits innovation and the flexibility necessary to effectively operate under conditions of uncertainty. Contingency theory is the alternative organizational model for environments where Weberian bureaucracy falls short. The discussion on contingency theory can be summarized in the following propositions:

1. There is no "one best way" to organize.
2. The nature of an organizations interdependency can either inhibit or enable effectiveness; no single rule applies to all situations.
3. The organization must flexibly harmonize with the capabilities of its members as well as with the fast-changing external environment.
4. To cope with change, enhanced diagnostic skills are essential in order to be proactive or preemptive.
5. Unstable environments where problems and requirements for action arise that cannot be easily broken down into specific tasks and distributed within a clearly defined hierarchy necessitate decentralized management.
6. The more complex the environment, the greater the need is for increased differentiation and coordination for effectiveness.

What implications can be drawn from the literature on innovation for waging unconventional warfare? The following propositions encapsulate the literature on military innovation:

1. Innovation in military organizations is difficult and often requires outside intervention.

2. Military organizations cope with uncertainty by developing standardized procedures and by distributing authority to enforce these procedures.
3. Those who hold power and authority in an organization have a vested interest in the doctrine associated with their status.
4. Innovation can be internally generated by the desire of professional officers to secure the state as well as by the promise of more resources.
5. Scientific entrepreneurship helps develop technologies that can instigate innovation.
6. Innovation is the result of individuals and their ideas.
7. Organizational culture can either facilitate or deter innovation.
8. Organizational culture is shaped by incentive structures that operate in the organization.
9. The interests of an organization determine what it thinks about a given innovation.

Reducing the bodies of literature on both organizational theory and processes of innovation to the few sentences above does an injustice to complexities of the subjects and to the people who study them. These few sentences represent only the tip of the iceberg. The analysis that follows will include a more detailed discussion on how these propositions affect the ability of DoD to conduct unconventional warfare.

A B-52 conducts "unconventional warfare." —*Defense Visual Information Center*

This is the now-famous photograph of a U.S. Army Special Forces NCO using a "new" means of mobility. —*Special Operations Command Public Affairs Office*

A Special Forces Operational Detachment Alpha poses at its firebase in Gereshk.
—*Special Operations Command Public Affairs Office*

A Special Forces medic provides aid and gathers local intelligence at the same time.
—*U.S. Army Special Operations Command Public Affairs Office*

Time was available for some friendly interaction with the locals. —*Defense Visual Information Center*

Soldiers from the 3rd Special Forces Group are shown on patrol. —*Defense Visual Information Center*

Members of 5th Special Forces Group pose amidst local leaders. —*U.S. Army Special Operations Command Public Affairs Office*

Fellow operators help a wounded Special Forces soldier who has just been evacuated aboard a Russian-made Northern Alliance Mi-8 helicopter. —*Special Operations Command Public Affairs Office*

Soldiers use a Special Forces combat vehicle they improvised. —*U.S. Army Special Operations Command Public Affairs Office*

Understanding the big picture is a necessary part of unconventional warfare. —*Defense Visual Information Center*

"New-age" Special Forces equipment carriers. —*Defense Visual Information Center*

Team members brainstorm an operation. —*U.S. Army Special Operations Command Public Affairs Office*

A two-thousand-pound Joint Direct Attack Munition hits a friendly base after incorrect GPS coordinates were given. —*Defense Visual Information Center*

Mazar E Sharif. —*Defense Visual Information Center*

Friend and foe. —*Courtesy of the author*

A Special Forces unit quickly discusses its options in the field. —*U.S. Army Special Operations Command Public Affairs Office*

Here, a Special Forces soldier plays a game of pool with local Afghani teens in a small village. —*Defense Visual Information Center*

A unit from the 3rd Special Forces Group, on patrol aboard an all-terrain vehicle, greets a group of local Afghani children on the outskirts of Kabul. —*Defense Visual Information Center*

New recruits assigned to the 1st Battalion of the Afghanistan National Army (ANA) practice marching at Kabul. The training program conducted by the 3rd Special Forces Group is designed to establish the core of the new ANA. —*Defense Visual Information Center*

During a search and destroy mission in the Zhawar Kili area of eastern Afghanistan, this large stockpile of ammunition and weapons used by Al Qaeda and Taliban forces was discovered in a cave. —*Defense Visual Information Center*

An Operational Detachment Alpha on patrol through the mountains near Urgun, in the Paktika province, move to establish an observation point to deny ease of movement to Taliban and Al Qaeda forces. —*Defense Visual Information Center*

Still more munitions are uncovered in a Zhawar Kili cave. —*Defense Visual Information Center*

The 3rd Special Forces Group instructs new ANA recruits on the operation of their AK-47 assault rifles on the range near Kabul. —*U.S. Army Special Operations Command Public Affairs Office*

ANA soldiers march to a training session near Kabul. —*U.S. Army Special Operations Command Public Affairs Office*

ANA soldiers return from a training session. —*U.S. Army Special Operations Command Public Affairs Office*

Chapter 4

Why Can't the United States Conduct Unconventional Warfare?
Implications of Contingency Theory

> Since being created by the Cohen-Nunn Amendment to the DoD Autho-
> rization Act of 1987, the U.S. Special Operations Command (USSOCOM)
> has provided highly trained, rapidly deployable and regionally focused SOF
> [special operations forces] in support of global requirements from the National
> Command Authorities, the geographic commanders in chief, and our Ameri-
> can ambassadors and their country teams.[1]

This statement by Gen. Peter J. Schoomaker's expressed to his U.S. Special Operations Command staff reflects the degree to which SOF have successfully responded
to the needs of other organizations. However, responding to the needs or desires of
others is not the same as responding to the changing nature of the strategic environment. Also, supporting the objectives of regional commanders is not necessarily
exploiting the strategic utility of special operations forces.

In September 30, 1986, the year before the Cohen-Nunn Amendment created
USSOCOM, the Goldwater-Nichols Department of Defense Reorganization Act
of 1986 became law, marking the end of one cycle and the beginning of another
in the long-standing debate about how to organize America's military forces and
command structure. Goldwater-Nichols was the culmination of more than four
years of passionate, often bitter debate dating to 1982, when former chairman of
the Joint Chiefs of Staff (JCS) Gen. David C. Jones called for fundamental change
in the operation of the JCS.[2]

The issues outlined by General Jones are instructive in assessing the ability
of the United States to wage unconventional warfare. For Jones, the tension that
existed between individual service priorities and those of the Joint Staff necessitated
an empowered Joint Staff to provide for the best security for the nation.[3] Today,
the tension that exists between USSOCOM and the Joint Staff with respect to
conventional versus unconventional operations often results in suboptimal solutions

to important issues of national security. SOCOM often ameliorates this tension by unwittingly refraining from offering an unconventional warfare (UW) option.

Furthermore, the services have a great deal to say about SOF structure and doctrine, both of which are designed to support large-scale conventional operations. In other words, the potential to conduct unconventional warfare is adversely affected by a conventionally oriented Joint Staff and by individual service concepts of how SOF is to support large-scale conventional operations. We are at the end of a cycle just as we were prior to Goldwater-Nichols.

DUEL HATTING

In the pre-Goldwater-Nichols era, General Jones identified the problem of "dual hatting" a service chief as a JCS member. The old system called on the JCS member to transcend his own service's interests and develop policy advice from a unified military perspective—a "national" viewpoint. Yet, as a chief of a service, the same individual was looked upon as its principal advocate. Theoretically, joint responsibilities were supposed to take precedence over service responsibilities. In reality, the primary loyalty of top officers remained with their respective parent services, which provided them with a political and budgetary power base that a relatively abstract group such as the JCS could not duplicate.

Bilateral loyalties also put America's top military advisers in a difficult position. No chief could rationally advocate additional divisions, ships, or planes as a service spokesman and then recommend reductions during JCS review. Siding with his service might temporarily imperil a chief's rapport with JCS compatriots, but disapproving proposals by his service even once on important matters could cost him permanent loss of its confidence.[4]

Today, the "national" viewpoint of the Joint Chiefs is unified, but conventional. The Joint Chiefs are the individuals from each service who have been identified through a lifetime of exceptional performance to lead their services into the future. These individuals also represent their services' past. They are products of organizational cultures and the prevailing assumptions, ideas, and norms that guide actions within their services. These men come from their organization's center and represent that center. Unconventional warfare is not a part of mainstream warfare. Consequently, the Joint Chiefs do not, and cannot represent an unconventional warfare approach.

One would think that USSOCOM, a four-star unified command, could advance unconventional warfare options to the president and the secretary of defense. The reality is quite different. In fact, the creation of a special operations unified command conceals the problem and compounds the inadequacy of the Joint Staff with respect to unconventional warfare.

This shortcoming manifests itself in two ways. First, the SOCOM commander and his service component commanders have bilateral loyalties similar to what existed before Goldwater-Nichols. The services promote and select the officers who will command both SOCOM and its service components. Additionally, the services provide the majority of the standardized equipment and institutional support to SOCOM units. Based on our discussion of organization theory in chapter 3, this creates a dependency relationship between the SOF and their respective services and makes the services stakeholders in the way SOF perform their assigned missions. The stakeholder aspect represents the second shortcoming.

DEPENDENCY

Officers depend on their service for advancement and command opportunities. To be sure, the services also depend on their officer corps to provide for national defense. However, the individual officer needs his service more than the service needs the individual officer. This situation is simply a function of the availability of alternative supply—many officers, one service. The service has power over individual officers, because it always has alternative sources of supply. As a result, the services have power over their officers and can impose elements of structure on them.

STAKEHOLDERS

The sets of entities in an organization's environment that play a role in the organization's health and performance, or that are affected by the organization, are called stakeholders. Stakeholders have interests in what the organization does and may or may not have the power to influence the organization to protect their interests. Stakeholders are varied, and their interests may coincide on some issues and not others. Therefore, you find stakeholders both cooperating with each other in alliances and competing with each other.

The services benefit more when the SOF directly support large (conventional) concepts of warfare. Special operations that are conducted independent of larger conventional operations are viewed as a threat to a service's long-term health and relevance. The services, therefore, have an important interest—a stake—in the roles and missions of their special operations components. The services protect their interests by controlling doctrine (and personnel assignments and promotions as noted above). Accordingly, doctrine almost always places the SOF in a supporting role in all conflict scenarios.

This explains why, as the war in Afghanistan became increasingly unconventional, the command and control arrangements became more conventional. After being confronted with a drastically altered operational setting, the command arrangement evolved into a large and complex structure that could not adequately respond to the new unconventional setting. The war no doubt would have started with this complex command structure if it could have been rapidly organized and deployed. Fortunately, this was not possible.[5]

This new structural arrangement was in sharp contrast to the early stages of the campaign, where the Joint Special Operations Task Force (JSOTF) headquarters effectively communicated directly with Gen. Tommy Franks, commander USCENTCOM (U.S. Central Command), through a daily video teleconference (VTC) link. This unorthodox arrangement gave a relatively low-level commander a direct link to the theater commander. This proved effective in the fight that led to the collapse of the Taliban.[6]

DESIRE FOR UNANIMITY

Jones also cited a desire for unanimity as an obstacle to effective JCS operation. In practice, the JCS believed that its recommendations carried more weight if they reflected the agreement of all the chiefs. Rather than offer policy alternatives, the chiefs considered it their responsibility to debate the options and refine them into a single recommendation. This meant that JCS advice on any controversial issue almost invariably reflected the lowest common denominator of what the services agreed on. Jones described the advice provided by the JCS as "not crisp, timely, very useful or very influential. And that advice is often watered down and issues are papered over in the interest of achieving unanimity." He concluded that the "resulting lack of credibility has caused the national leadership to look elsewhere for recommendations that properly should come from the JCS."[7]

The relationship that existed between the JCS and the services prior to Goldwater-Nichols is analogous to USSOCOM's current bargaining positions with the JCS and the regional combatant commanders. To begin with, USSOCOM rarely plans and executes military operations. USSOCOM normally provides forces to the combatant commanders, who are responsible for planning and executing operations within their geographic areas of responsibility.[8] This means that any input USSOCOM offers regarding military operations cannot materially diverge from mainstream warfighting paradigms. This is exactly what appears to have taken place in mid-September 2001 as the Bush administration searched to find an appropriate military response to the terrorist attacks in New York and Washington. It was the CIA that introduced the unorthodox warfare approach that President George W. Bush approved. The Defense Department never developed a strategy to fight this "new and different" type of war. Moreover, the president commented to Vice President Dick Cheney and Deputy Secretary of Defense Paul Wolfowitz that he found the military options offered by the chairman of the Joint Chiefs "unimaginative."

Jones also noted that neither experience nor education had equipped most officers to perform well in the joint arena. Joint assignments were not considered stepping-stones to success. They diverted officers from the mainstream of their respective military services into channels where duties conflicted with narrow service interests.[9]

The issue of possessing appropriate relevant experience for duty with the SOF has not been completely solved, although much has been done. Key positions on SOF staffs are mostly filled by officers with special operations experience. That said, the commander of the U.S. Air Force special operations component during the peak of operations in Afghanistan never served in a special operations unit prior to his assignment. If we look closely at the unconventional warfare experience level of officers in key SOF positions, we see a more ominous picture.

To start with, none of the six men who have commanded USSOCOM had relevant unconventional warfare experience. In fact, none of the five army officers who have commanded USSOCOM were career special forces officers. The quality of these men was certainly very high—perhaps sufficiently high to warrant their selection over others to the position. Also, maybe the special forces branch was too new and immature to have seasoned generals to fill SOF's senior position.

The issue of experience in the unconventional realm within the special operations community has implications that affect the nature of special operations and the soul of its organization. John Collins noted in his assessment of special operations forces that army generals selected to command USSOCOM come from the Joint Special Operations Command (JSOC), the Ranger Regiment, or the 82nd Airborne Division. Their experience emphasizes direct action, or strike missions—missions that Thomas K. Adams says are conventional, though executed with a degree of precision not routinely observed in conventional units. Also, no active duty psyop or civil affairs officer has ever been promoted to general officer. Even within the U.S. Army Special Operations Command, the home of U.S. Army Special Forces, only two of the six previous commanders were career special forces officers. The others had backgrounds in direct-action operations. Finally, air force generals in SOF positions often arrive via conventional routes.[10]

If we look closely at special operations in Afghanistan, we see an emphasis on direct-action or strike missions aimed at capturing or killing senior Taliban and al Qaeda leaders. Bringing these senior leaders to justice was, and is, important. However, the nature of the threat after the disintegration of the Taliban was actually more complex than it was prior to their collapse. The new operating environment called for counterinsurgency operations, which encompass a broader array of activities than is needed for successful strike missions. The political-military nature of counterinsurgency is more closely related to unconventional warfare than it is to direct-action operations.

Why did the commander of the special operations component of USCENT-COM (COMSOCCENT) remain oriented on strike when the environment called for a more comprehensive response? The answer appears straightforward—the training and experience of this very talented officer was in direct-action missions. He had been handsomely rewarded for his performance by promotion to flag rank. In fact, even before the September 11 attacks, COMSOCCENT had been developing a theater crisis response element (CRE) to respond, preemptively, against terrorists. It was clear the threat in the region was increasing. General Franks backed the concept. In addition, top CIA officials were briefed and were enthusiastic about the plan's potential. The ability to preempt, instead of respond to events such as the attack on the USS Cole and the U.S. embassy bombings in Africa was what the CIA was looking for. According to Director of Central Intelligence George Tenet and his counterterrorism chief, Cofer Black, the CRE gave the Agency an in-house "door kicking" capability that eliminated the need to rely on host-nation forces that were often undependable.[11] Direct action turned heads. It was simple, straightforward, and did not necessitate a combination of programs that required a long-term commitment and could be construed as nonmilitary.

One can easily, and appropriately, conclude that the rewards for being experienced in the direct-action realm of special operations exceed the rewards afforded those who develop unconventional warfare expertise. The incentive, therefore, to become accomplished in unconventional warfare is less than that for direct action. This would not be very important if it did not have the effect of slowly breeding out true unconventional thinking in the special operations community. This lack of unconventional thinking was clearly demonstrated by the Defense Department's inability to present an alternative strategy to the president and secretary of defense for prosecuting the war in Afghanistan.

The overall effects of the changes made to the JCS system as a result of Goldwater-Nichols have been modest. They have improved U.S. military capabilities and enhanced the prospects for success on the battlefield. That, however, is a narrow perspective. By choosing to focus primarily on military effectiveness, policy makers ignored a more important dimension, strategy. Senior civilian officials, therefore, often relied on civilian staffs and other experts for advice that should be provided by professional military officers. Perhaps this explains why unconventional warfare options seem to originate from outside the DoD. The DoD occasionally is pushed to consider an unconventional method, but an unconventional or unorthodox method is not unconventional warfare.

In sum, current DoD structure, leadership, and control mechanisms do not allow for alternative options that fall outside of conventional warfare paradigms. Structurally, unconventional warfare concepts are unlikely to survive the routing from originator to national-level decision maker. Current senior leaders value special operations that support conventional war. As a result, special operators who excel in direct-action missions—the missions that are conventional in nature and best understood by senior military leaders—will be rewarded through promotions and selection to command positions. Last, the services will continue to hold at least partial control in the way the SOF operate through the promotion and selection processes, through providing major items of equipment and by producing doctrine that will keep SOF in a supporting role to conventional operations.

THE NEED TO FOCUS ON AND UNDERSTAND THE EXTERNAL ENVIRONMENT

The UW operational environment consists of microclimates, which are defined by geography, history, ethnicity, religion, and politics. Geography must be understood in at least three contexts: political, cultural, and physical. The political is constantly changing.

The cultural geography is important in a tribal context. Who are the tribesmen and what do they do? How do they live? Who do they associate with? The physical geography concerns the specific ground on which operations will occur. What is the terrain like? How will the weather affect operations? What constitutes key terrain? What characteristics about the terrain will limit the effectiveness of modern technology and level the playing field for the enemy? History tells us that those who become involved in irregular wars without knowing the history of tribal conflict in the area are headed for trouble. Ethnicity is another powerful consideration. Ethnicity is often enough to determine where a given group will line up in a conflict, determine recruitment potential, or shape political alignments and alliances. Religion is another powerful force. It can reinforce ethnicity but by itself is too simplistic to be a useful guide. After all, Muslims have fought Muslims, and Christians have fought Christians. Understanding local politics is vital. This type warfare is an extension of local feuds, betrayal, and unpaid old debts. Former speaker of the U.S. House of Representatives, Tip O'Neil, once said that "All politics are local." This statement is especially true in unconventional warfare. Understanding these external factors is a necessary condition for success in unconventional warfare.

Attrition v. Maneuver

The old saying goes: "If you don't know what to do, do what you know." The U.S. military style of planning and operational control is well suited for front-opening campaigns on the scale of Normandy in June 1944 and Iraq in March 2003. When the scale is reduced, the efficient and effective standard model rapidly becomes dysfunctional. Edward Luttwak addressed this issue in his commentary about the nature of the attrition-versus-maneuver approach to war in the context of irregular warfare. Luttwak claims that a military's position along the attrition-maneuver continuum is "manifest in their operational methods, tactics, and organizational arrangements, but especially in their methods of officer education."[12]

When victory is a product of an operational concept that transforms superior material resources into firepower by the application of the latter upon the enemy, the closer this military is to the attrition end of the continuum. An armed force of this kind wins wars by focusing on its internal processes to maximize operational efficiencies. Logically, this type of well-managed military force with a high attrition orientation cannot be very adaptive to the external environment.[13]

Alternatively, when victory is to be obtained by identifying specific enemy vulnerabilities and then reconfiguring one's own capabilities to exploit those weaknesses, the closer this military is to the maneuver end of the continuum. Accordingly, this type of armed forces will tend to be externally oriented. Success becomes a function of the organization's ability to interpret the external environment and all its complexities, and then to adapt internally to suit the requirements of the particular situation. Logically, this type of military organization with a high maneuver orientation is unlikely to be able to maximize internal process efficiencies and cannot usually develop optimal organizational formats and tactics.[14]

The U.S. Military — Attrition or Maneuver

A state's military force finds its position on the attrition-maneuver continuum over time based on the perceived balance of military power. A wealthy state will usually choose the attrition model to minimize risk by developing a balance of power in its favor. Minimizing risk, however, comes at a high material cost. A poor state with large ambitions must resort to the maneuver model that offers low material costs and a high potential payoff in exchange for corresponding risks. For the United States, "the strategy of annihilation became characteristically the American way of war."[15] Attrition best supports a strategy of annihilation.

There is no inherent virtue to either attrition or maneuver warfare. However, any equality between these two approaches to war ends when the enemy chooses to fight in an irregular manner.[16] This is because the relevance of attrition declines as the targets become less defined and more dispersed. Simply put, even the best precision guided munitions are ineffective against an insignificantly disposed and untargetable enemy. The pursuit of attrition efficiencies against an irregular enemy can only be damaging to one's own cause. Generating greater firepower against an ill-defined and well-dispersed enemy is likely to be counterproductive by producing collateral damage, antagonizing the population, increasing the ranks of the enemy, and eventually demoralizing one's own forces as a result of increasingly well-coordinated attacks generated by an increasingly hostile population.[17]

Irregular Warfare as a Subset of Conventional Warfare
In theory, a competently led military force should be able to make the necessary adjustments according to the situation at hand to achieve the optimal position on the attrition-maneuver continuum. In practice, however, it is not so easy. The deep-seated influences of structure and education are so pervasive that they cannot be overcome. This was the case in Vietnam. This is also the case in Afghanistan.

The irony of the U.S. attrition model is that the SOF, by their nature, are adaptable and therefore follow the maneuver model. The existence of the SOF component within the U.S. military force structure is an implied recognition that irregular warfare is not a subset of conventional warfare. But, the maneuver model contradicts the dominant orientation of the U.S. military—that of attrition. This, in part, explains why the U.S. military, in spite of external conditions that are not conducive to attrition-based warfare, always wages war in the same, predictable manner.[18]

Attrition, Maneuver, and Afghanistan
Claims regarding the nature of the U.S. effort in Afghanistan consistently describe a "different kind of war." On numerous occasions, the defense secretary has characterized the U.S. strategy as both "unconventional" and directed against an "unconventional" enemy. If the U.S. military adjusted its warfighting organization and tactics based on the nature of the enemy, the approach to the campaign would have a high "maneuver" orientation. Although much of the early success in the campaign was the result of modified tactical procedures and organizational arrangements, the warfighting model at the operational level remained firmly at the attrition end of the attrition-maneuver continuum. As the war continued, this became increasingly evident, as discussed in Andrew Krepinevich in The Army and Vietnam:

> Some have stated that the strategy of attrition was not a strategy at all but actually reflected the absence of one. The sheer weight of American materiel and resources seemed sufficient to the military leadership to wear down the North Vietnamese and their VC allies; thus, strategy was not necessary. All that was needed was the sufficient application of firepower. It had worked against the Japanese and the Germans in World War II and against the Chinese in Korea. It would be tried again in Vietnam.[19]

Krepinevich's statement, which once held true in Vietnam, seems more relevant today when applied to the situation in Afghanistan. The coalition has relied on its overwhelming mass and superiority of firepower and technology to supplant a comprehensive and unified strategy for Afghanistan. In addition, differing perceptions on the nature and status of the conflict have resulted in an overall disjointed effort among government and military organizations, producing redundancy and neglect of the fundamental aspects of counterinsurgency. While efforts at a unified approach to reconstruction began in mid 2003 with the introduction of the provincial reconstruction teams (PRTs), this effort has yet to be applied as part of a systematic approach that expands upon its success, condemning it to irrelevance despite its isolated benefit.[20] The effort in Afghanistan remains disjointed and unfocused, dominated by a partial strategy that addresses a single aspect of the spectrum of counterinsurgency, resulting in a slow defeat from within as the insurgents expand their hold over an increasingly frustrated population.

On March 20, 2002, George Tenet, director of the CIA, warned the Armed Services Committee of the impending shift in strategy by Taliban and al Qaeda forces operating within Afghanistan: "You're entering into another phase here that actually is more difficult, because you're probably looking at smaller units that intend to operate against you in a classic insurgency format."[21] However, less than three weeks earlier, Secretary of Defense Donald Rumsfeld characterized the status of security in Afghanistan differently, stating, "[We] have concluded we're at a point where we clearly have moved from major combat activity to a period of stability and stabilization and reconstruction activities. The bulk of this country today is permissive, it's secure."[22] Differing perceptions on the nature of the threat as well as the phase of conflict have come to characterize thinking among senior leaders in the U.S. government. These differing perceptions have created disjointed policies that cascade downward into conflicting and overlapping efforts and the overall lack of a single unified and comprehensive plan for Afghanistan. As a result, government agencies have pursued individual agendas independent of the operations of other forces operating in the same theater.

The lack of a comprehensive plan is no more evident than in military operations in which the sole pursuit has been the counterforce aspect of counterinsurgency dominated by the strategy of attrition. This singular focus on the attrition of enemy forces has inhibited the successful conduct of operations in Afghanistan in three ways. First, the successful use of force has been constrained by the lack of intelligence and used as a reflexive action rather than a proactive measure or as a deterrent allowing the insurgents to retain the initiative. The ancient Chinese military strategist Sun Tzu highlighted the danger in the reliance on a reflexive strategy in response to an enemy that cannot be located except by their choosing, stating, "If I am able to determine the enemy's disposition, while at the same time I conceal my own, then I can concentrate and he must divide. And if I concentrate while he divides, I can use my entire strength to attack a fraction of his."[23] The Taliban have capitalized on this lesson by targeting smaller government outposts and forces as well as undefended aid workers to achieve maximum psychological impact on the population and the international community.

Secondly, this singular, reflexive pursuit of the insurgents reinforced by its relatively minor successes has dominated the focus of coalition commanders, preventing the systematic application of forces and effort and making commanders oblivious to other aspects of counterinsurgency. A deterrence capability requires a highly developed intelligence system, enlarged and improved paramilitary and police forces, and expanded engineering and medical units for civic action in remote areas, rather than conventionally armed and trained military units with heavy firepower. The lack of focus on the security of the population produced by this pursuit has allowed the insurgents to retain their hold over the population, detracting from the coalition's ability to move and operate freely among the population as well as gather the intelligence essential to the overall success of operations.

Finally, the focus on attrition, the lack of security, and the overriding force protection concerns have severed the link between coalition forces and the indigenous population, eliminating the most valuable source of operational intelligence—the population—and inhibiting the ability of the coalition to locate and destroy the insurgents. Intelligence is the principal source of information on insurgents, and intelligence comes from the population. But the population will not talk unless it feels safe, and it will not feel safe until the insurgent's power has been broken.[24] The continued efforts of coalition forces to acquire information on the insurgents from an unwilling population has resulted in a growing resentment and alienation stemming from the cultural insensitivity, mistakes, and duplication of effort of coalition forces. In a letter of protest to the United Nations' mission in Afghanistan, the villagers of Lejay wrote, "The Americans searched our province. They did not find Mullah Omar, they did not find Osama bin Laden, and they did not find any Taliban. They arrested old men, drivers, and shopkeepers, and they injured women and children."[25] The building resentment of the Afghan populace, reinforced by mounting civilian casualties and cultural insensibility, has shifted the Afghan popular perception of the coalition from that of a liberator to one of an invader.

The lack of unity of effort among government agencies further compounds this problem. Competing efforts among government and military organizations in the strategy of attrition have fostered a lack of cooperation among agencies operating within Afghanistan, resulting in a lack of intelligence sharing and conflicting actions and further diminishing the capability of the coalition to achieve its ends. The duplication of effort has resulted in additional burden placed on the population of Afghanistan, as wave after wave of coalition forces from different units and organizations invade their villages and towns in pursuit of the same objectives. Finally, reconstruction efforts remain independent of military operations, creating a fundamental disconnect between aid and security that allows insurgents to capitalize on relief efforts that occur in areas the insurgents control. Additionally, efforts are applied in a distributed manner without regard for capitalizing on previous success, producing limited, isolated effects. Coalition operations in Afghanistan are characterized by the lack of a unified effort, a disproportionate focus on the attrition aspect of counterinsurgency, and neglect of local security and control. These defining characteristics have stymied coalition efforts in what can only be referred to as an operational quagmire that will eventually lead to the collapse of the Afghan government through the lack of stability and control and the growing legitimacy of insurgent forces.

Afghanistan—Two Phases

The U.S. campaign in Afghanistan can logically be divided into two distinct phases. Phase one took place between October and December 2001 and involved the defeat of the Taliban. This phase can be characterized as a fight against a conventionally disposed enemy force. The method for achieving decisive results revolved around a precision bombing campaign. To be sure, special operations forces were key to identifying targets for precision bombing as well as to coordinate the efforts of a disparate Afghan resistance in order to form a viable and essential ground force. Phase one can aptly be described as SOF-centric.[26] This phase involved decentralized operations, a high degree of autonomy, and small unit actions all taking place in a dynamic environment. The SOF certainly seemed to be operating at the maneuver end of the attrition-maneuver continuum. And, this is exactly where the SOF should be expected to operate. However, at the operational level, the war involved converting material resources into firepower aimed at destroying the Taliban and eventually al Qaeda.

Phase two of the war began with the fall of the Taliban in December 2001 to the present. This second phase can be characterized as a fight against an increasingly unconventional enemy. The Taliban had disintegrated. Its remnants, along with what remained of al Qaeda, dispersed into the rugged Afghan countryside. As the need to adapt to an increasingly dispersed and untargetable enemy increased, the U.S. military seemed to gain traction and did what it knows best—execute warfare at the attrition end of the attrition-maneuver continuum. In March of 2002, the 10th Mountain Division assumed operational control of all operations in Afghanistan.[27] The SOF would now have to subordinate their activities to a conventional headquarters that represented, by its very nature, an attrition-based organization. In June of 2002, the 18th Airborne Corps headquarters relieved the 10th Mountain

Division and assumed control of operations and further consolidated its control and corresponding reliance on the attrition model of warfare. SOF operations could now be characterized by a complex command and control arrangement and exhibiting limited autonomy. The SOF were in support of a conventional headquarters operating under the attrition model of warfare.

A Comparison of the U.S. Military and Its Enemy

A quick analysis seems to show that the remaining Taliban and al Qaeda adapted to the environment after December 2002. However, the U.S. response evolved contrary to environmental considerations. Where the enemy has become more dispersed, the United States has become larger and more concentrated. The decision loop for the enemy is quick, where the U.S. decision loop has slowed. The enemy is operating "underground," while the United States is operating in the open. The enemy has folded back into the population, while the U.S. mode of operation has distanced the population from the U.S. military. The enemy can observe much of what the United States is doing, while the United States sees very little of what the remaining Taliban and al Qaeda do. In short, as the threat became more unconventional, the U.S. response became more conventional and correspondingly more attrition based. The U.S. military possesses a "DNA" that can only produce one solution, a conventional solution at the attrition end of the attrition-maneuver continuum.

The requirement to make adjustments is perhaps most obvious in the area of intelligence capabilities. We have an unequaled capability to strike terrorists, and the DoD is taking steps to improve that capability. But finding the terrorists is the problem. We are more visible to them than they are to us. This means that intelligence is the necessary basis for everything we do in the war on terrorism. Human intelligence is the critical kind of intelligence, because the terrorists' signature is less susceptible to technical collection means than the nation-state targets for which national technical means are optimized. The human intelligence problem is complex and obviously involves activities undertaken by agencies other than the DoD.

To understand intelligence in the war on terrorism and why we have difficulty in collecting it, we have to understand that terrorists operate in two worlds.[28] The two worlds are not geographic places, but social, economic, political, and informational systems. Nor are they necessarily completely distinct. On the contrary, they coincide to at least some degree almost everywhere, with some countries characterized more by one of the two worlds than the other. The United States, for example, is more "Western" than "non-Western." Nigeria is more non-Western than Western. Almost every country today has some elements of the two worlds within its borders. The United States has non-Western elements, mostly in recent immigrant communities, for example.

Our intelligence capability is optimized for the Western world. Terrorists can operate in both. This is true not just of al Qaeda but also, for example, of the IRA, which has relied on ethnic organizations and the Irish diaspora for fund-raising and recruiting. As we penetrate the terrorists' Western world of support, communication, influence, and control, they can revert to the non-Western. To prevail, we must be able to operate equally well in both worlds.

Operating well in the non-Western world requires that we recognize its operational dynamic. This world runs on personal relationships, which means relationships of trust based on blood relations or at least long acquaintance. It is true that in the Western world, it helps to know people, but it is possible, for example, to get services from government agencies without having any personal or familial or tribal relationships with the people who work in these agencies. Moreover, if service is not good, there are ways to make it better that also do not depend on personal relationships. Generally speaking, these things are not possible or are much more difficult to accomplish in the non-Western world without family or tribal connections.

Because threats to our security often arise from the non-Western world, we must establish a sustained presence in the non-Western sectors of selected countries overseas. It might be more accurate to say that DoD should develop a version of the intelligence-gathering capability that resides already in many large police departments.[29] Establishing such a presence will allow us to build the personal relationships and trust that are critical to operational success in the non-Western world. What we have in mind by trust is not some generalized feeling of good will toward the United States or its personnel but personal relationships of mutual confidence built through sustained face-to-face contact.

Once we have established that trust, we will find it easier to gather the intelligence we need to fight terrorism, because we will have entered the human world where the terrorists live and operate. As we build trust, we will also build our influence. As we build our influence and increase our intelligence, these efforts will begin to reinforce one another. They will work together to increase our security in two ways. First, as our influence in, and intelligence about, the non-Western world grow, terrorists will find it harder to take advantage of the largely non-Western areas where they have tended to plan and hide. Second, building long-term relationships of trust will increase the likelihood that we can penetrate terrorist organizations. Concentric circles of supporters and sympathizers surround the hard core that kills. U.S. strategy must ultimately focus on getting people to move from the inner rings of the circle to the outer rings to decrease the support and sympathy that people give the terrorists. With success in this endeavor, the hard core will also become increasingly exposed, isolated, and easier to destroy. At the same time as people move out and away from the hard core, if we have penetrated the non-Western world, we will increase the chance that we will be able to direct people under our control to move in from the outer rings toward the hard core at the center.

The Defense Department is well positioned to penetrate the non-Western world, because it already has the capability to do so, as rudimentary as this currently is. It is lodged in the unconventional warfare skills of the SOF.

To have a clear idea of the capability that currently exists for this task, the difference between direct action and unconventional warfare forces must briefly be reviewed. Direct action (DA) is the application of armed force, typically done in the SOF community by hyperconventional forces such as the Rangers and special mission units, but also by special forces and SEAL teams. Very little care is taken in how the local population might be affected by DA missions beyond avoiding casualties and unnecessary collateral damage. Essentially, those who wield armed force in the name of DA make no attempt to win over the local population. They arrive in time of crisis and then they go away. Building relations is anathema to them.

Building relations, however, is critical to generating the kind of intelligence needed so that hunter-killer teams can strike accurately and effectively. To build these relations in the way they are built throughout most of the world requires us to do things in a manner significantly different from the way DA teams operate and the way the SOF's UW capability is currently used.

The aim of an UW capability is to work by, with, and through indigenous personnel over the long term. They would develop long-term, long-standing person-to-person relations. Their presence and expertise would provide a permanent, trustworthy ear to the ground to ultimately capture or kill "high-value targets" through either local military or police operations or as a result of U.S. military operations. Moreover, locally executed operations conducted as part of a U.S. UW plan facilitates greater geographical coverage for the global war on terror at reduced cost. Solving this intelligence problem will require organizational and cultural changes within the U.S. military.

A Simple Chain of Command and Freedom of Action

> Confronted with a task, and having less information available than is needed to perform that task, an organization may react in either of two ways. One is to increase its information-processing capacity, the other to design the organization, and indeed, the task itself in such a way as to enable it to operate on the basis of less information. These approaches are exhaustive; no others are conceivable. A failure to adopt one or the other will automatically result in a drop in the level of performance.[30]

Command and Control

In the above quotation, Martin van Creveld is referring to two distinct manners of command. A system of command should properly distribute authority and responsibility among the various echelons of the military organization. Striking a correct balance between centralization and decentralization, discipline and initiative, and authority and individual responsibility is essential for military success.[31]

No single activity in war is more important than command and control (C^2). C^2 by itself will not destroy a single enemy target. It will not affect a single resupply. Yet, nothing in war is possible without effective C^2. Without C^2, military units degenerate into mobs, and the subordination of military force to policy is replaced by random violence. With C^2, the countless activities a military force must perform gain purpose and direction. Command and control helps commanders make the most of what they have—people, information, material, and time. In short, command and control is essential to all military operations.

Modern war is distinguished by its speed and by the need for close synchronization among many kinds of command and combat support functions. Accordingly, other factors being equal, a command system that allows for initiative at the lowest level is likely to be superior to one that does not. To put effective command and control into practice, we must first understand its fundamental nature, its purpose, characteristics, environment, and basic functioning.

The Nature of C^2

Sometimes C^2 takes the form of a conscious command decision—as in deciding on a concept of operations. Sometimes it takes the form of a preconditioned reaction—as in combat drills, practiced in advance so that they can be executed reflexively in a moment of crisis. Sometimes it takes the form of a rules-based procedure—as in the guiding of an aircraft on final approach. Other forms may require such a degree of judgment and intuition that they can be performed only by skilled, experienced people.

The Relationship between Command and Control

The traditional view of command and control sees "command" and "control" operating from the top of the organization toward the bottom.[32] The reality, however, is different. C^2 is a dynamic process that sees command as the exercise of authority, and control as feedback about the effects of the action taken. The continuous flow of information allows the commander to adjust and modify command action as needed. Feedback may come from any direction and in any form. Feedback allows commanders to adapt to changing circumstances, exploit fleeting opportunities, respond to developing problems, modify schemes, or redirect efforts.[33] Command

and control is thus an interactive process involving all the parts of the system and working in all directions. The result is a mutually supporting system of give and take in which complementary commanding and controlling variables interact to ensure that the force as a whole can adapt continuously to changing requirements.

War Is the Realm of Uncertainty

The defining problem of command and control that overwhelms all others is the need to deal with uncertainty. Were it not for uncertainty, C^2 would be a simple matter of managing resources. Uncertainty is what we do not know about a given situation. Uncertainty is doubt that blocks or threatens to block action. Uncertainty pervades the battlefield in the form of unknowns about the enemy, about the surroundings, and even about our own forces. Furthermore, the rapid tempo of modern operations limits the amount of information that can be gathered, processed, and assimilated in time to be of use. Command and control thus becomes a race against time. So, the second requirement in any C^2 system is to be fast, at least faster than the enemy.[34]

The resulting tension between coping with uncertainty and racing against time presents the fundamental challenge of command and control. This is perhaps its single most important challenge. Fortunately, the enemy faces the same problem. The object of the successful commander is to achieve some relative advantage.

The C^2 Spectrum

As Creveld noted in the quotation at the beginning of this section, there are two basic responses to the fundamental problem of uncertainty—to pursue certainty as the basis for effective command and control or to accept uncertainty as a fact and to learn to function in spite of it. The first response is to try to minimize uncertainty by creating a powerful, highly efficient C^2 apparatus able to process large amounts of information in order to minimize all unknowns. The result is complex and detailed command and control. Such a system stems from the belief that if we can impose order and certainty on the disorderly and uncertain battlefield, then success will result.[35]

This type of C^2 can be coercive in its attempt by the commander to achieve unity of effort. In such a system, the commander holds a tight rein, commanding by personal direction or detailed directive. C^2 tends to be centralized and formal. Orders and plans are detailed and explicit. Their successful execution requires strict obedience and minimizes subordinate decision making and initiative. Detailed command and control emphasizes vertical, linear information flow. Information flows up the chain of command, and orders flow down. Discipline and coordination are imposed from above to ensure compliance with the plan.[36]

In a system based on detailed C^2, the command and control process tends to move slowly. Such a system does not generally react well to rapidly changing situations. Nor does it function well when the vertical flow of information is disrupted. This approach represents an attempt to overcome the fundamental nature of war. Detailed command and control risks falling short of its desired result. The question is whether it nears the desired result enough to achieve overall success.

By contrast, "mission command" and control accepts the turbulence and uncertainty of war.[37] Rather than try to increase the level of certainty, mission C^2 attempts to reduce the degree of certainty that is needed. Mission C^2 is not the product of conformity imposed from above but of the unpremeditated cooperation of all the elements of the force.[38] Subordinates are guided not by detailed instructions and control measures but by their knowledge of the requirements of the overall mission. In such a system, the commander holds a loose rein, allowing subordinates significant freedom of action. Because it grants subordinates significant freedom of action, mission C^2 demands more of leaders at all levels and requires rigorous training and education.[39]

Mission C^2 tends to be decentralized, informal, and flexible. Orders and plans are as brief and simple as possible, relying on subordinates to effect the necessary coordination and on the human capacity for implicit communication based on a mutual understanding of the requirements. By decentralizing decision-making authority, mission command and control seeks to improve the ability to deal with fluid and localized situations. Moreover, with its reliance on implicit communications, mission C^2 is less vulnerable to disruption of the information flow than is detailed command and control.

The two approaches to the problem mark the theoretical extremes of a spectrum of command and control. In practice, no commander will rely entirely on either purely detailed or purely mission methods. Exactly what type of C^2 will be used in a particular situation should depend on a variety of factors, such as the nature of the action, the nature and capabilities of the enemy, and, perhaps most of all, the qualities of the people undertaking the task. This is not to suggest that the two types of command and control are of equal value and merely a matter of personal preference. While detailed command and control may be appropriate in the performance of some tasks, it is less than effective in the overall conduct of military operations in an environment of uncertainty, friction, disorder, and fleeting opportunities in which judgment, creativity, and initiative are required.

How to Organize

Organization is an important tool of command and control. How one organizes can complicate or simplify the problems of execution. By organizing military forces into capable subordinate elements and assigning each its own task, a mission is organized into manageable parts. The organization of a military force, then, should reflect the conceptual organization of the plan.[40] In other words, organization should dictate the chain of command as well as the command and support relationships within the force. Similarly, organization should ensure that a commander has authority over or access to all the resources required to accomplish the assigned mission.

Narrowing span of control, that is, lessening the number of immediate subordinates, means deepening the organization by adding layers of command. But the more layers of command an organization has, the longer it takes for information to move up or down. Consequently, the organization becomes slower and less responsive. Conversely, an effort to increase flexibility by eliminating echelons of command, or flattening an organization, necessitates widening the span of control. The commander will have to resolve the resulting tension that exists between organizational width and depth.

What Should Such a C^2 System Look Like?

Initiative is an essential element of mission command and control, because subordinates must be able to act without instructions. Current warfare doctrine emphasizes seeking and rapidly exploiting fleeting opportunities, possible only through low-level initiative. Initiative hinges on distributing the authority to decide and to act. C^2 should be biased toward decision and action at all levels. All commanders within their own spheres should act on the need for action rather than primarily on orders or explicit approvals from above.

It is important to point out that initiative does not mean that subordinates are free to act without regard to guidance from above. In fact, initiative places a special burden on subordinates, requiring that they always keep the larger situation in mind and act in consonance with their senior's intent. The freedom to act with initiative thus implies a greater obligation to act in a disciplined and responsible way. Initiative places a greater burden on the senior as well. Delegating authority to subordinates does not absolve higher commanders of ultimate responsibility. Consequently, they must frame their guidance in such a way that subordinates are provided sufficient understanding to act in accordance with their desires while not restricting freedom of action. Commanders must be adept at expressing their desires clearly and forcefully.

C^2 in the Information Age

Many of the factors that influence C^2 are timeless—the nature of war and of human beings and the problems of uncertainty and time, for example. Conversely, war cannot help reflect the characteristics of the period. As war has evolved, so has command and control. War has become increasingly complicated, and so have the means of control. Technological improvements in mobility, range, lethality, and information gathering continue to compress time and space, creating a greater demand for information. The more quickly the situation changes, the greater the need for continuously updated information and the greater the strain on command and control.[41] But technology is not without its dangers, namely the overreliance on equipment on the one hand and the failure to fully exploit the latest capabilities on the other. It is tempting, but a mistake, to believe that technology will solve all the problems of command and control. Many hopes of a decisive technological leap forward have been dashed by unexpected complications and side effects or by the inevitable rise of effective countermeasures.[42] Moreover, used unwisely, technology can be part of the problem, contributing to information overload and feeding the dangerous illusion that certainty and precision in war are attainable.

A Final Thought on Command and Control

In general, we should take a flexible approach to organization, maintaining the capability to organize forces to suit the situation that might include the creation of nonstandard and temporary task forces. However, the commander must reconcile this desire for organizational flexibility with the need to create implicit understanding and mutual trust that comes with standing military organizations. Mission C^2 requires the employment of self-reliant military units capable of acting semiautonomously. By organizing into self-reliant groups, we increase each commander's freedom of action and at the same time decrease the need for centralized coordination of support. We also reduce synchronization across an extended battlefield. We should seek to strike a balance between "width" and "depth" so that the organization is suited to the particular situation. The aim is to flatten the organization to the greatest extent compatible with reasonable spans of control. Commanders should have the flexibility to eliminate or bypass selected echelons of command or staff as appropriate in order to improve operational results.

A word is in order about the size of staffs. The larger the staff, the more information it requires to function. This increase in information, in turn, requires an even larger staff, and the result is a spiraling increase in size. However, the larger a C^2 organization, the longer it generally takes that organization to perform its functions. In the words of Gen. William T. Sherman, "A bulky staff implies a division of responsibility, slowness of action and indecision, whereas a small staff implies activity and concentration of purpose."[43] Also, a large staff takes up more space, creates a vulnerable target, and is often a political liability. A large staff may be more capable of detailed analysis and planning than a small one, but speed and agility are generally of greater value than precision and certainty. Under certain conditions, the ideal staff might be so austere it could not exercise fully detailed command and control.

Finally, in a decentralized command and control system, a common vision is essential to have a unity of effort. Without a common perspective and understanding of the battlefield, the various actions will lack cohesion. If the commander does not clearly express a common vision, there simply can be no mission command and control.

SOF C² in Afghanistan

The beginning of this section started with a quotation from Martin van Creveld. Creveld states that there are two alternatives for command and control of military operations. One is to create staffs with enormous information-processing capacity and the capability to precisely manage subordinate units; the second is to design the organization and divide the task itself in such a way to enable subordinate units to operate with less information. The first alternative necessitates tight control by higher headquarters of subordinate elements; the second necessitates loose control. Creveld also tells us that a failure to adopt one of these two alternatives will result in diminished combat performance.

Up until the fall of the Taliban in December 2001, the second of the two alternatives best describes the C² process in Afghanistan. The commander of Task Force (TF) Dagger (essentially the 5th Special Forces Group plus supporting units) was in direct contact with General Franks, the combatant commander. The subordinate elements of TF Dagger had the most current and accurate intelligence about the situation on the ground. It was impossible for anyone in Washington or Tampa to have a better sense of what needed to be done. Therefore, by accident more than by design, control was loose and even the smallest special forces elements were able to respond quickly to the exigencies of the battlefield.

In early 2002, the C² process changed. As soon as the conventional military was able to gain traction, command and control began to resemble the first alternative. According to Creveld, either alternative can produce acceptable results. What was actually developed was quite different from either alternative. It appears that the conventional military created what appeared to be Creveld's first alternative. However, a dangerous and inoperative hybrid of both alternative C² options emerged. Higher headquarters seemed to understand that the war had to be fought at the local level and that each town and province had unique geographic, political, and security issues. Accordingly, bottom-driven operations became the expectation of both CJTF-Mountain and subsequently CJTF-180.[44] Higher headquarters seemed to be moving toward Creveld's second alternative C² process. At the same time, however, CJTF-180 adopted tight controls that reflected the first C^2 process. The result was a large, higher headquarters that didn't (and couldn't) acquire or process the large amounts of information needed to generate combat operations and subordinate elements without the necessary authority to act in a timely manner to emerging situations. This hybrid produced paralysis in the forward-based special forces teams. It also generated operations directed by CJTF-180 based on intelligence that was old and no longer valid.

A quick look at the U.S. military in-country personnel strength figures helps us understand why the military felt a need to adopt tight controls. Troop strength steadily increased each month except in the December–January time frame, which can be explained by a liberal Christmas holiday leave policy, and briefly in April–May 2003, during major combat operations in Iraq. By June 2003, in-country troop strength had recovered and exceeded pre-Iraq war numbers. The following personnel strength figures were obtained from the Directorate of Personnel at CENTCOM Headquarters.

U.S. Service Personnel in Afghanistan

January 2002: 4,024	October 2002: 9,427
February 2002: 4,156	November 2002: 9,509
March 2002: 5,052	December 2002: 9,662
April 2002: 6,980	January 2003: 9,021
May 2002: 7,010	February 2003: 9,583
June 2002: 7,251	March 2003: 9,587
July 2002: 7,884	April 2003: 9,502
August 2002: 8,102	May 2003: 9,344
September 2002: 9,028	June 2003: 9,787

As of November 2005, approximately 18,000 U.S. service personnel are in Afghanistan. This number has remained constant since June 2004.

Lt. Gen. Paul Mikolashek, the land component commander for the initial combat phase of operations, did not ask for or want another large headquarters to run operations in Afghanistan. His intention was to forward deploy a small element of his own headquarters to Bagram Airbase to facilitate command and control. However, the army pressured General Franks to permit the deployment of a division headquarters to oversee all operations in Afghanistan. One general officer commented that the army had to prove itself. The defense secretary had questioned the relevance of the army in dealing with future threats to American interests. Afghanistan was landlocked, so there simply had to be a key role for a division headquarters.

The 10th Mountain Division assumed control of operations in Afghanistan in March 2002. Every four hours the division operations center would have a "huddle" to assess the situation since the previous huddle and to review future activities. The "huddle" routinely contained seventy people, most who had something to say about ongoing operations. To be clear, the seventy people represented only a fraction of the headquarters staff, the "key" people. This large group seemed to contribute more to the fog and friction of war than did the enemy. In June 2002, 18th Airborne Corps took over control of the Afghanistan theater of operations, adding yet another layer of supervision. Now, a special forces detachment's request to conduct an operation could conceivably have to be processed through six levels of command before being approved. One general officer summed up the situation nicely, "Too much overhead!"[45]

Viable C^2 was also affected by the fact that headquarters staff update briefing slides were sent directly to the secretary of defense. At one staff update, the chief of staff of 10th Mountain stressed the importance of consistency among the various staff sections so that the secretary would "get the right story." One admiral stated that Secretary Rumsfeld routinely required commanders to answer tactical questions. These requirements often resulted from the staff update slides that were sent to the secretary, but were also to help prepare the defense secretary for his numerous media presentations. This forced staffs at all levels to focus a considerable amount of effort on providing information up the chain of command. Higher-level staffs were able to cope with Washington's insatiable appetite for information. However, the distraction was nontrivial, especially at the lower levels, where large staffs were nonexistent. Rather than facilitating operations, higher staffs were placing demands on subordinate units that undermined effective combat operations.

Tight command and control paralyzed initiative. Reports from members of the 3rd Special Forces Group in Afghanistan indicate that U.S. forces must obtain approval from the CJTF headquarters before conducting operations six kilometers beyond their firebases. Additionally, all "named" operations (all those other than routine travel) require approval from the CJTF-180 headquarters, which may take up to forty-eight hours. Special forces members in Afghanistan describe the CJTF-180 planning and approval process as "too slow and too large for all operations" and state that "the formal planning process demanded for all operations diminishes responsiveness to the point of inefficacy."[46] The net effect of these restrictions is to impede the flexibility and response of the SOF, thereby surrendering the initiative to local insurgents. The lack of responsiveness of U.S. forces has allowed insurgents to conduct operations unimpeded, thereby diminishing security and control by the central government.

The absence of local security coupled with the lack of contact between U.S.

forces and the population driven by overzealous force protection measures diminished the ability of the coalition to obtain operational intelligence. Force protection measures have limited the beneficial contact between the SOF and the population. Limiting contact with the local population to strictly military ventures such as sweeps en masse seriously impeding efforts to gather vital information necessary to locate and destroy insurgent forces. The use of sweeps has produced the alienation of the local populace, fostering mistrust and creating a further impediment to intelligence collection. Additionally, interviews with several military intelligence officers serving in Afghanistan reveal that that there exists no integrated intelligence collection plan or matrix to divide intelligence requirements among the collection agencies, further convoluting efforts to collect vital intelligence. An intelligence officer operating out of Kandahar Air Base stated, "The CJSOTF has no intelligence collection plan and does not pass down requirements, resulting in insufficiently developed intelligence for certain operations such as no name or picture of the target."[47]

How Could This Happen?

How one organizes can complicate or simplify combat effectiveness. Organization is a function of how a particular problem is diagnosed. A faulty diagnosis will almost always lead to a poor operational plan. Yet, the organization of a military force typically reflects the conceptual organization of the operational plan. In other words, not understanding the post-Taliban situation, yet reflexively organizing according to a traditional military model, created a complex C^2 arrangement incapable of conducting military operations suited to the environment. The Defense Department's organizational culture could only reproduce an offspring that was compatible with its DNA.

An operational plan, organizational structure, and command and control process are inextricably related to one another. To some extent, the genesis of the C^2 problem began with the nation's response to the 9/11 attacks. The CIA, not the DoD, developed the war plan that was approved by the president. In fact, the CIA sent a liaison officer to Fort Campbell to brief the 5th Special Forces Group on the plan. Yet, the DoD provided almost all of the resources for the war. The operational azimuth initially set by the Agency became difficult to overcome. At one point, even Secretary Rumsfeld questioned who was in charge of the war effort. But the initial plan worked; and it worked quicker than almost anyone had anticipated. The quick victory seemed to eliminate any incentive to carefully assess post-Taliban Afghanistan and produce a modified plan, force structure, and appropriate C^2 arrangement.

A Conventional Headquarters in Afghanistan

Afghanistan is a landlocked country. For the U.S. Army, that was a signal that warfare in such a domain was an army responsibility. The U.S. Army was also in the middle of a bureaucratic struggle to demonstrate its future relevance to a defense secretary who was intent on reducing army force structure. The quick victory in a SOF-led war that combined U.S. air power and a ragtag indigenous force highlighted the "relevancy" issue. The army leadership continuously pressured General Franks to get a division headquarters into the fight. Franks would support this important request even though his land component commander located in Uzbekistan, General Mikolashek, didn't want or need a division headquarters. And if a division headquarters was not needed, how was it that after a brief four months, a corps headquarters replaced the division? Simply put, a force structure was decided upon before an assessment of the situation was conducted and a plan was developed. Rather than a plan, appropriate forces, and logical C^2 flowing from a careful diagnosis of the situation, the plan and C^2 flowed from the political imperative of getting a large army headquarters into the fight.

The decision to introduce a large army headquarters into Afghanistan resulted in a chain reaction that conventionalized a war against an enemy that had become very unconventional.[48] A large conventional headquarters requires a lot of support. A large support group requires additional support for sustainment. The result is a spiraling increase in size. Much of the staff effort is devoted to internal management, not the external dimension that includes the war effort. In fact, during a period in March 2002, C–130 cargo aircraft were delivering refrigerators and water heaters to Bagram, while special forces teams waited for airlift to get them to their base camps. Furthermore, conventional units wage conventional war. Their doctrine, training, education, and experience cannot help but produce conventional solutions. One might think that a well-trained army is flexible enough to make the needed adjustments to a new setting. This is not the case. The commander of CJTF–180 commented that existing army doctrine was inadequate to provide a solid basis for action in Afghanistan. A doctrinaire approach to military operations is by definition conventional.

SOF Command and Control
The SOF chain of command created their own problems that were magnified by conventional force C^2 inadequacies. The special operations component commander in CENTCOM (COMSOCCENT) directed that four separate joint special operations task forces be formed.[49] SOCCENT also established its own headquarters in Qatar. The special operations support structure is not designed to support five separate JSOTFs simultaneously. And arguably, there was no need to establish so many commands. The results of the decision to form multiple JSOTFs forced the SOF to rely excessively on conventional support structures. More important, JSOTF

commanders did not have authority over special operations aviation support necessary to conduct operations. Conventional aviation support was available. However, the SOF commanders did not have control of these assets, nor were the conventional aircraft and pilots capable of providing the type of aviation support that was routine for special operations aviation.[50]

COMSOCCENT's decision to establish his headquarters in Qatar also had serious, and perhaps unforeseen, harmful operational consequences on the war effort in Afghanistan. To be sure, COMSOCCENT had regional responsibilities that went beyond the war if Afghanistan. But executing special operations within the region could have been managed from within Afghanistan after December 2001. In addition, Afghanistan was the main effort. COMSOCCENT never really exercised operational control of the SOF inside Afghanistan. The commander of TF Dagger communicated directly with General Franks prior to the fall of the Taliban. COMSOCCENT was a bystander. With the initial phase of the war won and the introduction of a large conventional headquarters into Afghanistan, it was easy and logical to fold the SOF under the conventional umbrella.[51] Simply put, SOCCENT, the special operations component of CENTCOM, relinquished its role in shaping operations in Afghanistan.

The dominating nature of a large conventional headquarters could not help but affect special operations. CJTF-180 did the best they could to establish a common vision for how the war would be prosecuted. Because their assessment of the situation was faulty, the common vision was faulty. If COMSOCCENT was in charge of SOF (or even all military) operations in Afghanistan, it is plausible that its assessment of the problem would have differed from that of CJTF-180, and therefore, that a more appropriate vision would have emerged. To illustrate, SOCCENT's initial plan to defeat the Taliban was classic in its unconventional approach. The plan closely adhered to the doctrinal phases of a U.S.-sponsored unconventional war. The plan never made it to Secretary Rumsfeld's desk. Either the CENTCOM staff or the Joint Staff eliminated it as a viable course of action.[52] If COMSOCCENT had been charged with the conduct of the war, the unconventional warfare plan developed by the staff and internalized by subordinate units likely would have affected the strategy and the operational and tactical dimensions of the campaign. Unfortunately, this was not to be. The war's strategy logically reflected the nature of its controlling headquarters. Conventional headquarters fight conventionally. Their men and women are educated, trained, and equipped to defeat conventional threats. Their experience produces a strategy in line with general-purpose-force capabilities. The SOF simple became another maneuver force to support attrition warfare.

Tight control of all military activities became routine as soon as CJTF-180 took charge. Part of the tight control was the result of the nature of modern conventional operations that requires complex synchronization of many actions. Part of the need for tight controls also seemed to be a by-product of demands from Washington. The secretary of defense continually sought tactical information to help him prepare for his twice-daily press conferences. The defense secretary's requests became the priority effort rather than focusing on combat operations.[53] It is likely that tight controls on combat operations had to be established to allow senior commanders and staff members to keep pace with operations while answering the secretary's queries. At one operations briefing inside CJTF-Mountain's Joint Operations Center (JOC), the task force chief of staff stressed that the briefing slides had to be accurate and consistent, because the slides were sent directly to Secretary Rumsfeld's office unaltered. The implied message was to keep the slides simple and accurate, and operations should follow the slide presentation that went to the secretary. Also, the task force judge advocate general stated that sensitive operations required the secretary's approval, although General Franks could authorize an operation if there was insufficient time to get Washington's approval and the window of opportunity to engage the target was closing. To an extent, tight controls on operations were an inadvertent by-product of trying to create a common operating picture of the battlefield from the foxhole to the Pentagon.

Force Protection

Force protection consists of activities to prevent hostile actions against DoD personnel and equipment. These actions are designed to conserve the force's fighting potential so it can be applied at the decisive time and place while degrading opportunities for the enemy.[54] One seemingly innocuous directive from CJTF-180 that greatly affected SOF operations was a requirement to use armored Humvees when leaving firebases. The purpose of the directive was to minimize the risk while moving on roads within Afghanistan. Some people had been killed while using commercial SUVs to conduct business. Nevertheless, this simple control measure meant that anytime SOF units left a firebase, there was a clear and easily identifiable signature to warn hostile forces. The effect of the directive was to forfeit the element of surprise and to increase the overall danger to the SOF. This is an example of a control measure, appropriate for a conventional force, that significantly undermined the ability of special forces teams to conduct effective operations.

Another control measure designed to allow the JSOTF to scrutinize the activities of forward-based teams was a requirement to submit a written concept to move beyond a three-kilometer radius of a firebase. This requirement should not be confused with a logical requirement to get formal approval to execute deliberate combat operations. A formal approval from higher headquarters was needed to conduct routine business with local military forces or village elders or simply going into town to see what was going on. In other words, special forces teams needed prior authorization for every military action they took. This frustrated the very soldiers who needed the flexibility to move about freely. Furthermore, reacting to fleeting opportunities became impossible. Good intelligence had a life span of about thirty minutes, and getting approval to move beyond the immediate vicinity of a firebase could take more than a day.[55]

Psychological Operations and Civil Military Operations
Psychological operations and civil military operations (CMO) command and control are lacking in at least two aspects. First, they receive little direction from their respective commands. A civil affairs officer operating in Kandahar Province put it this way: "We have the tool but no blueprint. We are conducting civil affairs for the sake of civil affairs." The joint civil military operations task force (JCMOTF) is located in Kabul, separated from all military headquarters involved in prosecuting the war.

According to reports from members of 3rd Special Forces Group operating in Afghanistan, there is a fundamental disconnect between aid programs and military operations. Despite the lack of intelligence cooperation with the military forces by the villagers, military commanders remain unable to stop the flow of aid and benefits to the villagers as a form of carrot and stick approach. This inability produces misperceptions between the villagers and the military and civil affairs and demonstrates that, despite the lack of cooperation and continued attacks on Western personnel, the benefits will continue. A civil affairs officer operating out of a firebase near the city of Deh Rawod stated, "People feel no obligation to the U.S. for CA projects. If a CA team is hit with a mine, the villagers will not give up the names [of the attackers] or intelligence. Even if we stop work in the village, this has little to no impact on the villagers, because they [the villagers] do not feel security comes from the U.S. but from local warlords."[56] Additionally, independent civil relief actions by aid organizations remain autonomous of large-scale planned relief and reconstruction efforts.

Provincial reconstruction teams (PRTs) represent the first truly integrated program implemented by the coalition in Afghanistan. The program combines security with civil action to facilitate reconstruction in a secure environment. The PRTs have three purposes: "To provide a safe environment for humanitarian activities; exchange information between the central government, the army, and nongovernmental organizations; and help the Afghan government project its presence outside of Kabul."[57] U.S. Ambassador to Afghanistan Robert P. Finn said, "There are ongoing security problems. We want to provide a safe platform for other peacetime activities."[58] The program has addressed the concerns of nongovernmental organizations (NGOs) that have been increasingly targeted throughout 2003 by insurgent forces seeking to demonstrate to the population the lack of government progress. The teams are composed of a joint civil-military effort of 50–100 military and civilian personnel tasked to provide relief and facilitate economic development in areas with ongoing security problems through projects such as building schools, repairing damaged bridges, establishing medical clinics, or digging water wells.[59] As of September 2005, PRTs have been established in twenty-two Afghan cities. Some of these teams are led by New Zealand, Lithuania, Germany, Italy, Canada, Great Britain, Netherlands, and Spain.[60] However, the news reports in the latter half of 2003 indicate that the teams have had some success and fostered renewed faith in the Hamid Karzai regime and coalition forces. Muhammed Dalili, governor of the Paktia Province, was quoted as saying, "The suspicion between the local people and the central government has lessened because of the coalition PRT. They see that the central government is working to reconstruct their country, and because of the security forces, there is now a sense of security here among the people."[61]

Despite the limited success of this initiative, the overall effort faces several issues impeding its effectiveness. NGOs have expressed opposition to this program, stating that PRTs blur the line between the military and civil relief and aid projects, resulting in increased targeting of the NGO aid workers. Denis McClean, a spokesman for the International Red Cross and Red Crescent Society, has stated, "We don't believe that military forces should have any part in the delivery of humanitarian aid, or be involved in it—unless in very extreme and difficult circumstances. And we feel that when people see soldiers throwing aid out the back of a truck and providing humanitarian assistance, it blurs the lines of distinction between humanitarian aid workers and the military."[62] Additionally, a State Department representative states that the teams maintain "storefronts" in numerous towns, but do not provide permanent security. Provincial reconstruction teams operate over a wide area containing several villages and towns. The lack of permanent security that results allows criminals, warlords, and insurgents to reclaim areas once the PRTs have moved, allowing them to reap the rewards of the PRTs' efforts. Political, social, economic, and other reforms, however much they ought to be wanted and be popular, are inoperative when offered while the insurgents still control the population. Additionally, the operations needed to relieve the population from the insurgents' threats and to convince it that the counterinsurgents will ultimately win are necessarily intensive in nature and endure for a long time. They require a large concentration of efforts, resources, and personnel. This means that the efforts cannot be diluted all over the country but must be applied successively area by area. While initial efforts have capitalized on the relative security of the cities and provinces in which they operate, attempts to expand these efforts into less-secure areas will result in the insurgents exploiting or mitigating the benefits provided by the PRTs.

The establishment of PRTs represents the first step in the development of an integrated effort to facilitate reconstruction at the local level. However, the lack of a comprehensive plan has resulted in insufficient coalition resources to provide permanent security over the entire area of coverage, while the dispersion of effort has impeded the ability of the coalition to expand on the local success of the individual teams. The plan requires further integration with efforts to train and equip local law enforcement forces that can gradually supplant coalition security forces, thereby allowing the PRT to create stability and security that will remain after the PRT has moved to the next area without fear of the original area returning to the control of criminals and insurgents. Until such efforts are consolidated and focused by a comprehensive plan to systematically expand security and stability and integrated with other programs to foster permanent security, the effects of the PRTs will remain limited and local.

Psyops C^2 is also difficult to unravel. The joint psychological operations task force (JPOTF) is located in Tampa. It is unclear in the minds of psyop officers operating in Afghanistan exactly who approves the various psyop products. While some products are approved in Afghanistan, others must go to Tampa. Additionally, some of the product development is done by the 4th Psychological Operations Group located at Fort Bragg, North Carolina, while other products are developed in country. Additionally, contract professors from the University of Kabul check some products but not others. Also, the U.S. embassy in Kabul sees some products and not others. According to an officer from the 3rd Special Forces Group, there is no coherent psychological operations plan or counterpropaganda plan to relay the progress made by the central government or to counter the claims of the insurgents as to the corruption and lack of progress of the Karzai regime. Because of the lack of psyops activities, insurgents convey their propaganda unopposed, allowing them to dominate the beliefs of a population that is isolated from the rest of the world. Maj. Mohammed Issaq, commander of the Afghan National Army (ANA) unit in Qalat, stated, "If we had a radio station in this province, we can [sic] tell people what the government is doing for them. As it is now, the Taliban can get the word out and tell people whatever it likes."[63]

The vast majority all of psyops and CMO personnel are from the reserve components. While, in most cases, the individual soldiers are highly motivated and qualified in these components, the headquarters elements and communications equipment necessary to establish adequate C^2 are lacking. The separated and inadequate psyops and CMO C^2 results in a poor integration of these important activities into military operations. The whole winds up being much less than the sum of the special operations parts.

Technology

The proliferation of technologies provides nonstate actors with access to capabilities previously attainable only by states. This has the effect of compressing time and space and increasing the demand for information. The information age has had a profound effect on C^2, not all of which is positive. Focusing on equipment has had a tendency to create an illusion of sophistication. While technology might be advanced, its use is not necessarily sophisticated. To an extent, advanced technologies have replaced sophisticated thinking about important issues. One army general officer has commented that we were "too technologically proficient. The quest for perfect knowledge has generated equipment, people, more equipment and more people. Everyone between the most forward-deployed unit and Washington wants information just in case it is needed."[64] Feeding this information-hungry system often becomes the burden of the forward elements. The insatiable appetite for information can paralyze warfighting efforts.

Next, secure e-mail has become a substitute for the more cumbersome Joint Operations Planning and Execution System (JOPES). E-mail is faster and easier, but its informal style leaves out much of what is required to properly coordinate and execute a military operation. Additionally, e-mail invariably does not get distributed to everyone who has a role in an operation. The overreliance on secure e-mail without carefully determining how best to exploit its capabilities was potentially risky. Similarly, the extensive use of secure video teleconferences involving limited personnel created similar risks.

A Final Thought on C^2

An essential part of every successful command and control system is to have a unity of effort that results from a common vision. Many of the shortcomings in C^2 might have been significantly reduced with a less liberal personnel rotation schedule. The U.S. military, including the SOF leadership, seems to think that it is more important to get the troops home for rest and recuperation than it is to effectively prosecute a war. The conditions in Afghanistan are harsh, but not that harsh. Almost to the man, special forces soldiers interviewed in Afghanistan would have preferred to stay until the job was complete. Most were on their second or third tour anyway and were extremely frustrated to find that the progress they had made during their first deployment was no longer visible. They had to start from the beginning and cover much of the same ground that was previously covered. Also, all situations change over time. Consequently, it took time for returning special forces teams to get reoriented to new developments. Continuity on the ground may ameliorate some of the troublesome C^2 issues. Liberal troop rotation policies compound command and control issues and adversely affect the ability of the United States to make significant progress against an enemy that has time on his side.

Our C^2 must improve our ability to generate more successful action than the enemy. It should help us adapt to rapidly changing situations and exploit fleeting opportunities. C^2 should help provide insight into the nature of the problems faced and into the nature and designs of our enemy. It should help us to identify critical enemy vulnerabilities and should provide the means for focusing our efforts against those vulnerabilities. It should help establish goals that are both meaningful and practicable, and it should allow the monitoring of events closely enough to ensure proper execution, yet without interfering with subordinates' actions. C^2 should help us communicate instructions quickly, clearly, and concisely and in a way that provides subordinates the necessary guidance without inhibiting their initiative. We have much room to improve in this vital area.

THE IMPORTANCE OF AN INCENTIVE STRUCTURE TO OUTPUT

An incentive is any factor that provides a motive for a particular course of action, or counts as a reason for preferring one choice to the alternatives. Since human beings are purposeful creatures, the study of incentive structures is central to the study of human behavior both in terms of individual decision making and in terms of cooperation and competition within a larger institutional structure.

A Strategic Rewards System

It should come as no surprise that organizational actors seek information about what activities are rewarded and respond accordingly. Incentive structures are designed to motivate individual and collective action toward attaining established goals and objectives. Incentive structures consist of a set of processes that include goal setting, measuring and assessing action outcomes, judging contributions, distributing rewards, and providing feedback. Incentive structures serve a motivational function that collectively induce actions to shape and maintain desired outcomes.[65]

The military services have well-established incentive structures that are understood by their members. These structures are central to an organization's collective behavior. An incentive structure is (or should be) specifically designed to set a strategic course for the organization. Incentives also shape attitudes. Organizational actors enter into an implicit exchange relationship; they act in ways that contribute to organizational goals in return for rewards provided by the organization.[66]

Incentive structures create expectations in the organization's members. People become forward looking in that they are concerned about the rewards and punishments their behavior will produce. Often, in very subtle ways, people construct definitions of their situations to accommodate organizational goals and individual professional concerns. This does not mean that people necessarily compromise professional concerns for the material rewards associated with conforming to recognized incentive structures. The incentive structures of organizations are more complex than the simple exchange relationship. The outcomes of individual actions result in learned behaviors. These results, and the actions that caused them, are disseminated throughout an organization's population. People respond to rewards. Successes, rewards, and recognition all satisfy an important need in most people. This is part of human nature.

As previously mentioned, incentive structures are designed to set a strategic course for an organization. But how is a strategy determined and communicated? Ideally, an organization's strategy is written and available to all organizational members and stakeholders. Sometimes, strategy is implied. Occasionally, it is revealed over time. Most often, it is a combination of the three. But, evaluating actions and not words is key to assessing a strategy. Strategy is the pattern of decisions by an organization that reveals its true objectives, produces its principal policies, defines the range of acceptable ways for achieving objectives, and identifies the value of its human capital and the nature of the overall contribution it intends to make to its employees, stakeholders, and community.[67] Strategy and incentive structures are best assessed by evaluating an organization's actions over time.

Aligning Strategy and Incentive Structures within the Organization
Can a single organization accommodate multiple strategic concepts and multiple, distinct incentive structures without adversely affecting the organization or its subordinate parts? It seems logical that if incentives are designed to focus the energy of an organization for strategic purpose, the incentive structure should be as clear and unambiguous as possible. Multiple incentive structures within a single organization are likely to reduce clarity and increase ambiguity. Multiple incentive structures may be accommodated, but at a cost—the lessening of the organization's strategic focus and a decrease in clarity in the organization's incentive structure. Military organizations are not likely to accept this cost or, at least, impose it on themselves.

An organization that attempts to establish multiple incentive structures faces a significant challenge. Though separate incentive structures may appear equal, the organization will eventually reveal its true preferences through its policies and pattern of distributing rewards. As a result, a single incentive structure will eventually emerge that reflects demonstrated organizational preferences. Assuming that separate incentive structures are intended to induce actions to shape and maintain different outcomes, the defacto elimination of one incentive structure, united with the preeminence of another, can only result in the elimination of the outcome that the purged incentive structure was designed to produce.

UW and Afghanistan

The fact that the unconventional plan for Afghanistan that was approved by the president was crafted by the CIA cannot be ignored. Though CENTCOM had developed their own UW plan, it was not presented to either the secretary of defense or the president. Why was the DoD not able to generate an unconventional option for presentation to the commander in chief? The former commander of the SOF in CENTCOM insists that General Franks was a strong supporter of UW and that the Joint Staff had to be the organization that filtered out CENTCOM's unconventional warfare recommendation.[68]

Whether it was the Joint Staff or the CENTCOM commander who derailed the presentation of the unconventional option is less important than the fact that UW could not gain traction within the Defense Department. This is because the service incentive structures have demonstrated a clear preference for conventional operations. Unconventional thinking has been bred out of the officer corps as a result of a strategic alignment of a warfighting concept and a system of rewards that motivates individual and collective action toward attaining conventional military goals and objectives. The fact that the DoD's objectives and rewards system seem to be properly aligned is admirable. It is also important to maintain this alignment because of its obvious important contribution to national security. Yet, the option of unconventional warfare can also strongly contribute to national security and therefore needs its own viable structure to thrive.

USSOCOM, Incentives, and UW

Members of the SOCOM community are first members of their parent service. The services promote and select officers for key positions. As a result, incentive structures within SOCOM do not displace long-standing service incentives. Consequently, senior SOF leaders are conditioned by service preferences through a well-understood system of rewards. It is important to understand that from the viewpoint of the conventional military, the SOF is useful only in so far as it supports conventional operations. This is an understandable position. But this thinking, coupled with the present incentive system, severely impedes SOCOM's ability to cultivate unconventional thinkers.

This shortcoming became clear after Defense Secretary Rumsfeld announced that he had given new authorities to SOCOM to kill and capture al Qaeda operatives and other terrorists.[69] Rumsfeld was dissatisfied with the pace of the war on terror and felt that the global nature of the war, the nature of the enemy, and the need for fast, efficient operations in hunting down and rooting out terrorist networks required an expanded role for special operations forces.[70] Hunting down terrorists is obviously an important element of the war on terror. SOCOM made it clear that the new authorities required additional resources. This is a reasonable reaction, but it is the nature of the resources identified by SOCOM that is instructive.

Pentagon officials estimate that SOCOM will receive a $7 billion increase to buy new weapons and equipment and to accommodate new personnel. SOCOM will get an additional 4,000 personnel. Most will be assigned to the Tampa command or to theater special operations commands. The army will expand its 160th Special Operations Aviation Regiment, which flies U.S. Army Special Forces troops into battle. The regiment has a strength of 1,400 and will add about 900, along with thirty-five helicopters. The navy will increase its SEAL force, which has 2,200 men, although the exact number and timetable is uncertain. Also, the navy is considering recommissioning an aircraft carrier or coming up with another ship that could be used as a staging base for special operations forces.[71] The air force wants to provide additional training between its pilots and the combat controllers who teamed up with special forces and SEAL teams to call in air strikes in Afghanistan, using handheld lasers or radios. The air force also wants to accelerate the purchase of high-tech equipment for the combat controllers—specifically, a handheld device that would determine the coordinates of a target and electronically beam them to an aircraft overhead. Additionally, SOCOM intends to increase the capability of its C–130 fleet by converting an additional four to AC–130U gunship aircraft. Furthermore, the MC–130 aerial refueling system acquisition will be accelerated to acquire twenty-four new systems by the end of 2005. The army wants more training involving its special forces and conventional soldiers, who are working together closely in Afghanistan, where there is no clear battlefront.[72]

What is interesting was that the new authorities were not new. SOCOM had previously operated in a manner that Secretary Rumsfeld was searching for, as the supported commander. The new authorities were perhaps more a message from an aggressive defense secretary to a status quo headquarters than an expansion in authority to hunt down and capture or kill terrorists. Most compelling is that SOCOM's response seemed to revolve around equipment and increases in staff personnel. A new operational concept was not presented.[73] The additional resources SOCOM wanted directly support the ability to strike terrorist as well as conventional targets, something conventional forces can use. Again, there is nothing wrong with this approach, but it is not unconventional; it is conventional or perhaps hyper-conventional. More important, the ability to strike was not the shortfall. The U.S. military has an unequaled capability to strike. Developing indigenous capabilities and acquiring high-fidelity intelligence are the issues. This necessitates an unconventional approach that appears absent from SOCOM's thinking. Strike operations against terrorists can drive many of the undecided into the terrorist camp if conducted without considering many of the variables that are relevant in unconventional warfare. New equipment is unlikely to be decisive. The U.S. military and the SOF already have more resources available than any potential foe. An unconventional warfare concept has not emerged from SOCOM.

What conditions must exist to encourage and sustain an unconventional warfare capability? To be sure, the best organizational design (and commensurate rewards system) may enhance performance in one area and detract from performance in another. Edward Lawler, a leading authority in the subject of strategic incentives, claims that there are two aspects of a rewards system that directly affect organizational performance. First, incentives shape an organization with the capabilities and competencies needed to accomplish stated objectives; second, incentives motivate the members of an organization to use the competencies and capabilities in a way to enhance organizational performance.[74]

It is a nontrivial task to create a rewards system that both helps the organization develop the right competencies and stimulates the appropriate strategic behavior. Reward systems affect both individual and organizational performance through the effect that they have on people's beliefs and expectations about how they will be rewarded. Beliefs and expectations are largely influenced by past practices and behaviors of the organization. Expectations influence behavior as well as have an important effect on organizational culture. Organizational culture is critical to attracting and retaining the right people.[75] Regardless of what an organization says about its rewards practices, people will form beliefs about how rewards are administered. Individuals will try to make sense of their surroundings by making adjustments to foster a satisfying and rewarding work environment.[76] In other words, despite SOCOM's requirement to be capable to wage unconventional warfare, the organization's incentives are directly linked to a revealed preference for strike operations. The resulting organizational culture attracts those who prefer strike operations and subtly encourages others to conform. The outcome is inadequate performance in the conduct of unconventional warfare.

Performance means that an organization works well on every level. Clearly, creating high-performance organizations is not simple. Often there are conflicts and trade-offs. Still, one thing is certain—people understand that a line of sight exists between their performance and the desired reward.[77] With separate personnel appraisal, ranking and rewards systems, unconventional thinking (and doing) will probably accelerate rapidly. Enthusiastic, smart special operators in the field will deliver all the innovation and risk taking a president and aggressive defense secretary could ever hope for or expect. Until then, there is little incentive to do so.

CONTINGENCY THEORY HAS ITS LIMITS

A theory can be described as a logical model of a system comprising a set of variables and a set of constraints. Contingency theory, like all other theories, is applicable only under a given set of conditions.

Unconventional Warfare Needs an Enemy with Exploitable Vulnerabilities

Every combatant has vulnerabilities that theoretically could be exploited. However, some vulnerabilities are best exploited by the SOF. Successful UW benefits from a stupid enemy unable or unwilling to learn from its mistakes, or unable to reduce its vulnerabilities. The repressive, repulsive, and racist nature of the Taliban produced the geopolitical conditions that supported military operations in Afghanistan, in general, and specifically, special operations aimed at forging a ground force coalition composed of indigenous military forces. The Taliban could not defend the country and could not rely on the population to thwart the strategic effects of special operations. Additionally, the insular nature of the Taliban regime made it extremely difficult for the Taliban to learn from its own mistakes. This greatly contributed to the strategic utility of SOF. The Taliban was exceedingly limited in its ability to protect itself from special operations.

UW benefits from an oppressive enemy. It is difficult to operate in your opponent's territory if the population is sympathetic to his cause. The relationship between an enemy state and its people usually defines the limits of UW. Since an oppressive enemy will generate opposition to its rule, it follows that it is usually in our interest if the enemy is oppressive. Exceptions to this include the possibility that enemy oppression may be so effective that it crushes local resistance. Also, there is the moral consideration that the pursuit of our strategic interests may exacerbate oppression. The nature of the Taliban was certainly oppressive as well as capable of crushing local resistance and increasing oppression against those who might welcome a change of regime. Fortunately, the Taliban disintegrated rapidly. As a result, it did not have a chance to crush potential local support.

Similarly, the shape of Afghan economic, social, and political development had a significant influence on the state's vulnerability to special operations, including psychological warfare. Increased exposure to advanced society in the last century expanded the potential for UW. As the Taliban pursued goals with little concern for the well-being of the Afghan people, the vulnerability to special operations increased. The characteristics of modern society are features that attract the UW planner and the terrorist who, to a notable degree, share a similar tactical outlook.[78]

The SOF need a substantial and accessible enemy area in which to operate to conduct unconventional warfare. Long-term occupation of enemy territory increases an opponent's vulnerability to a wide range of special operations. But, long-term occupation is a two-edged sword; it can set the stage for guerrilla operations against an occupying force. This cautionary note is reflected in the increasingly insurgent nature of the current Afghan campaign. As foreign troop strength in Afghanistan increases, it appears that Taliban and al Qaeda remnants are stepping up attacks on coalition forces. In fact, the sophistication of the attacks and the quality of the weapons used against coalition forces is improving.[79] In other words, the favorable conditions for waging UW comes with its own vulnerabilities that must receive proper attention for UW to succeed.

Lessons of Contingency Theory

Organizational theorists have not been able to identify the best organizational structure to guarantee success. Furthermore, success cannot be sensibly reduced to a formula. Likewise, the conditions for successfully waging unconventional warfare cannot be presented in a strategist's cookbook. Also, success can happen in the absence of these conditions, because the performance required of friendly forces is dramatically affected by the competence of the enemy. Still, the conditions presented below are extracted from the discussions in this chapter about the war in Afghanistan and appear to be necessary, though not sufficient by themselves, to wage successful unconventional warfare.

Necessary conditions for successful unconventional warfare:

- UW needs its structure, leadership style, and control systems to be adaptive to the prevailing situation.
- UW requires a focus on and thorough knowledge of the external environment (area of operations).
- UW requires a simple chain of command and freedom of action extended to the smallest forward-based units.
- Maintaining the capability to conduct UW requires an incentive structure that promotes UW.
- UW needs an enemy with exploitable vulnerabilities.

Chapter 5

Why Can't the United States Conduct Unconventional Warfare?
Implications of Processes of Innovation

STEPHEN PETER ROSEN defines "major innovation" as:

> a change that forces one of the combat arms of a service to change its con-
> cepts of operation ands its relation to other combat arms, and to abandon or
> downgrade traditional missions. Such innovations involve a new way of war,
> with new ideas of how the components of the organization relate to each
> another and to the enemy, and new operational procedures conforming to
> those ideas. They involve changes to critical tasks, the tasks around which war
> plans revolve.[1]

Even the most cursory survey of military history illustrates the critical importance of technological and tactical innovation. Sometimes the vision of the innova-
tors is beyond the capacity or willingness of other to fully comprehend. Yet without
such visionaries and without irnnovation, a nation's way of war becomes predictable; and predictable means vulnerable.

THOSE WHO HOLD POWER IN AN ORGANIZATION HAVE A VESTED
INTEREST IN THE DOCTRINE ASSOCIATED WITH THEIR STATUS
The issue of dependency was discussed in chapter 3. The military, like many large
organizations, is a giant network of units linked by relationships that can be beneficial, detrimental or neutral. Every military unit is dependent on its higher headquarters for authority, material resources, and money. To the extent that a unit needs
its headquarters less than the headquarters needs the unit, the unit has power. That
is, power is a function of asymmetric mutual dependence. Dependence is itself a
function of available alternatives. Organizations that have power over others are able
to impose constraints on them.

There are numerous historical examples of the SOF being committed to combat situations for which they were not suited. The U.S. Army Rangers at Cisterna

and U.S. Special forces along the border in South Vietnam to control infiltration are examples of misuse of SOF. Arguably, the inappropriate employment of these forces was a function of the dependency relationship between the SOF and their controlling conventional headquarters. In the above two cases, the conventional headquarters certainly had options besides the SOF. Alternatively, the Rangers and special forces were anchored to the conventional structure. Orders and resources came from one sponsor. There was no other channel to pursue to check questionable orders or to acquire needed resources. The SOF did not have alternatives and therefore paid a heavy price in blood without amassing the expected benefits of their operations.

SOF Independence

The use of the SOF in Afghanistan was unique in many ways. One unique aspect of the conflict that is rarely discussed is the degree of leverage the SOF had in the early days of the war. Interestingly, the notion that the SOF was the force of choice by senior military leaders is not correct. The SOF would not have played a key role if Gen. Henry H. Shelton remained chairman of the Joint Chiefs, according to the officer who was the chief of the Special Operations Division of the Joint Staff during the first year of the war. Shelton's retirement and Air Force Gen. Richard B. Myers's assumption of the chairmanship were important to crafting the SOF's role in the war. Shelton, though a former commander of USSOCOM, was first and foremost a conventional army general. Employing the SOF as the primary ground element was incongruous to Shelton's education and experience. For Shelton, a war required conventional ground troops and the SOF would support as needed. Myers was an air force general. His education and experience left open the SOF option. Simply put, Myers's inexperience in ground operations resulted in the SOF being an early option against the Taliban and al Qaeda.[2]

To be sure, there were other important factors that allowed for the SOF alternative. The initial war plan approved by the president was a CIA initiative and required special forces soldiers to support Agency operatives. The Defense Department did not offer an acceptable course of action to the president and secretary of defense. The DoD needed months to get ready to go, while the president and secretary of defense were thinking in terms of days and weeks. Also, the defense secretary, Donald Rumsfeld, was a forceful and impatient man, who was determined to get U.S. military troops on the ground in Afghanistan quickly. The SOF were his only option.

This situation reversed the dependency relationship between the Joint Staff and the special operations community. As a consequence of the president's approval of the CIA's plan, the SOF were not exclusively sponsored by the DoD. Furthermore, the DoD did not have a viable alternative (other than the SOF) that would satisfy the president and secretary's demand for swift retribution. Special forces had what everyone needed, and special forces was the only source of supply. The result was an empowered SOF, at least for a while.

The 5th Special Forces Group (SFG) was essentially in charge of the ground war in its earliest phases despite the fact that there were levels of command between the 5th SFG and the commander of CENTCOM. But the 5th group commander had his forces fighting and in place. The forward-operating elements were "educating up." There wasn't a headquarters or senior officer in a position to have a better judgment about the situation than the sergeants and young officers on the ground. Additionally, a well-used video teleconference (VTC) link between 5th SFG and USCENTCOM further empowered the SOF relative to other military stakeholders. In this "different kind of war," senior officers were, in many ways, no more experienced than junior officers who were seeing combat for the first time. This reversed the traditional dependency model. Higher headquarters was dependent on the SOF in the field to make judgments that would have operational and perhaps strategic implications. A colonel had unfiltered access to the theater commander by means of VTC at least once a day. The results of this dependency anomaly were impressive—in a short few weeks, small, distributed special operations teams conducted a low-cost, high-leverage campaign that resulted in the complete disintegration of the Taliban and delivered a severe blow to al Qaeda's ability to export terrorism to the United States.

SOF Dependence

As early as late September, the army decided a conventional headquarters would be needed for command and control of ground forces in Afghanistan. The 3rd Army, located in Uzbekistan, had been the land component headquarters for operations in Afghanistan. The commander of 3rd Army, Lt. Gen. Paul Mikolashek, had not asked for a division headquarters to run operations in Afghanistan. He only needed a small element from his own headquarters, forward based and augmented by additional personnel to help coordinate operations. But at the highest levels of the army, it was decided that a division headquarters would go into Afghanistan. According to Maj. Gen. Frank Hagenbeck, the 10th Mountain Division commander, the army hierarchy expected that the SOF would work with the Northern Alliance until perhaps early spring, and then hand off ground operations to the conventional army. Getting the big army into the fight was key, perhaps more for political reasons than for operational reasons. Hagenbeck also pointed out that the army had anticipated the use of conventional forces from the start of the war. The conventional military was getting the traction they could not develop in the days after 9/11. Now there would be division headquarters located in Afghanistan.[3]

By late February 2002, the 10th Mountain Division headquarters was up and running in Bagram. It was preparing for what would be one of the largest and most costly operations in the war—Anaconda. U.S. SOF had been monitoring a large-scale pocket of al Qaeda forces in the Shi-e-Kot Valley, southeast of Gardez, for more than a month. The 10th Mountain, now designated CJTF Mountain, conceived a classic "hammer and anvil" maneuver to clear the valley of the al Qaeda threat. SOF and Afghan forces would be key in the operation. Unity of command would also be a key issue, not only for Anaconda but also for all future operations in Afghanistan. Special operations in Afghanistan would now be under the operational control of CJTF-Mountain.[4] The SOF in Afghanistan were now dependent on the 10th Mountain for operational direction and mission approval. In other words, the SOF would now have limited direct influence over Gen. Tommy Franks at CENTCOM headquarters in Tampa, because two operational headquarters separated the SOF from the theater commander. The dependency created by this command arrangement would alter the effectiveness of SOF-centric, distributed small teams conducting a low-cost, high-leverage campaign. Now, deep institutional barriers would stand in the way of the United States conducting irregular warfare.

SCIENTIFIC ENTREPRENEURSHIP DEVELOPS TECHNOLOGIES THAT CAN INSTIGATE INNOVATION

The "Defense Planning Guidance" (DPG) for 2004 to 2009 aims to replace a Cold War–era strategy of being able to fight two major-theater wars nearly simultaneously with a more complex approach aimed at dominating air and space. The plan directs the military to focus more of its spending to combat Afghanistan-style threats and weapons of mass destruction and to develop even greater precision-strike capabilities.[5]

The new DPG represents acceleration in the shift toward the high-tech gadgetry of warfare on which the Pentagon has relied since Desert Storm in 1991. The classified document requires the military services to further develop the capability to launch preemptive strikes, a new doctrine outlined by President George W. Bush in the current national security strategy. The DPG also sets specific goals, such as the development of a squadron of a dozen unmanned fighter jets by 2012 and a "hypersonic missile" that can travel 600 nautical miles in fifteen minutes by 2009.[6]

The plan seems to codify the military transformation that Defense Secretary Donald Rumsfeld has touted since he took over the Pentagon. It places emphasis on capabilities such as surprise high-volume precision strikes, and calls for laser and microwave-powered weapons and nuclear-tipped "bunker buster" bombs capable of striking deeply buried cave complexes such as those in the mountains of Afghanistan. The document also calls for the services to make cyber warfare a "core competency." It further calls for protecting critical U.S. computer networks and destroying the enemy's networks.[7]

SOF, Innovation, and Technological Assistance

Tactical and technological innovations are not new impulses for special operations forces. In fact, the SOF have historically been a laboratory for procuring and testing lightweight equipment, radios, night-vision devices, specialized weapons, and demolitions. During World War II, the British Combined Operations Directorate was especially innovative in developing support procedures between Orde Wingate's Chindit Special Forces in Burma and the U.S. Army Air Corps Air Commandos.[8]

The impulse for innovation and technological advantage for SOF is easy to understand. Colin Gray expresses this idea nicely: "Strategic utility rests upon tactical feasibility, and tactical feasibility for handfuls of heroes who are hugely outnumbered requires technical assistance."[9] Even a minor deficiency in equipment or procedure can have disproportionately large negative consequences for a special operation that, by definition, is taking place at the edge of the envelope of military feasibility. In addition to better training, better equipment and operational techniques are necessary to offset the extreme nature of special operations missions.

Historically, conventional forces have often adopted techniques and equipment perfected by the SOF. Today, the magnitude of technological innovation throughout the U.S. military greatly outpaces the ability to properly integrate emerging technologies into doctrine. When the SOF operate within the narrow parameters of a limited duration, special operation, with limited interaction with conventional units, the troublesome effects of technology proliferation are manageable. However, all of the adverse consequences of using emerging technologies are fully experienced when the SOF operate with conventional forces and under their control. Consequently, technologies used in Afghanistan, whether by conventional forces or the SOF, affected the SOF. Therefore, the use of advanced technologies in Afghanistan must be viewed in context with the overall operation and not just from a SOF perspective.

Military Transformation

Military planners have been throwing the word "transformation" around for years. It is clear that transformation involves making use of the best technologies to conduct warfare. Military planners are also quick to note that transformation is more than exploiting technology—it includes how we think about war and how we educate the next generation of military leaders. The evidence and budget priorities seem to suggest that the transformation agenda is strong on enabling technologies and weak on developing military leaders who are skilled in military operational art.[10]

Perhaps new and powerful technologies for waging war reduce the importance of military operational art. The British historian Michael Howard, in his well-known paper "The Forgotten Dimensions of Strategy," for example, argues that the logistics, technological, and social dimensions of military success are at least as important as the operational dimension.[11] Edward Luttwak, in his insightful essay, "Notes on Low-Intensity Warfare," says that powerful countries that have powerful militaries tend to

> be focused on their own internal administration and operations, being correspondingly less responsive to the external environment comprising the enemy, the terrain, and the specific phenomena of any one particular conflict. . . . Victory is to be obtained by administering superior material resources, by their transformation into firepower, and by the application of the latter upon the enemy, the armed forces of that kind should concentrate on their own inner workings to maximize process efficiencies all around.[12]

The Gulf War is of particular interest here and seems to support Howard's and Luttwak's points. In spite of the well-documented allied flanking maneuver that broke the Iraqi Republican Guards, what was most impressive and decisive in retrospect for the allied victory happened in the dimensions of logistics and technology, not in operations. Indeed, it could be argued that the war's outcome indicates how unimportant operational art and military leadership are becoming.[13]

But is military leadership and operational art less important as a result of ever-increasing technical capabilities? A closer look at the Gulf War reveals a failure of operational art and leadership at senior command levels, which greatly affected the war's strategic outcome. The flanking maneuver to close the ring on the Republican Guards failed to permanently eliminate this force. This error was certainly compounded at the level of political-military decision making. The premature halt of the ground war for public relations reasons, the signaling of the U.S. intent to withdraw from Iraq without a quid pro quo, the abandonment of the Kurds and Shiites, and the obvious absence of any serious planning for the war's endgame all helped turn a remarkable feat of arms into something considerably less than a strategic victory.[14]

U.S. military actions over the last decade strongly suggest that the Gulf War was not an exception. From Somalia to Bosnia and Kosovo, American political and military leadership has often been inadequate and shortsighted in its strategic thinking. There are few signs that the technical revolution is easing the requirements for strategy and operational art. U.S. military actions in Iraq and Kosovo as well as in Afghanistan point to the futility of revolution in military affairs (RMA) style precision bombing, absent appropriate operational concepts and serious thought about strategic outcomes.[15] Technology cannot substitute for an appreciation of the logic of war. In fact, the responsibility of senior military officers becomes greater when the logic of war is lacking in civilian leaders. Furthermore, a case can be made that the evolving technologies are likely to centralize control at senior levels, which could concentrate strategic, operational, and tactical planning. How would this consolidation affect strategic thinking?[16]

Technology Cuts Both Ways

A logical argument against the quest for technological superiority cannot be made. At the same time, we should be skeptical about the dividends technology may be expected to deliver. In 1995 I had the privilege of spending a few days with the late Trevor Dupuy, the distinguished military historian. We were discussing the RMA. Dupuy, a consummate gentleman, pulled a lengthy report he had written from his briefcase and showed me that the rates of advance of armies in contact have not changed in four thousand years. He then asked me to detail for him why I thought the next twenty years would alter this historic phenomenon. After describing most of the newest technological advances, I couldn't convince Dupuy that the RMA would truly have revolutionary effects on the ground, the domain where military success or failure is ultimately measured. Dupuy's point was simple—technological and doctrinal advances are quickly and relatively inexpensively countered.[17]

Old Tricks for New Times

It should not surprise anyone that human beings make mistakes. It should also not surprise anyone that during war, deception is used to induce human error.

In preparation for the Normandy invasion during World War II, the allies made good use of simple inflatable rubber tanks, airplanes, and armored cars (as well as other deception schemes) to convince German intelligence that the main allied invasion would hit at the Pas de Calais and not at Normandy. German reconnaissance and surveillance assets were not able to uncover the fact that the "main" attack force was composed of inflatable rubber decoys.

It would be a mistake to assume that this type of deception could not happen today with the sophisticated sensors available to modern militaries. During NATO's air war in Kosovo, crude decoys routinely fooled modern bombers into dropping costly ordinance on plywood and log mockups of tanks and artillery batteries. This scenario was repeated in Afghanistan.[18]

New Technology Offers New Opportunities for Deception

The successful use of decoys in Kosovo reaffirmed that modern technology can be thrown off track by old deceptive techniques. It appears that new technologies offer more, not fewer, opportunities for deception. For example, with U.S. forces closing in on him during the battle of Tora Bora in late 2001, Osama bin Laden employed a simple feint against sophisticated U.S. spy technology to vanish into the mountains that led to Pakistan and sanctuary. A Moroccan who was one of Bin Laden's longtime bodyguards took possession of the al Qaeda leader's satellite phone on the assumption that U.S. intelligence agencies were monitoring it to get a fix on their position. The bodyguard moved away from Bin Laden and his entourage as they fled. He continued to use the phone in an effort to divert the Americans and allow Bin Laden to escape. The bodyguard, and Bin Laden's phone, were tracked and captured at Tora Bora—the al Qaeda leader was not tracked and was safe elsewhere.[19]

Yet, human error exists without the assistance of enemy deception measures aimed at inducing incorrect actions to create a disadvantage for friendly forces and an advantage for enemy forces. For instance, consider the numerous cases of "friendly fire" accidents in Afghanistan. In perhaps the most publicized case, U.S. forces were tracking legitimate al Qaeda targets when an air force AC-130 gunship opened fire on a group that was celebrating a wedding. The assault killed forty-eight civilians.[20] Also, an F-16 fighter pilot from the Illinois Air National Guard reported weapons fire below and moments later radioed that he was attacking in self-defense. The 500-pound, laser-guided bomb was deadly accurate, but it didn't hit the enemy. Instead, it landed on the Princess Patricia's Canadian Light Infantry, killing four soldiers.[21]

Friendly fire has always been an element of war. Those who study it remind us that Confederate General Thomas "Stonewall" Jackson was mortally wounded by his own men at Chancellorsville. For years, the military accepted the idea that friendly fire would cause 2 percent of casualties in any war. Recent reviews of World War II and Korean War casualty records suggest the correct figure might be as high as 15 percent.[22]

Another tragic example of just such a mistake occurred in December, when three U.S. soldiers and an estimated twenty-five Afghans died after a satellite-guided bomb struck their position. The bomb, dropped from a B-52, was supposed to hit target coordinates sent to it by a forward ground controller. But after sending the coordinates, the controller reportedly stopped to change the batteries in his handheld satellite navigation unit. When he restarted it, the unit defaulted to the controller's own position, inadvertently redirecting the bomb back to him.[23]

Why have discussions about friendly fire changed? There is no simple explanation, but military analysts say that fratricide is climbing, because American weapons have become more complex and more accurate, inviting human mistakes and eliminating the margin for weapons error. Modern weapons go exactly where they are told to go. It is human error that results in increased fratricide. A munition may be smart, but it is not intelligent. It cannot correct for faulty input. Furthermore, the relatively low numbers of Americans killed by hostile fire in both the Gulf War and Afghanistan also serves to highlight the friendly fire deaths. So far, at least ten incidents of "friendly fire" have been investigated in Afghanistan.[24]

The Age of the Unmanned Aerial Vehicle

Since the dawn of warfare, military commanders have felt they lacked the proper information to direct their forces. In ancient times, everything over the next hill was often a mystery. Now, Predators can let them peer over that hill and the one after that. The problem is how to sift through the information quickly and find what is useful. Since the United States military campaign began in Afghanistan, the unmanned aerial vehicle (UAV) has gone from a bit player to a starring role. Rather than searching out the enemy by more traditional means, commanders made use of the Predator not just to find the enemy but, for the CIA, to fight them too.

Predator unmanned planes have given commanders around-the-clock video views of the battlefield. But the introduction of this machine also has a negative side. Predator gave generals and civilian leaders back in Washington something they had never seen before—a continuous live view of Americans in ground combat in the mountains of Afghanistan, ten time zones away. Cameras on the twenty-seven-foot drones beamed back dramatic scenes from the heat of battle in the Shi-e-Kot region, notably the killing of a Navy SEAL commando. Never before had an extended battle by U.S. forces been piped into U.S. command centers around the globe in hour after hour of real-time video that made distant officials feel unusually close, perhaps too close, to the battlefield. Pictures from the Predators have been distributed to a variety of command posts around the world, including the air operations center in Saudi Arabia; Central Command headquarters at MacDill Air Force Base, Florida; and the Pentagon and CIA headquarters in the Washington, D.C., area.[25]

According to several 10th Mountain Division officers, the Predator was more trouble than it was worth. Soldiers involved in the battle said the live video links gave them little useful information and were sometimes a distraction, encouraging higher-level military staffs to try to micromanage the fighting.[26] In fact, the video tends to be seductive, fixing the attention of its viewers on whatever it shows. At times, the Predator seemed like entertainment for senior people at CJTF-Mountain headquarters.[27]

Maj. Gen. Franklin L. Hagenbeck, the commander of U.S. ground forces in Afghanistan from February to June 2002, said the biggest problem with Predator was that its transmission of real-time images made staffs above his feel they were in a position to get involved in the battle. The Predator had the effect of making every senior headquarters with a video feed a consumer of information. Senior staff officers continually asked for information they presumed their bosses would want to know. This diverted attention from everyone directly involved in the real action on the ground. Hagenbeck noted that during the first days of the Shi-e-Kot battle, people at higher level staffs would call down to the 10th Mountain staff to get information and make suggestions. In this respect, the Predator proved to be disruptive.[28]

To be fair, Predator is a new system, and the introduction of any radically new technology requires a settling-in process. Higher headquarters certainly didn't help to facilitate a smooth integration of Predator into existing doctrine. As previously discussed, they might have even adversely affected ground operations. But frontline units also created their own operational inefficiencies by overrelying on Predator.[29] The intelligence collection plan for CJTF-Mountain seemed to be built around the UAV. Typically, intelligence-collection plans use many information collection assets to find answers to specific intelligence questions in order to facilitate combat operations. Predator seemed to be the focus of the CJTF-Mountain intelligence staff. They would follow the Predator video as long as the drone was aloft. As for intelligence collection plans, when several CJTF-Mountain intelligence personnel were interviewed, they said that none existed. This was also the case in SOF intelligence sections. From an observer's point of view, it seemed that, at times, the Predator was leading the army around the battlefield. The Predator was running the show.[30]

Command, Control, and Video Teleconference

Some in the U.S. military are concluding that the sprawling command structure used in the war in Afghanistan, with units getting orders through video teleconference from half a world away, has been cumbersome and has created unnecessary friction between senior military leaders and commanders on the ground.[31] In an official report, the Marine Corps depicts Central Command, based 7,000 miles from Afghanistan in Tampa, as a distant and troublesome overseer. This command structure has been a unique feature of the Afghanistan campaign, departing from past conflicts, including the Gulf War, in which U.S. military commanders moved their headquarters closer to the battlefield. The time differences wore down staffs in the war zone region. The almost never-ending workday was largely the result of the need to interface with multiple staffs in different time zones. VTCs were scheduled twice daily at times convenient to Tampa and Washington. "This was simply a fact of life, said Rear Adm. Craig Quigley, a spokesman for the Central Command. To keep the Pentagon and White House informed, he explained, "every forward-deployed element . . . needed to adjust their daily battle rhythm, to some extent, to accommodate this reality."[32] If this is true, it is a remarkable shift in the "reality" of combat shifting from the battlefield to command centers far removed from the fighting.

Not everyone in the war found the command structure troubling. Col. John Mulholland, who spent six months in and around Afghanistan as commander of the Army's 5th Special Forces Group, said the distant command did not hurt his ability to fight.[33] Why did Mulholland's view differ from those of so many others? One explanation could be the nature of Mulholland's initial relationship with General Franks that was created by the VTC. The 5th Special Forces Group was the first U.S. military unit to enter Afghanistan and the first military unit in Afghanistan to create tangible successes against the Taliban. During this initial period, General Franks and Mulholland would communicate directly with one another through VTC. Although others would participate, not everyone involved in the campaign was connected to the VTC. For Mulholland, a colonel, but nevertheless the senior commander in Afghanistan, the direct link to the theater commander was extraordinarily useful. As the ground commander, Mulholland would obviously inform Franks of his immediate needs, and Franks would direct that Mulholland receive what he asked for. After all, the 5th Special Forces Group was the only significant military unit operating in Afghanistan. Those who would replace Mulholland would not have this unique relationship with Franks. Afghanistan quickly became filled with units, all competing for limited resources and "air time" with the theater commander.

The miracle of VTC technology also had the unintended effect of creating uncoordinated actions. A simple comparison of the cumbersome, unpopular, but effective Joint Operations Planning and Execution System (JOPES) to the VTC will illustrate this point. JOPES is exactly what its title suggests—a standardized planning and execution system for military operations. Some suggest it is cumbersome because it requires that written messages be used to coordinate the efforts of every organization that has a role in the operation. Changes and modification to initial plans generate additional written messages. The written messages, which do take time to write, are quickly disseminated to all organizations that have a role in, or have a need to know about, the operation. The written message is usually clear and not subject to interpretation. Additionally, the process of writing orders requires an internal logic often absent from verbal communications. As a consequence, JOPES facilitates the coordination process.

Conversely, the VTC is usually quick and certainly easier than converting verbal instructions to written orders. But the VTC (at least for now) is not disseminated to all organizations involved in the operation. Only selected organizations are involved, leaving the others uninformed or at the mercy of receiving orders indirectly, and perhaps interpreted by the deliverer of the order. Worse yet, the order may never get to an organization that has a role in the operation, or it may arrive too late to receive proper attention.

The VTC phenomenon was compounded by the introduction of secure e-mail. Secure e-mail accounts were used to facilitate operational planning. This had effects similar to those created by the VTC—not everyone received copies of the e-mails to facilitate coordination of operations. Even trying to research the history of the Afghan campaign is difficult, because individual e-mails and VTCs are difficult, if not impossible, to access.

In sum, advanced technologies may not be a necessary condition and are certainly not a sufficient condition, for military success—though they can enhance the likelihood of success. The VTC and secure e-mail, like the Predator, are fraught with both blessings and curses. These systems will become more beneficial once the settling-in process is complete. Technology must be subordinate to a sound framework for action. But doctrine will continually try to catch technology. This problem is likely to become more severe with technology advancing along a geometric curve. Also, defeating sophisticated technologies is much easier than creating those technologies. Therefore, defaulting to one's most advanced capabilities must be carefully considered. Perhaps Trevor Dupuy was correct—be wary of the payoffs from technological advances. While technological advances are inevitable and solve old problems, they also create new problems that keep war much like it has always been.

ORGANIZATIONAL CULTURE IS SHAPED BY INCENTIVE STRUCTURES THAT OPERATE IN THE ORGANIZATION

Is it possible to teach people to think unconventionally? What role does an organization's structural design play in generating "unconventional" thinking? The discussion in chapter 3 on organizational theory and processes of innovation strongly suggest that within organizations, innovation is difficult to accomplish (though not impossible), and the organization has operating parameters that shape and control the behavior of its members. If unconventional warfare is, as some claim, merely a subcategory of conventional warfare, a single military structure and culture would probably suffice. But the majority of military leaders today, even those who believe the role of SOF is to support conventional war, acknowledge that special operations are qualitatively different from routine military endeavors. Therefore, a separate and different organizational culture is necessary for special operations forces in order to maximize their strategic utility.[34]

For the U.S. military, strategy and doctrine flow from the interpretations of the writings of Carl von Clausewitz and Antoine Henri Jomini.[35] It is questionable to what extent this understanding of warfare remains relevant for acts of terrorism, insurgencies, and post–Cold War internal wars such as those fought in Bosnia and Herzegovina, Somalia, Rwanda, and Haiti. The characterization of future (and current) wars may not deal with realpolitik. Hatred, jealousy, and greed rather than strategy may more accurately frame the terms of the struggle. As we have seen in Africa, wars may become oddly nonmilitary with the systematic murder and terrorizing of civilian populations passing for "military action."[36]

The phenomenon is not new, though insufficient attention has been paid to what some military thinkers refer to as "small wars." The British soldier-scholar, Col. Charles E. Callwell, was among the first to write about "small wars"—wars fought between regular and irregular (tribal, partisan, perhaps nonstate) forces. Callwell wrote about uncivilized warfare, even savage warfare, and asymmetric warfare. Although Callwell first published his classic work, *Small Wars: Their Principles and Practice,* in 1896, it explains, with penetrating insight, the full range of issues faced today in unconventional operations. Callwell cautions those who think the Clausewitzian model has universal application:

> The teachings of great masters of the art of war, and the experiences gained from campaigns of modern date in America and on the continent of Europe, have established certain principles and precedents which form the groundwork of the regular warfare of to-day. Certain rules of conduct exist which are universally accepted. Strategy and tactics alike are in great campaigns governed, in most respects, by a code from which it is perilous to depart. But the conditions of small wars are so diversified, the enemy's mode of fighting is often so peculiar, and the theatres of operations present such singular features, that irregular war must generally be carried out on a method totally different from the stereotyped system. The art of war, as generally understood, must be modified to suit the circumstances of each particular case. The conduct of small wars is in fact in certain respects an art by itself, diverging widely from what is adapted to the conditions of regular warfare, but not so widely that there are not in all its branches points which permit comparisons to be established.[37]

Callwell's point is key: small wars have their own grammar and logic that diverge from the rules of regular warfare.

Unconventional Minds
Irregular warfare does not show strategy the door. On the contrary, it demands the strategist work smarter. Conventional strategy seeks to find the enemy and defeat him. Waging irregular, guerrilla, partisan, or other unconventional warfare is a strategic choice most often made by a militarily weaker party to avoid major battle that would result in defeat. This creates a dilemma for the conventional strategist. A solution to this problem has been elusive. As Clausewitz points out, "Everything in strategy is very simple, but that does not mean that everything is very easy."[38]

The difficulties associated with a single military organization dividing its intellectual creativity between conventional and unconventional warfare are great—apparently great enough to overstretch its human and organizational talent.[39]

The effectiveness of unconventional warfare is ironically linked to its limitations.[40] To illustrate, those initiating unconventional warfare usually must confront an enemy that is superior in overall mass and firepower. This requires thorough knowledge of the enemy in order to strike at precisely the right time and place, while being able to withdraw and disperse quickly and effectively, and to reform and strike again when the enemy shows a vulnerable spot. Even the effectiveness of a conventional force is linked to its limitations when it performs a counterinsurgency function. This is because the insurgent has (or should have) the advantage of terrain, intelligence, and local popular support. This demands that the counterinsurgency force significantly change its structure and normal mode of operation. The effectiveness of this force is no longer based on the unit's original organization and standing doctrine.

In other words, unconventional warfare requires a different mental framework as well as unique tactical skills. Recruiting, training, and ultimately employing elite warriors is not sufficient for winning wars. The realm of modern strategy has been reluctant to accept the uniqueness of unconventional warfare and to avoid conventionalizing the unconventional. The SOF has sufficient tactical doctrine and manuals on tradecraft. What is lacking is relevant strategic theory for exploiting the skills of the special forces warrior. History is filled with cases of misuse of special operations forces as elite shock troops. Arguably, these failures were the result of insufficient unconventional thinking on the part of military leaders, to include the special operators themselves. Unconventional war is a state of mind as well as a mission and a distinct set of tactics.[41]

The Unconventional Afghanistan

Three weeks after the attacks of September 11, preparations started for the war. Before deployment, all the teams were sequestered at Fort Campbell or Fort Bragg, North Carolina, to focus on mission preparations. No team knew another's mission. In a period ranging from two days to three weeks, they learned about the local culture, the key players, the terrain, and the vegetation. Some studied the local languages, Pashtu and Dari. The teams didn't mingle with anyone else in order to preserve operational secrecy. They traveled separately to bases in the region. At night, the special forces teams helicoptered into various parts of Afghanistan to link up with the local anti-Taliban fighting forces.[42]

Soon after arrival, most shed their uniforms and wore nonmilitary clothes; some adopted Afghan dress. One wore his Red Sox cap; others wore Harley Davidson caps. Many grew beards. They wanted to blend in (at least from a distance), but they also wanted to be readily identifiable by other team members to protect themselves. In a firefight no one wanted to be confused with the enemy.[43]

Their first job was to establish trust with local commanders. In the process, they established rules of engagement. Almost all the possible air raid targets would be double-checked by the local Afghan commander, civilian areas were to be avoided, and targets were to be military. When the special forces captain who commanded ODA 574 received intelligence about a potential target in the middle of the night, he would see his local commander, Hamid Karzai, who became the interim leader of Afghanistan. "I would wake Hamid up," the ODA commander said." I would say, these are the targets we are looking at now; is this valid? What do you want me to do? He would say, this is a legitimate target, and this isn't. Hamid was very careful. If there was any doubt, we wouldn't bother killing it. I could afford to let a few guys go if I wasn't sure. Hurting the populace hurt our own cause."[44]

The Conventional Afghanistan

The soldiers, weighed down under their helmets, bulletproof vests, and load-bearing equipment and weapons, walked within the secure Kandahar compound from their tents to the latrines and to the mess halls. The 101st Airborne Division (Air Assault) soldiers wore their full battle dress everywhere. The brigade commander insisted the troops under his command wear their full protective gear everywhere. As Sean Naylor wrote in the *Army Times*,

> The whole purpose of the vest and the Kevlar helmet is to provide protection to the most vital areas of the human body, that if hit with the smallest element, could cause death. The uniform you see us wearing is the uniform of the 101st Airborne when it crosses Range Road and goes to the field. This is the way we go to train, and ... we train the way we're going to fight.[45]

The commander of the 19th Air Support Operations Squadron, a unit attached to the 101st, ordered his airmen to follow the same uniform policy as the 101st troops. "It's all about being a team player. It's all about solidarity."[46]

Unconventional Meets Conventional

The 82nd Airborne conducted a well-publicized military operation, Mountain Sweep, in August 2002 that demonstrated what the brigade commander from the 101st meant by "we train the way we're going to fight." What this statement implies is that a unit also fights the way it is trained, unaffected by externalities that significantly differ with the training setting.

Operation Mountain Sweep was a week-long hunt for al Qaeda and Taliban fugitives in eastern Afghanistan. One afternoon in August, a U.S. Special Forces team knocked at the door of a mud compound in the Shi-e-Kot Valley. The man of the house, an elderly farmer, let the special forces soldiers in as soon as his female relatives had gone to a back room, out of the gaze of strange men. The team leader asked if there were any weapons in the house. The farmer showed them his only firearm, a hunting rifle nearly a century old. When the team had finished searching, carefully letting the women stay out of sight, the farmer served tea. The special forces team thanked him and walked toward the next house.[47]

Not long after the special forces team left the home, six paratroopers from the 82nd Airborne, also part of Mountain Sweep, were positioned outside the farmer's house, preparing to force their way in, the way they are trained to do. The paratroopers kicked in the door. The farmer panicked and tried to run, but one of the paratroopers slammed him to the ground. The soldiers from the 82nd attempted to frisk the women. The family was in a state of shock. The women were screaming. The elderly man was in tears. He had been dishonored.[48]

The official story from 18th Airborne Corps headquarters, the command in charge of operations in Afghanistan, was that Operation Mountain Sweep was a resounding success. Several arms caches were found and destroyed, and at least a dozen suspected Taliban members or supporters were detained for questioning. But according to special forces teams that remained near the Shi-e-Kot Valley and had daily contact with Afghan villagers and local officials living in or near the valley, the mission was a disaster. The Afghans claimed that American soldiers simply terrorized innocent villagers. Equally significant, the operation was a blow to the rapport the special forces had built up with local communities during the previous six months. Special forces soldiers reported that after Mountain Sweep, they were getting rocks thrown at them on the road in Khowst. Special forces members said that Mountain Sweep probably set back their counterinsurgency and intelligence operations by at least six months.[49] Officers in the 82nd insist their men did nothing wrong. In response to media queries, public-affairs officers characterized the special forces soldiers involved in Mountain Sweep as "prima donnas," who were damaging the war effort by raising objections to the procedures used by the 82nd. Yet, Operation Mountain Sweep raises serious questions about the best strategy for fighting the type of war faced in Afghanistan.[50]

The above contrast between the unconventional and the conventional is deliberately sharp and even somewhat unfair to conventional forces. The requirements for discipline and standardized procedures for conventional units populated by young soldiers calls for clear and simple rules. However, contrary to the statement of the commander of the 19th Air Support Operations Squadron, it is not about "being a team player" or about "solidarity." Those are internal issues. The heart of the matter consists of the external issues. Organizations where internal administration and operations receive the most attention are much less responsive to the external environment composed of the enemy, terrain, and the specific phenomena of any one particular conflict. Therefore, a well-managed force of this kind is significantly less adaptive to the external environment.[51]

Both the 101st and the 82nd Airborne are typical U.S. military organizations. They *can* focus on their internal machinery, because their internal capabilities will almost always exceed the capabilities of opponents. Said another way, superior internal standardized procedures will lead to a quick victory by applying overwhelming power quickly and decisively. Yet, the enemy is faced with a deadly situation only if he chooses to fight conventionally. If the enemy chooses insurgency, the United States is faced with a deadly paradox—maintain control over complex terrain using conventional military tactics and accepting heavy casualties (with CNN recording daily tactical defeats), or wage counterinsurgency that requires a keen awareness and ability to manage the external setting—unfamiliar ground for conventional forces.

What happens when a small organization that is externally oriented is placed under the control of a large organization that is internally oriented? The answer is obvious—the orientation of the larger, more dominant organization prevails. This is precisely the situation faced by the SOF in Afghanistan after the disintegration of the Taliban. By February 2002, special forces units in Afghanistan were essentially working for the 10th Mountain Division commander. The 18th Airborne Corps headquarters assumed control of the SOF when the 10th Mountain was relieved and returned to Fort Drum. The standard doctrinal command relationship for the SOF would have had the Theater Special Operations Command (TSOC) in charge of special operations. Although doctrine does not preclude a unit like 10th Mountain or 18th Airborne Corps from controlling the SOF, the arrangement comes at a hefty price—the conventionalization of the SOF and the operations they perform. It is important to point out that many special operations commanders view subordinating the SOF to conventional commanders as useful. For them, it does, in fact, demonstrate being a "team player" and showing "solidarity."[52] Therefore, many special operations leaders play a role in the conventionalization of the SOF. After all, it is the "big" military that decides who gets promoted and who is selected to command.

Top-Driven Conventionalism

It seems that SOF professionals grow increasingly conventional as they progress up the promotion ladder. Junior officers and enlisted men had an exceptional grasp of the Afghan operational environment. The lieutenant colonels and colonels understood but were forced to balance what they might have been able to do with what a conventional operational chain ordered. This is a reasonable course for a commander who must balance competing issues and who is bound to obey legal orders. But there is little evidence that SOF commanders pushed unconventional solutions. This, of course, was compounded by the command arrangement that placed SOF under the control of a conventional command. The special forces have often had a stormy relationship with the rest of the army. Conventional commanders sometimes regard the elite fighters as arrogant cowboys. Lt. Gen. Dan McNeill, the commander of 18th Airborne Corps, made a point of "getting everyone under control" when he took charge in Afghanistan.[53]

Curiously, at the senior-most levels within the Defense Department, the thinking was also conventional, notwithstanding the rhetoric about a "different kind of war." Pentagon brass and civilians alike were asking why terrorist leaders like Osama bin Laden and Mullah Mohammed Omar were still running loose. Defense Secretary Donald Rumsfeld reportedly dressed down General McNeill in July 2002 for failing to capture more "high-value targets."[54] Such impatience was likely a factor in launching Operation Mountain Sweep. It's the victory of form over substance; it is substituting action for results that is valued, especially when viable alternatives are not presented. Rumsfeld was correct in wanting results. However, the military, in general, and the special operations community, in particular, failed to present an unconventional alternative for consideration.

No Military Cultural Melting Pot

Although special operations can be complementary to conventional warfare, unconventional operations challenge the foundation of traditional military ethos and standard ideas about the conduct of regular military operations. A detached observer or historian will have difficulty grasping just how alien and even distasteful unconventional operations are viewed by those trained and socialized in conventional military behavior. This point is key and mostly overlooked. The possibility of an unconventional option that taps the strategic utility of the SOF is not likely to reach senior-level decision makers when special operations rest in the hands of military officers who have attitudes, interests, and a conception of warfare unfriendly to the potential of unconventional warfare.[55]

Thus, what are the essential conditions for special operations to succeed? First, military and political leaders must be willing to allow the SOF onto the playing field and must understand their potential and limitations. Special operations do not offer leaders a free lunch. Second, special operations are more a state of mind than a laundry list of primary and collateral missions. Unorthodox thinking, drawing on a thorough understanding of war, demography, human nature, culture, and technology are part of this mental approach. The answers to special warfare challenges will rarely be found in military manuals. Finally, special operations are political-military activities specially designed to achieve specific objectives. Special operations units must be outwardly focused in order to adapt, with great flexibility, to the requirements of each new mission. Instead of having a standing list of assigned missions, special operations should be viewed as an infinite realm of missions for which the SOF provide the capabilities most likely to result in a successful military operation. Developing mission areas first results in the SOF developing their own rigid doctrine that tends to contradict or stifle the heart of the matter—developing a true unconventional ethos.[56]

The 82nd was the wrong military force to send into Shi-e-Kot. The remaining al Qaeda and Taliban forces retreated into the mountains or melted into the civilian population after the Taliban disintegrated in December 2001. Since then, the Afghan war has become a guerrilla conflict, a counterinsurgency, with Taliban and al Qaeda fighters operating in small cells, emerging only to lay land mines and launch nighttime rocket attacks before disappearing once again. The special forces were created to deal with precisely this kind of enemy. They patrol isolated villages, working closely with local forces in ordinary Toyota pickups and talking to the inhabitants. They have been trained to assimilate local customs and sensibilities as carefully as possible. Many of them sported full beards until someone decided it did not look good. A shaven adult male is a strange sight for rural Afghans. Villagers made no secret of that unhappiness.

In short, unconventional warfare prescribes that special forces soldiers must be diplomats, doctors, spies, cultural anthropologists, and good friends—all before their primary work comes into play. The organizational culture necessary to develop a true unconventional mind-set cannot flourish in the giant shadow of the conventional military organizational culture. More important, the senior political and military leaders will not receive viable, alternative military options without an organizational culture free to develop such options and deliver them unimpeded.

"An Irish guy with a beard is still an Irish guy," proclaimed the conventional base commander in Kandahar when questioned about the order for special forces to shave and get into standard military uniforms. "I don't know what they are trying to achieve."[57] He was absolutely correct on both counts.

THE NEED TO THINK STRATEGICALLY

It is normal after military success to look back and to ask how victory was achieved. Operation Enduring Freedom (OEF) poses an additional question—where has victory delivered us? In two short months, OEF transformed the strategic landscape of not only Afghanistan, but also Central Asia, South Asia, and the Middle East. It did so in ways that were largely unforeseen at the outset of the war. Seldom has the gap been so great between the clarity of battlefield victory and the uncertainty that followed that victory. The Taliban has been driven from power and al Qaeda has been scattered to the hills, but Afghanistan is not a stable place. Many contend that there would be considerably less uncertainty today if the war had been approached using a true unconventional warfare model.

When it was launched, OEF was categorized as a "new kind of war," which gave its architects considerable freedom to play it by ear.[58] Actually, what was new was not the war but the scale and audacity of the attack that America suffered on September 11.[59] In the wake of this attack, the push to war overwhelmed the attention that might have been given to the war's possible broader effects. Once war commenced, the measure of success in Afghanistan came to focus narrowly on battlefield gains. The rush into an ambitious and complex operation so soon after September 11 made adequate political preparation impossible, and this produced the operation's shortcomings. So, it should come as no surprise that we found ourselves unprepared for political realities.

U.S. Military Engagement

OEF certainly advanced the U.S. position in Afghanistan and Central Asia. It also has strengthened the U.S. hand in Pakistan, with the Pervez Musharraf regime now substantially dependent on U.S. support. It has also created a new basis for cooperation with India. Russia's influence in Afghanistan also has advanced substantially. Russia will contest U.S. advances in the region; so will China and Iran. America's new ties to Pakistan and India may involve the United States in their dispute. Pakistan's increased dependency on the United States will undoubtedly necessitate supporting Musharraf against internal opponents. In sum, translating the improved U.S. regional position into long-term gains will require substantial additional investments, commitments, and involvements, and it will entail a significant risk of future conflict, perhaps on a large scale.[60]

The Taliban regime, which absorbed most of our attention, had little relationship to al Qaeda's activities outside of Afghanistan. Most of al Qaeda's capabilities to conduct international terrorist acts resided and resides outside of Afghanistan, and thus fell beyond the scope of Operation Enduring Freedom. Therefore, the unintended negative side effects of OEF have had little to do with the requirements of taking quick action against al Qaeda. Instead, they resulted from the decision to focus the operation on the Taliban government with the aim of toppling it as a first order of business, and the operation's heavy reliance on aerial bombardment. Less costly and less destabilizing approaches were available, although these would have required greater patience, restraint, imagination, and unconventional thinking. Such a campaign would have produced results, not quickly, but reliably and with a minimum of negative side effects.[61]

Resolving the broader problems of Afghanistan might have required a major military operation, but this could have been delayed until an adequate political framework was in place. A few months of intensive diplomatic, intelligence, and military preparations between special forces and anti-Taliban forces would have made a significant difference in terms of the impact, effectiveness, and broader repercussions of a military operation aimed at bringing stability to Afghanistan. Such preparations might even have obviated war or allowed a reduction in its scale.

After September 11, the Bush administration declared various near-term military objectives with regard to Afghanistan. Among these was to bring the leaders of al Qaeda to justice and destroy their organizational capacity. For many observers, this implied a carefully focused response involving special operations units and limited air strikes targeting Bin Laden and the al Qaeda network in Afghanistan. The notion of a low-profile operation with a reduced risk of collateral casualties had strong appeal for most allies, and especially Pakistan. It appealed to many unconventional warfare experts as well.[62]

In the weeks leading up to the war, the Bush administration was unclear about the goals and nature of the prospective military operation in Afghanistan. Of course, Bin Laden was in the crosshairs. Regarding the Taliban, however, the administration publicly emphasized that the Taliban must comply with American demands in order to obviate a strike.[63] But there was little hope that the Taliban would or even could comply. The demands made of the Taliban leadership were both substantial and nonnegotiable—turn over Bin Laden and the al Qaeda cadre, shut down all their camps and sites, and open Afghanistan to U.S. inspections. Even had the Taliban leadership been ready to rid themselves of Bin Laden and his top associates, the nature of the U.S. ultimatum made their compliance unlikely.

Although before the war the Bush administration had publicly emphasized the "punish and coerce" option for the Taliban, it also began soon after the September 11 attack to build support among its European allies for the more ambitious goal of forcing a regime change in Afghanistan. By late September, the administration was openly encouraging indigenous resistance to the Taliban and pledging indirect support without naming the Northern Alliance as the intended beneficiary.[64] What remained to be determined was who or what would replace the Taliban and how the administration would effect the change. As it turned out, battlefield exigencies would make both decisions for the administration during the first month of war. In other words, war would determine politics and tactics would define strategy.

Initially, the goal of regime replacement did not imply unleashing the Northern Alliance or completely uprooting the Taliban in the south. Instead, the United States aimed to pressure and weaken the Taliban through a combination of air attacks, special operations, and limited support to the Northern Alliance. The United States hoped to induce a split in the Taliban by killing off the most dogmatic elements of the movement and those linked closely to Bin Laden.[65] A more amenable Taliban might then mix with other Pashtun elements being assembled by the United States and Pakistan. The final step would be the creation of a government incorporating the Northern Alliance, all under the tutelage of King Zahir Shah and the auspices of the United Nations, perhaps freeing the U.S. from long-term commitments.

Romancing the Taliban

The U.S. plan came together hastily in the aftermath of September 11. It proved impossible to quickly assemble a Pashtun alternative to Taliban power while conducting military operations that were killing hundreds of Pashtuns, aiding their northern adversaries, and exacerbating a humanitarian crisis in Afghanistan.[66] King Zahir Shah's office, including Hamid Karzai, felt undersupported. Afghan expert Barnett Rubin's assessment of the effort made on the political side is harsh:

> They've got one part-time upper-middle-level figure [Richard Haass] working on the political side, and they've got all of the Joint Chiefs of Staff working on the military side. And they can't find half the price of a cruise missile to support Zahir Shah's office in Rome.[67]

Many elements of the Taliban's domestic coalition might have defected to a viable alternative Pashtun coalition if one had been available. But none could be constructed in the time allotted. This much is clear, there were deep divisions within the Taliban that could have been exploited through a political-military effort that is the essence of unconventional warfare.

The Initial Air Campaign—A Hammer without an Anvil

Through the end of October, the air campaign failed either to compel Taliban cooperation or destroy the movement.[68] What should have been clear from the experience of Operation Allied Force was that the "hammer" of air power requires an "anvil" on the ground.[69] The available ground anvil in Afghanistan, the Northern Alliance, was regarded initially (and accurately) as unlikely to produce the desired political outcome if victorious. Thus, support for the Alliance's war effort was minimally configured to sustain their front and pressure the Taliban without enabling a rapid Alliance sweep. Of course, the only completely reliable anvil would have been U.S. troops on the ground in large numbers. Practical problems precluded this option, at least in the chosen time frame.[70]

For its part, the Northern Alliance was reluctant to risk its troops in vigorously attacking well-defended Taliban positions unless the United States provided more air support. The apparent resilience of the Taliban prompted a process of questioning and reorienting America's efforts. The administration's initial response to the difficulties during the second week of war was not to unleash the Alliance but to increase the intensity of bombing all around. This also increased the rate of civilian casualties and elicited a new round of international criticism. The war effort became a race between the cumulative effects of bombing and the international condemnation that this course incurred. Through the end of October, the air campaign was ineffective.[71]

Defense Secretary Rumsfeld routinely responded to criticism about civilian casualties by arguing that the United States had taken great pains to limit collateral damage but that some amount of it is inevitable in war. Rumsfeld's defense begged the question of whether the response to the September 11 attacks should have taken a different form—in other words, an unconventional approach.[72]

A Shift in Targeting Strategy

For the Bush administration, the darkest moments of the war came between its third and fifth week. Indications of the apparent troubles on the battlefield was obvious in press coverage, as indicated in the following article titles:

> "Taliban Hang On; U.S. Finds They Are Not So Easy to Defeat" (*Newsday*, October 26);
> "Big Ground Forces Seen as Necessary to Defeat Taliban; Bombing Has Left Militia Largely Intact," (*Washington Post*, November);
> "The Week It All Went Wobbly for the West" (*Sunday Times*, London, 4 November, 2); and,
> "U.S. Adjusts Battle Plans as Strategy Goes Awry" (*New York Times*, November 9).

The bombing campaign had been intensified during the second week. Daily sorties rose from about twenty-five to ninety after the Taliban had proved more resilient than initially expected and the Northern Alliance had failed in its initial effort to take Mazar-i-Sharif. But this was still consistent with hopes that the Taliban might be split. The significant shift was the decision to cast America's lot with the Northern Alliance military effort.[73] This gained substance during the last week of October, when B-52s began to carpet bomb Taliban positions opposite the Northern Alliance and U.S. Special Operations troops assumed a bigger role in guiding both the air attacks and the Alliance's efforts. Throughout the first ten days of November, air support for the Alliance grew in tandem with criticism of the war's slow progress and its mounting civilian costs.

U.S. air power found its required ground anvil in the Northern Alliance's troops. But it was a devil's bargain that cost the United States leverage and control at the strategic level. The contradiction inherent in fully supporting the Northern

Alliance military effort was two-fold. First, the Alliance's goals, beyond defeating the Taliban, were not the same as those of the United States. Second, U.S. leverage over the Northern Alliance would decrease as Alliance troops closed in on the victory that U.S. air power made possible. Thus, fully supporting the Alliance meant losing control over it. The Alliance, fully aware of both these facts, quickly discarded its promise of restraint once it became possible for it to ride into Kabul and into power without further American assistance.[74]

A Theater Redefined

The sudden disintegration of the Taliban and the Alliance victory profoundly altered the national and regional strategic situation in several ways—the most significant being the releasing of tendencies throughout Afghanistan that gave warlordism, banditry, and opium production a new lease on life. This erased the one positive feature of the Taliban period. An immediate effect was the aggravation of the country's humanitarian crisis. A longer-term effect was greater difficulty in building a unified polity and resilient civilian authority.[75]

Additionally, the increased salience of ethnic and tribal divisions also increased the pressures on the international coalition supporting the operation. Notably, the Alliance victory had substantially increased Russian influence in Afghanistan, contrary to U.S. interests and to the dismay of both Pakistan and Iran. Indian interests (tied to the Tajik militias) also advanced substantially. These developments increased the prospects for future intensified regional contention over Afghanistan.[76]

These outcomes were largely the result of America's having augmented and unleashed the Northern Alliance, a force over which it had insufficient control. This policy shift indicated the extent to which military expediency had come to dominate U.S. strategic calculations. The Bush administration first sowed the seeds of this problem when it decided in September to pursue ambitious war objectives without giving enough time or attention to political preparation—the foundation of unconventional warfare.

The Structure of Postwar Afghan Instability

The potential for instability in post-Taliban Afghanistan resides in three systemic features of the new strategic environment. First, the present distribution of national and provincial authority in Afghanistan bears little relationship to the balance of interests and resources within and around the country. Instead, it is a by-product of Operation Enduring Freedom. Long-term local and regional players disfavored by the war's outcome will likely mobilize resources and try to compel an adjustment. Second, the post-Taliban balance between warlords and civilian authority decisively favors the former. Finally, no central or single indigenous military authority yet exercises either reliable or predominant control over the country, which remains a patchwork of fiefdoms and contested or lawless areas. These features of post-Taliban Afghanistan imply a significant potential for internecine conflict, including terrorist activity.[77]

The diffuse character of military power in post-Taliban Afghanistan constitutes a substantial limitation on the government's effective authority. Of course, the Karzai government can call on U.S. support whenever it needs it. But U.S. priorities are not identical to those of the interim government. Principally, the United States is engaged in a punitive expedition and a manhunt first, a nation-building exercise second—maybe. The long-term stability of Afghanistan, the authority of its government, the relief of its humanitarian crisis, and the country's prospects for reconstruction and recovery all depend on reversing the decentralization of military power.

U.S. and Afghan Interests Diverge

The collapse of the Taliban dramatically altered the context and meaning of Operation Enduring Freedom. Inside Afghanistan, the military priorities of the United States and those of its indigenous allies began to diverge in critical ways. For our Afghan allies, the end of the Taliban and flight of al Qaeda meant the end of the war and the beginning of a postwar period governed by its own imperatives. Allied militias increasingly turned their attention to building their ethnic and factional power bases. Consequently, conflict and cooperation no longer followed a simple Taliban versus anti-Taliban dichotomy. Ethnic and tribal allegiances became more important.[78]

America's terminal goals were to capture and imprison the top Taliban leaders and all al Qaeda cadre. Moreover, the United States wanted those rank-and-file Afghan Taliban who did not defect to be disarmed; foreign fighters generally were to be disarmed and interned. From the U.S. perspective, there was no acceptable alternative to these terms.

At the national level, Afghan leaders responded to the Taliban surrender of power by shifting their emphasis to the goals of conflict limitation, reconciliation, and reconstruction. The new Afghan leadership supported the capture and imprisonment of remaining al Qaeda leaders and cadre, but not with the single-mindedness exhibited by the United States. Instead, they gave priority to the tasks of building government legitimacy, averting communal violence, and relieving the nation's humanitarian crisis. No Afghan leader, national or local, demonstrated a willingness to risk much political, human, or material capital in efforts that did not conform to postwar imperatives.[79]

In sum, behind the post-Taliban divergence of priorities among the allies is the reality that the U.S.-Afghan coalition had significant differences from the start. Efforts converged, however, when the United States decided in late October to throw its support fully behind the Northern Alliance. This convergence facilitated the Taliban's defeat, gave Afghanistan to its present rulers, and won for the United States greater freedom to pursue Bin Laden throughout the land. But the close parallel of U.S.-Afghani efforts ended with the Taliban's defeat. Since then, the United States has been increasingly on its own, pursuing its terminal goals in a manner that affects some part of Afghanistan every day, but that bears little positive relationship to what Afghanistan's new rulers view as their most pressing problems.

A Failure to Adjust

The divergence of priorities within the U.S.-Afghan coalition has been especially disruptive to the U.S. campaign, because it was premised on close cooperation between U.S. and Afghan forces. More than cooperation, the effort required a degree of dependency on unfamiliar local fighters that set it apart from any of America's recent wars, including Vietnam. This dependency virtually guaranteed that, should priorities diverge, U.S. mission capabilities would be seriously compromised. The problem lies not with the concept of cooperation, but rather with the expectation that a strong basis for cooperation, trust, and combined operations can be established overnight.[80]

The change in strategic circumstances that followed the Taliban's demise challenged Operation Enduring Freedom in other ways as well. With the collapse of the regime, the immediate mission of U.S. forces changed, exposing weaknesses in America's operational concept. The combination of U.S. air power and thousands of mediocre allied militia supplemented by U.S. Special Forces had been sufficient to drive the Taliban from the field and from government. However, the combination was much less effective in capturing or killing the majority of al Qaeda cadre once they had dispersed. Defeating large units that are attempting a positional defense and toppling a regime is very different from interdicting small bands of guerrilla fighters that have gone underground or have "taken to the hills."

What was needed after December 2001 was a greater emphasis on U.S. Special Operations troops, supported by light infantry, conducting counter-insurgency operations. Aerial bombardment should have become a rare thing. Several of the controversial attacks in which dozens of civilians were killed—for instance, the December bombings of a convoy in Paktia Province and the village of Qalaye Niazi—would have been better handled by ground operations using U.S. Special Forces.[81]

The failure to adjust U.S. operations in line with the post-Taliban change in theater conditions cost the United States some of the fruits of victory and imposed additional, avoidable humanitarian and stability costs on Afghanistan. Why the United States failed to adjust is unclear. One possible explanation is that the administration may simply have failed to notice that strategic conditions had changed, or it may have failed to appreciate the significance of these changes. Most likely, the failure to adjust to an environment that was growing increasingly unconventional was a predisposition on the part of U.S. military planners for conventional operations.

The Path Charted by Enduring Freedom

The clearest achievement of Operation Enduring Freedom was forcing the Taliban from power. But this goal was secondary to the one of destroying the al Qaeda network, which is down but not out. Despite the change of government in Kabul, Afghanistan is less stable today than before the operation. The Taliban-al Qaeda bond has been displaced by a potentially more serious one, regional interstate contention over the direction of an unsettled Afghanistan.

The war also left Pakistan and its president in a precarious position, and it may have contributed to a dangerous escalation of the Arab-Israeli conflict. Finally, the operation, especially the bombing campaign and the postwar treatment of prisoners, has fed anti-American sentiments throughout the Arab and Muslim world. The various effects of the campaign combine to give the impression that the war is precisely what the Bush administration says it is not, an assault on Arab and Muslim interests. Indeed, the war's inadvertent effects may be more significant than we think.[82]

Defense Secretary Rumsfeld has signaled a willingness to deploy to other countries in pursuit of terrorists. But the method and path charted by Enduring Freedom would lead the United States into a thicket of civil, ethnic, and interstate conflicts involving much more than the issue of terrorism as is already the case in Afghanistan. In such complex circumstances, the single-minded exercise of U.S. military power is bound to produce inadvertent and chaotic results. Moreover, it will implicate the United States as a partisan in local disputes in ways not originally intended.[83]

The Triumph of Expediency

Enduring Freedom was also distinguished by the degree to which military expediency determined strategic choices—such as the decision to unleash the Northern Alliance. This feature of U.S. decision making in the war contributed to the preponderance of inadvertent outcomes. The U.S. relationship with the Northern Alliance was governed by a mutual opportunism. Tactical alliances are not, of course, unusual in war. But the degree of U.S. dependency in this case and the differences in the broader goals, interests, and values that separated the United States and its battlefield partners ensured that the U.S. victory would not be complete.[84]

The administration's focus on state actors comports well with the structure of U.S. military power and with prevalent concepts about its proper use of decisive force and traditional notions of deterrence. But the U.S. paradigm marginalizes subnational and transnational dynamics, the locale where most of the answers regarding the new terrorism reside. Effective action against terrorism depends on a unique synergy of military and nonmilitary measures—the latter including diplomatic, humanitarian, informational, development, peace-building, and law-enforcement efforts. Military efforts serve to guarantee nonmilitary measures and help maintain the conditions that ensure stability and that does not leak terrorism. It is in the integration, balancing, and pacing of military and nonmilitary, unilateral, and cooperative initiatives that Operation Enduring Freedom has fallen short, and the result is greater instability in Afghanistan. The final outcome of the war in Afghanistan has yet to be determined. In fact, what seems positive in the short term may be potentially explosive in the long term.

Understanding the Potential and Limitations of Unconventional Warfare

Understanding the nature of a conflict is fundamental to developing a winning strategy. Unconventional warfare can produce great strategic utility under the appropriate circumstances. Spectacular success enhances the status and power of a nation. Conversely, spectacular failures produce the opposite affect.

Unconventional Minds

The range of activities that seem to be identifiable as unconventional warfare is broad. This is partly because of the increasingly large number of military units that now fall under the operational control of USSOCOM (and consequently, by definition, are special operations forces) as well as paramilitary organizations belonging to other government agencies that claim to conduct UW.

The complexity of most conflicts often disguises the nature of the conflict. Therefore, conceptual clarity in analyzing a conflict is exceedingly important. For instance, in Vietnam, U.S. Special Forces, by default, assumed a key role in a war that was devoid of a comprehensive strategy. Was the war an unconventional one because of a key role played by SOF? In contrast, British regulars and Malayan forces carried out counterinsurgency operations in Malaya in the late 1950s. Was the British approach conventional or unconventional?

Any inquiry into the dynamics of a particular war must first begin with a proper assessment of the threat followed by an examination of one's own capabilities. A faulty diagnosis of either of these variables can be costly. There is a great deal of tactical doctrine for SOF but virtually no relevant strategic theory or history.

There is an immense library of colorful narratives of stirring deeds in special warfare by men such as Maj. Robert Rogers of Rogers's Rangers who carried out daring raids during the French and Indian War and T. E. Lawrence, whose exploits during World War I have become legend. But a history that explains the effects of special operations on the course and outcome of a war is not available. Similarly, strategic theory that would help explain what small teams of special warriors can accomplish would help educate potential clients about the services provided by special operations forces.[85]

The history of the twentieth century is strewn with cases of the misuse of SOF as elite shock troops, as well as with opportunities for special operations, arguably lost, because no one, including the special warriors themselves were sufficiently unconventional in their thinking. The conduct of unconventional warfare carries heavier demands than the wearing of a beret and the mastery of unusual firearms. Unconventional warfare is a state of mind as well as mission and a distinctive set of tactics.[86]

What Must Political and Military Patrons Understand about UW?

Before discussing some general points that help us understand the potential of unconventional warfare, it is important to note that the use of unorthodox methods, or the introduction of a new operational concept, does not necessarily mean that unconventional warfare is being waged. Furthermore, warfare, even where SOF play a key role, is not inevitably unconventional.[87] Finally, strategy much more than tactics, defines the nature of a war.

It has always been a military virtue to achieve maximum results with minimum effort. In military language, this virtue is commonly referred to as economy of force. SOF can wage war economically. Detachment 101 in Burma, the SAS (Special Air Service) in North Africa in 1942, and the SOE (Special Operations Executive) in France all illustrate this point. SOF can conduct operations at a fraction of the cost of conventional forces. But special operations are not cost free. Special operations, which by definition are small, almost always require the support of national assets. Furthermore, the scale of investment necessary to develop and maintain a capable special operations force is significant. UW capabilities that are not properly developed, understood, and employed can result in tragic failure. The foreign policy disaster that resulted from the Bay of Pigs fiasco in 1961 is a classic case of not understanding the nature and limitations of unconventional warfare. The Bay of Pigs case did show that unconventional warfare (especially when improperly applied) is high risk and that failure could have far-reaching affects.

Second, there are situations where brute force is not applicable. These situations may be suited for the agility, maneuver, and finesse that characterize UW. SOF function as force multipliers in UW. Their language capabilities and cultural knowledge help develop a synergism among local forces. However, it is unlikely that this style of warfare will bring immediate effects on a battle, on a campaign, or on a war. Often, success will be measured by the absence of a particular outcome. Positive strategic results can occur, but it will require patience.[88]

Third, the warrior virtues of SOF entice leaders to employ elite forces during desperate circumstances that can lead to catastrophic results. Elite units have often been assigned missions suitable to their warrior virtues, though not to their numbers, their firepower, or their ability to sustain high casualties. This inappropriate use of SOF can be attributed not only to the ignorance of the senior commander but also to insecurity within the SOF, which encourages the acceptance of all missions, appropriate or not.[89]

Fourth, UW must take a holistic approach to conflict. Focusing on any single aspect of a war would leave friendly forces vulnerable. As Clausewitz observed: "But in war more than in any other subject we must begin by looking at the nature of the whole; for here more than elsewhere the part and the whole must always be thought of together."[90] Therefore, UW must address issues beyond those normally considered by conventional forces. The nature of the enemy, his strategy, the psychological vulnerabilities of friend and foe, and economic and political considerations all require attention.

Fifth, UW can have positive strategic value whether they are used on independent missions or they coordinate their actions with conventional forces. Partisan operations in World War II by Detachment 101, the SAS, and the OSS all support the claim that UW can prepare the battlefield for the success of future conventional operations. Recent special operations in Iraq also support this claim. Alternatively, UW can succeed independent of conventional operations. Arguably, U.S. success in El Salvador resulted from a handful of special warriors working closely with local military, political, economic, and psychological forces to defeat a well-organized communist insurgency without introducing U.S. conventional forces to the conflict.

Sixth, UW is an alternative use of force that expands the options available to political and military leaders. The indirect nature of UW makes it politically attractive when circumstances preclude a conventional option. In theory, there are always alternatives to the use of force. However, in practice, power remains the currency of international relations. The credible capacity to use coercion is enhanced by an unconventional warfighting capability that provides flexibility to political and military leaders.[91]

Finally, UW can help shape the future course of political events. By helping to shape people's views about our collective enemy, and by providing unwavering support, we can assist a future ally to wage war against an unjust regime. UW can assist a disadvantaged people to remain politically viable and to fight against a common enemy. UW is a clear message of commitment and shows a continuing political interest in an area. In fact, employing SOF may be a more impressive gesture of political interest than using conventional alternatives. Helping a people defeat a stronger opponent can result in strong political ties advantageous to the United States.[92]

A Balanced Assessment

Any military action that has the potential to achieve political success also has the potential to produce political failure. The risk to national standing increases when a special operation is launched because conventional alternatives are not viable. Said another way, successful UW can enhance U.S. standing, but failure will correspondingly reduce political respect. Furthermore, failure will be magnified when it is America's elite that produced the defeat.

Next, UW is ultimately aimed at replacing an existing regime with a politically and militarily viable opposition that has been nurtured by SOF.[93] Whenever UW is applied against an enemy, the possibility exists that rather than softening him up, the reverse will occur—his resolve will be strengthened. Government reprisals against an opposition can generate hatred not only against the government, but also against the country that set in motion the events that resulted in reprisals.

Third, UW designed to pave the way for conventional operations has the potential to alert the enemy to the prospect of direct attack by conventional forces. If an enemy can determine the purpose of an upcoming military operation, he can prepare his defenses accordingly and increase the cost for a U.S. victory. Clandestine and covert operations are becoming more difficult to execute in a world that is increasingly transparent.

Finally, claims that the SOF are so special that they can do almost anything demanded of them is not only wrong but fraught with peril. There is no free lunch. SOF have limitations. It takes good leaders who understand the special operations business to protect the nation from the fantasies of political and military leaders. Furthermore, special operations leaders themselves may have limited or dated special operations experience, or for political reasons may be reluctant to speak about SOF limitations.[94]

These four caveats are simply warning for political and military leaders and are not intended to detract from the tremendous potential of unconventional warfare. Success in UW depends on favorable conditions. Assessments about the conditions as well as the capabilities of the SOF can only be made by an educated patron.

Assessing UW in Afghanistan

The common view is that the war in Afghanistan has been unconventional. The war has been different from recent wars, and aspects of the war seem to conform to the joint doctrinal definition of UW. However, the complexities of many conflicts, and the conflict in Afghanistan in particular, can disguise the true nature of the war. Furthermore, the response to the threat more accurately defines how the threat was diagnosed. How a nation responds to a threat is a function of many factors, but two are paramount—the assessment of the threat and an examination of one's own capabilities. Both of these factors must be constantly reevaluated.

The assessment of the threat from Afghanistan in the period immediately after the 9/11 attacks was relatively straightforward. Al Qaeda was behind the attacks that killed roughly three thousand Americans. Al Qaeda's corporate headquarters was in Afghanistan and was provided with safe sanctuary by the Taliban regime. The Taliban would not turn over the al Qaeda leaders to the United States, so the Taliban would have to be destroyed in the U.S. pursuit of al Qaeda. The task of destroying the Taliban and al Qaeda was simplified, because they were almost indistinguishable from one another.

The assessment of U.S. capabilities to respond to the threat was more challenging. Political leaders demanded a quick military response. They also demanded a response that would be qualitatively different from those of the Bill Clinton administration. Cruise missile attacks or bombing alone would not do. The glacial speed of major troop deployments would not satisfy the need for the quick, lethal response demanded by the president and defense secretary. Fortunately, the inadequacy of the Taliban's military and the existence of the Northern Alliance allowed the U.S. military to rapidly deploy special forces teams into Afghanistan to masterfully orchestrate a ground campaign by the Northern Alliance supported by overwhelming U.S. air power. The Taliban was crushed and literally driven to the hills along with the remaining al Qaeda. The campaign started slowly, stalled a bit, then accelerated geometrically to bring victory to the coalition before any serious thought could take place about the type of peace that would follow. Where the initial diagnosis of the threat and the response proved accurate, subsequent assessments have missed their mark.

Instability and Insecurity after the Fall of the Taliban
To be sure, the Taliban did enforce law and order (though harsh and in violation of human rights) in Afghanistan. The destruction of the Taliban generated instability and insecurity. In the capital, an interim national government had been formed. Hamid Karzai, the interim leader, was to maintain law and order in Kabul through a seven-thousand-strong international security force. However, at the periphery, local thugs with private armies were now able to dominate local politics. Many of these

thugs were men who fought alongside the United States to defeat the Taliban. Many were also appointed by Karzai to govern the various provinces. For some Afghanis, the harshness of the Taliban was preferred over the lawlessness that resulted from their fall from power.

U.S. Diagnosis of the Post-Taliban Threat

The United States was committed to rebuilding Afghanistan with the help of the international community. Much was at stake in this commitment. Bin Laden and others tried to portray the war as an assault on Islam. U.S. actions in Afghanistan would either reinforce Bin Laden's claim or demonstrate that the United States was waging war against terrorists and not Islam.

Factionalism, and politics in its most basic form, are parts of the enduring tapestry of Afghan life. These constitute the greatest threats to the national government. Political power is directly related to one's credible (and demonstrated) capacity to coerce. The national government is secure as long as the international community maintains a dominating security force in Kabul. Equally important, international recognition of the government is tied to Hamid Karzai, the charismatic president of Afghanistan. Keeping Karzai alive and keeping the government viable is a priority of the United States, even if it results in discounting the future for the present.[95]

Factionalism and politics within Kabul represents only one significant threat to the future of Afghanistan. The second, and perhaps greater threat to Afghanistan's future is the centrifugal forces from the provinces that can render the national government irrelevant.[96] These centrifugal forces are directly tied to the instability and insecurity that exists in the provinces. Creating a stable environment and securing the population from lawlessness should be the highest priority of the U.S.-led military coalition. However, the focus of the coalition, to include U.S. SOF, remains to kill or capture high-value targets and other elements that oppose coalition operations in Afghanistan. Senior SOF leaders quickly dismiss any actions that hint of nation building as not being part of their mission.[97] Misdiagnosing the problem has resulted in military operations that are undermining U.S. political objectives in Afghanistan.

UW, Stability, Security, and Intelligence

UW can help shape the future of political events. The views of the Afghan people will ultimately be shaped by whether local governance is perceived as legitimate. Focusing on any single aspect of the war such as killing, capturing, and disrupting, leaves friendly forces and potentially friendly populations vulnerable to the advances of factions that want power for selfish reasons. Without the aid of precise, multisource intelligence, SOF operations to kill and capture selected enemy personnel are producing little. More important, these imprecise operations are moving U.S. forces across the line from liberators to occupiers. This problem is exacerbated by the fact that senior SOF leaders in Afghanistan do not routinely meet with local leaders.[98] SOF leaders must take a holistic approach to conflict and address issues normally beyond the consideration of conventional thinkers.

Stability, security, and intelligence are related to one another in a dynamic way. Moreover, the milieu generated by the skillful manipulation of these variables will result in capturing and killing those wanted for conducting or supporting terrorism more effectively than the single-dimensional approach of terrorist hunting. This idea requires further explanation.

The idea that to succeed against terrorism we must do more than just catch terrorists should not be interpreted to mean that we must appeal to or even appease terrorists or their supporters. On the contrary, intimidation and fear can be highly effective tools. Indeed, experience suggests that what is needed is some blend of cooption and coercion—or sticks and carrots—the proportion impossible to specify in the abstract but to be adjusted as the campaign goes forward, and according to the character of the target audience. Whatever the mix of rewards and punishments, the point should be to direct them not only to the terrorists, but beyond them to their sources of support.

Intelligence is decisive, because in struggles such as the one we are engaged in with al Qaeda, the enemy operates clandestinely in small groups, without the infrastructure of established military organizations, and can easily blend in with ordinary populations. Yet, while our technical means of collection are unparalleled, impressive, and useful, they are also limited. Our best sources of intelligence are likely to be the layers of people among whom the terrorists hide. Gaining their cooperation and eliciting the intelligence they hold is another reason to work on the terrorists' supporters and sympathizers. Peeling them away will not only get us closer to the terrorists themselves, but also will limit terrorists' operational effectiveness. It is here that SOF, operating in a true unconventional warfare mode can make their greatest impact.

There are a number of ways to think about unconventional warfare. Beyond the official definition, members of the special forces often boil UW down to any effort in which they work by, through, and with indigenous forces. From a special forces perspective, the goal of UW is to help win a war by working with—as opposed to neutralizing or fighting around—local populations. UW represents a classically indirect, and ultimately local, approach to waging warfare. It demands that efforts at all levels—strategic, tactical, and operational—be coordinated. To work with indigenous forces, SOF must win their trust. To do this, they live with them, eat with them, and share the same living conditions. Building trust invariably takes time, but the payoff comes in a better understanding of the operational environment, and the ability to solicit the kind of solid intelligence that enables operations to succeed.

Civic action is closely related to, indeed, an unavoidable part of such efforts. According to Col. Edward Lansdale, who claimed to have coined the term in the Philippines in 1950, civic action describes soldiers' "brotherly behavior."[99] Certainly, U.S. soldiers sent abroad appear to intuitively understand the value in helping improve conditions of indigenous populations. It earns them gratitude, if not friends. This becomes key to any UW effort, because friends won't let friends get hurt. Civic action thus doubles as force protection. It also helps dry up the sea of supporters in which opposing forces swim by providing a more stabilized, improved, and secure local environment. The safer and more secure citizens feel, the more committed they become to staying secure. The exchange relationship is such that the fewer the population's causes for legitimate grievance, the fewer inroads insurgents or terrorists can make. Or, said another way, by implicitly trading security for local assistance, civic action can yield militarily useful results, particularly in the realm of intelligence. But here, too, there is a catch. What composes civic action in a particular locale can usually only be determined once units are on site. To identify the most pressing local needs and determine what will earn a team the most bang for its buck invariably takes time. One size will not fit all circumstances.

Often, civic action will require a "tough love" approach in lieu of the "brotherly behavior" espoused by Edward Lansdale. One special forces team sergeant knew exactly how to balance the two approaches. The team sergeant's orders were to kill or capture selected Taliban and al Qaeda leaders. Master Sergeant "M" deliberately chose to accomplish his task indirectly by stabilizing the area and establishing a secure environment. He was conducting UW.[100]

In March 2002, Master Sergeant M was operating in the vicinity of Urgun. He and his detachment made a point of staying in close contact with the local population and especially the local elders. Zakim Kahn (ZK), a warlord with significant influence in the neighboring Paktia and Paktika provinces, had moved to establish his control in the area around Urgun. ZK came to Urgun with three hundred armed fighters and took charge of a few government buildings and warehouses that were filled with weapons and ammunition. ZK felt it was his prerogative to reclaim these facilities, because he was an acknowledged political leader in good standing with the government in Kabul. Further solidifying ZK's claim of legitimacy was the fact that the CIA was paying him $20,000 a month to maintain himself and his private army of one thousand men. ZK, however, was in business for himself, though his men were supposed to provide local security.

ZK quickly moved to take control of the local customs house and to establish checkpoints that extorted tolls from vehicle traffic. The tax revenue raised was pocketed by ZK or used to help fund ZK's fight against his rival, Pacha Kahn, who operated out of the Khowst area. Little, if any, of the taxes raised in Urgun benefited the people of Urgun. Even the money the CIA was giving ZK to maintain his army was not all getting into the hands of the soldiers. ZK was collecting taxes for himself and skimming CIA money intended to maintain a militia friendly to U.S. interests. Master Sergeant M clearly saw ZK as an obstruction to local stability, security, and legitimate governance, and ultimately, to capturing or killing Taliban and al Qaeda leaders.

Master Sergeant M quickly moved to have the CIA funnel ZK's monthly payment for maintaining the three-hundred-man security force through him. M told ZK's troops that they would receive their full pay if they worked for him. Only ten men stayed with ZK. The remaining 290 would now work for Master Sergeant M. Next, M seized the government facilities that ZK was occupying, including the weapons and ammunition. Without his militia and a facility to operate from, ZK returned to his own area in Paktia Province. ZK was driven out of town by a special forces detachment.

ZK was gone, but the issues of stability, security, and legitimate governance needed immediate attention. The militia M now controlled would provide local security for the time being. But the CIA funding would not last indefinitely.[101] A more permanent solution was necessary. Also, M wanted to be careful not to create a situation where the population continuously turned to him to solve local problems. Consequently, M assembled the local elders to establish a Shura, a consultative, decision-making council to exercise legitimate local governance.

The "force in being"[102] Master Sergeant M, his detachment, and the 290-man militia established permitted the Shura to begin addressing community issues that required attention. Urgun needed a local police force. M was asked to assist in establishing a police department. Once the size of the force was determined, the Shura was asked to identify men, ensuring proportional representation from the ethnic groups living in the area, to be trained to perform police duties. Master Sergeant M and his team equipped and trained a credible local police force responsive to the governing Shura. But the police needed to be paid. The special forces team was not authorized to pay local police. After consultation with M, the Shura established a system to tax the population as well as raise revenue by setting up road tolls. The money was used to pay the police and to hire workers to repair the roads around Urgun.

Next, the Shura identified a need to establish a local clinic. Master Sergeant M had to stretch the funding rules to support this important need. The special forces teams had operational funds but their use was restricted. They couldn't use the operational fund to build a clinic or pay doctors, but they could use the fund to pay for the destruction of confiscated weapons. M saw an opportunity that required great discretion. He used the fund to pay locals to cut apart Taliban tanks, thus destroying the weapons systems. The scrap metal was hauled to Pakistan and sold. The money was used to pay for the clinic. Everyone was happy, though Master Sergeant M would most likely have not received permission for his scheme had he asked for it. He knew better than to ask the question.

Master Sergeant M and his detachment worked closely with the Shura and police to stabilize the area and establish a secure environment. Even carrying weapons in town was outlawed. At one point, the population wanted to make M the local warlord. Most significant, however, the town was moving in the direction of self-sufficiency. They were able to solve their own problems and protect their property. Taliban and al Qaeda leaders could not find sanctuary in Urgun. The area was thoroughly pacified.

Unfortunately, the story does not end here. Master Sergeant M and his detachment returned to the United States. A mixture of conventional forces and SOF rotated through the area for several months. Urgun regressed. The time that was needed for the UW operation to fully take hold was cut short by a self-induced administrative need to get the boys home. The protracted nature of UW is inconsistent with the U.S. way of war, including modern special operations.

UW Needs to Be Understood at the Highest Levels

Master Sergeant M demonstrated the potential of UW to shape the course of political events. Imagine his success multiplied by the number of special forces teams that have been deployed to Afghanistan since the Taliban was defeated in December 2001. There would be little room, geographically and politically, for al Qaeda or Taliban leaders to maneuver. But, a UW strategy at the CJSOTF, CJTF-180, or combatant-command levels does not exist. M produced maximum results with a minimum of effort. Brute force, in the traditional sense, was unnecessary. The SOF functioned as a force multiplier by training and equipping local military and police forces and subjecting their use to the oversight of the local, legitimate Shura. Master Sergeant M took a holistic approach and created an environment inhospitable to our common enemies.

Unfortunately, Master Sergeant M's approach was not the norm. The focus on "killing or capturing" becomes more important as you move up the SOF chain of command.[103] Perhaps the warrior virtues of SOF entice leaders to default to employing elite forces for direct-action or hyperconventional missions even though, in the case of special forces, their competitive advantage lies elsewhere. Conversely, maybe special forces feel insecure in a special operations world that is dominated by leaders who have been shaped by the hyperconventional side of special operations.

In observing and talking with special forces leaders in Afghanistan, it clearly appears that the force suffers from "Delta envy."[104]

Lessons of Processes of Innovation

Scholars who study military innovation have not been able to specify the circumstances that guarantee successful innovation. Successful innovation is too complex to be sensibly reduced to a formula. Likewise, the conditions for successfully waging unconventional warfare cannot be presented in a strategist's cookbook. Also, success can happen in the absence of these conditions, because the performance required of friendly forces is dramatically affected by the competence of the enemy. Still, the conditions presented below are extracted from the discussions in this chapter about the war in Afghanistan and appear to be necessary, though not sufficient by themselves, to wage successful unconventional warfare.

Necessary conditions for successful unconventional warfare:

- UW needs a separate and different organizational culture.
- UW capability must not be dependent on conventional sponsorship.
- UW can benefit from advanced technologies.
- Waging UW requires political and military patrons who understand its potential and limitations.
- Waging UW requires civilian and military leadership that possess a strategic mentality.

Chapter 6

⁞ Conclusions and ⁞ Recommendations

AL QAEDA OPERATIVES WHO FOUND REFUGE in Pakistan have largely regrouped and moved back into Afghanistan. This was accomplished within a year after a successful U.S. military campaign forced them to flee their onetime sanctuary by the thousands. The influx back into Afghanistan has created new dangers. Al Qaeda members have launched numerous small attacks against U.S. forces and may have been behind an attempted assassination of the Afghan president, Hamid Karzai. The return of many al Qaeda operatives thus represents a serious threat to the American-backed Karzai government, which has been unable to gain effective control of the Afghan countryside.

While U.S. military might smashed al Qaeda's training camps and terrorist infrastructure in Afghanistan after the terrorist attacks on New York and Washington in September 2001, al Qaeda quickly adapted. It has transformed itself into a more mobile, flexible, and elusive force than ever before. Management books talk about "learning organizations." Osama bin Laden has built something that is a learning organization. It is changing and adapting to the loss of its infrastructure. Al Qaeda has shown remarkable resilience in the face of the worldwide pressure applied by the U.S.-led counterterrorism campaign, and it retains a lethal capacity to mount attacks against U.S. interests. Alliances formed with leaders of other Islamic radical groups before September 11, including members of the Philippines-based Abu Sayyaf group, the Islamic Movement of Uzbekistan, and the Egyptian Islamic Jihad, also helped al Qaeda weather the U.S. assault.[1]

U.S. officials say they have reports showing that al Qaeda operatives are still trying to develop rudimentary chemical weapons, even while they are on the run, using their training in how to make weapons out of commercially available goods. Additionally, al Qaeda has adapted not only by seeking new ties with other Islamic radicals, but also by promoting from within, finding new leaders to step in for others who have been killed or captured. "As people have been killed or captured, we have seen temporary blips in al Qaeda operational activity, but not an overall decline," said one American official. "They continue to conduct operational planning even after a leader has been removed, which suggests that they have real depth."[2] Al Qaeda has adapted in remarkable consonance with changes in its operational environment. Can the same be said of the United States?

THEORETICAL PROPOSITIONS—CONTINGENCY THEORY AND PROCESSES OF INNOVATION

Here are the starting propositions from the literature on contingency theory and processes of military innovation identified in chapter 3:

1. There is no "one best way" to organize.
2. The nature of an organization's interdependencies can either inhibit or enable effectiveness; no single rule applies to all situations.
3. The organization must flexibly harmonize with the capabilities of its members as well as with the fast-changing external environment.
4. To cope with change, enhanced diagnostic skills are essential in order to be proactive or preemptive.
5. Unstable environments where problems and requirements for action rise that cannot be easily broken down into specific tasks and distributed within a clearly defined hierarchy necessitate decentralized management.
6. The more complex the environment, the greater the need is for increased differentiation and coordination for effectiveness.
7. Innovation in military organizations is difficult and often requires outside intervention.
8. Military organizations cope with uncertainty by developing standardized procedures and by distributing authority to enforce these procedures.
9. Those who hold power and authority in an organization have a vested interest in the doctrine associated with their status.
10. Innovation can be internally generated by the desire of professional officers to secure the state as well as by the promise of more resources.
11. Scientific entrepreneurship develops technologies that can instigate innovation.
12. Innovation is the result of individuals and their ideas.
13. Organizational culture can either facilitate or deter innovation.
14. Organizational culture is shaped by incentive structures that operate in the organization.
15. The interests of an organization determine what it thinks about a given innovation.

This study sought to use these propositions as a framework for assessing the DoD's ability to depart from convention, to adapt, and to win what President George W. Bush called "a different kind of war" fought by a new kind of enemy.[3] The following questions were addressed and I hope answers have emerged in the many pages that constitute this study.

- How should we characterize the Afghanistan campaign?
- How has the nature of the war changed?
- Has the United States made necessary adjustments to changing conditions?
- Are command and control arrangements adaptive to the nature of the environment?
- Do long-standing, administrative, organizational dependencies affect organizing for combat employment?
- Do other players and stakeholders influence operational designs?
- Do institutional norms constrain military operational art?
- Is the United States prosecuting a war in a manner that is likely to result in victory?
- Is the United States capable of waging unconventional warfare?

Finding—The Case of Afghanistan

A brief review of the case addresses both the propositions and questions listed above. After September 11, the United States focused on Afghanistan, which harbored Bin Laden under the Taliban regime. As a consequence of the need for action, and to preempt any further attacks against the United States, the U.S. government decided to wage war against al Qaeda in Afghanistan almost from the outset. The leadership of the al Qaeda was headquartered in Afghanistan, and the Taliban supported al Qaeda. Other states were known to harbor terrorist groups, but the head of the snake was seen to be in Afghanistan.

There have been what could be described as four segments to this war in Afghanistan. The initial segment of the war was a very short one, where we applied air power alone with very little success. The second segment was the introduction of special operations forces (SOF) to assist anti–Taliban forces. Combined with the ground operations of the Northern Alliance, equipped with Russian aid and American money, our SOF were successful in dislodging the Taliban and al Qaeda from their conventional defensive positions. The third segment was the operation in the Tora Bora Mountains, where we found that the combination of the SOF and reluctant allies was not enough to both seal the Pakistani border and take the battle to the enemy in their caves. The fourth segment started with Operation Anaconda, where we used conventional U.S. military forces along with a smattering of our closer allied special operations teams but ultimately had to call in the local Afghani warlord to help oust the enemy from the Shi-e-Kot stronghold. The enemy appeared to have been able to fade across the border into Pakistan.[4] Segment four continues with the manhunt to kill or capture key al Qaeda and Taliban leaders.

If examined through an objective lens, it becomes clear that Taliban and al Qaeda forces were not fighting a guerrilla war during the first two segments. They were in conventional defensive positions. Only after they were shoved out of power were they able to fight in the way that they are most effective, from the caves and in small groups against a conventional force.

So far, the most interesting aspect of the war has been the ability of the special operations forces to operate in this environment. The SOF were able to establish contact with the anti-Taliban forces and create a powerful force leveraging indigenous ground capabilities with U.S. air power. These special operations teams were adaptive and facilitated combat operations that resulted in a considerable victory. This remarkable achievement was enabled to a degree never before experienced by high technology (direct communications with air platforms and precision guided munitions). While we should not minimize the contribution of the new technologies, the fact is that the difference between the ineffective segment one and the highly effective segment two was "boots on the ground."

The absence of command rather than the presence of command is an interesting feature of the second segment of the war. While there were daily reports from Afghanistan, it was almost as if CENTCOM, located in Tampa, was waiting for SOF teams to report in through their channels before reporting to the world what was happening. The dramatic pictures of SOF soldiers in various stages of uniform disarray riding horses, donkeys, and all terrain vehicles (ATVs) across the high plains complete with laptops portrayed a situation where these teams, knowing what was required, exploited the seams of al Qaeda and Taliban wherever they could. Within days, the SOF and our newfound allies had achieved the equivalent of the German Blitzkrieg across the plains of France in World War II, albeit against a much more lightly armed enemy. The rapidity with which the SOF teams and allied fighters did this was amazing, but it has to be said that the Taliban and the al Qaeda were never trained or organized to fight the conventional fight.

The battle in the hills of Tora Bora did not demonstrate that the SOF were any better than the conventional forces used in Anaconda, but the promise of a small, versus large, U.S. footprint appeared to be the way to combat the enemy. More to the point, the Tora Bora and Anaconda operations both show that SOF were equally effective (or ineffective) as a larger U.S. force with all the command and control paraphernalia and posturing.

The question is, why do we want to commit a large conventional U.S. force to such battles? Part of the answer is that all good commanders seek to get into the battle whether or not they lead the best-suited force. If there is a battle, then ride to the sound of the guns. Furthermore, the army had been pushed to demonstrate its relevance in the emerging warfighting environment characterized as lighter, quicker, and more lethal. The army had to prove its manhood. The fight near Shi-e-Kot seemed like the opportunity it had been waiting for. Despite individual acts of heroism and uncommon bravery among the troops and unit leaders, it is clear that the army was ill-prepared for combat against an illusive enemy located in the high mountain caves and extreme cold of the Afghan mountains.[5]

Intelligence has revealed that Bin Laden was in the Tora Bora complex but escaped. It was speculated that the failure to capture or kill Bin Laden was because the United States did not commit conventional ground forces to seal the borders with Pakistan. While it is easy for armchair strategists to conclude that had there been forces guarding the border, Bin Laden would not have escaped, this conclusion is inconsistent with what we know about how an insurgent enemy operates. They have an uncanny ability to avoid contact when they want to avoid it. In that terrain and altitude, it would probably have taken several divisions to seal off the border while protecting our own rear from insurgent attacks from Pakistani soil. The real failure was in misreading the cultural intelligence that should have told us that our somewhat erratic allies were not up to this fight. Understanding the motivation of the friendly forces should have been a top priority. One suspects that our SOF advisers knew as much and probably reported it through the chain of command.

U.S. conventional military forces had been deployed to base areas in Afghanistan, but they had not been deployed into the combat areas. It was in the Shi-e-Kot Valley that senior U.S. military leaders had their first chance to plan and execute a battle of annihilation against mostly al Qaeda fighters using mostly U.S. troops. Unfortunately, it turned out that the "victory" of Operation Anaconda was more imagined than real. Too many of the al Qaeda forces escaped the noose again to claim anything but a hollow victory for the elements of the 101st Airborne and the 10th Mountain divisions and the allied special operations forces.

The al Qaeda fighters successfully ambushed and successfully escaped the clutches of the Americans. Anaconda was an attempt to create a linear battlefield by Clausewitzean-minded military leaders using heavy doses of attrition warfare on an elusive enemy. The U.S. military attempted to apply a conventional solution against an unconventional enemy much like it did in Vietnam, where it failed. In fact, it handed al Qaeda a moral victory, with many escaping or staying hidden.

Instead of adapting to the enemy, instead of being flexible with regard to the response, instead of recognizing our own inherent limitations, U.S. military leaders perceived a conventional Clausewitzian war that they could understand and fight. Battles were not lost; but the strategic initiative and momentum created in segment two was lost.

Senior military officers took control of media relations and spoke in the overoptimistic terms and "body count." Unquestionably, the troops that fought at Shi-e-Kot were well trained, but for what kind of war? The troops may not have been acclimated for the altitude and there may have been considerable difficulties supporting them, but there was plenty of heroism to go around for all. In one incident, a SEAL, PO 1st Class Neil Roberts, fell out of a MH-47 that had been shot up. Although he was captured and murdered, he was not left on the ground. His buddies went back for him. That is the mark of a well-trained, well-led, and cohesive force. But such bravery does not mean that our military forces are prepared to fight an unconventional foe.

While it is true that our soldiers are well trained, and while it is true that we have not committed large numbers of troops to Afghanistan, what we have not proved is that we can conduct unconventional warfare (UW). So far, special operations forces have only demonstrated that they can conduct maneuver warfare.

Before the U.S. military (including the SOF community) can conduct UW, it must first understand it. To understand UW requires study and thinking. There appears to be precious little thinking about UW going on in the institution of the profession of arms. The war colleges are dedicated to the principle of thinking, but they appear to have produced senior military leaders skilled in the art of attrition warfare, the warfighting approach that succeeded in two world wars, resulted in a stalemate in Korea, and lost in Vietnam. Our response to virtually every conflict is to liberally apply firepower.

Boots on the ground are important, but more important is having smart boots on the ground. Special operations forces are in high demand. Special operation forces have been training to operate in this type of environment; so it should come as no shock that these small teams of mature soldiers know their way around this different kind of battlefield. Their talented teams and capabilities will be able to do more in this type of environment than entire divisions of conventional forces that require large logistics footprints and become juicy targets. U.S. Special Operations Forces come with other important elements designed to help win wars and not merely defeat opponents—psychological operations and civic affairs units. Also, intelligence operations and special operations have traditionally worked hand in glove. This combination of capabilities at the operational and tactical levels provides a potent force with which to confront irregular threats. Conventional forces certainly have a role even in an unconventional setting, but their role is limited and subordinate to a distinctively separate warfighting construct—unconventional warfare. However, even SOF have been employed only to a fraction of their potential.

What would features of an unconventional warfare strategy look like? The list below is representative and not exhaustive:

- Undermine insurgent causes and destroy their cohesion by demonstrating integrity and competence of government to represent and serve the needs of the people
- Take political initiative to root out and visibly punish corruption and eliminate grievances
- Infiltrate guerrilla movements and employ the population for acquiring intelligence
- Deploy administrative talent, police, and roving counterguerrilla teams into affected regions
- Take and keep the initiative by relentless pursuit. Employ tactics of reconnaissance, infiltration, and ambush to keep insurgents off balance and to make their base areas untenable.
- Emphasize capture and conversion to the government cause instead of focusing on "body count" as a basis to undermine insurgent influence.
- Visibly identify the central government with local political/economic/social reform in order to connect the government with hopes and needs of people, thereby gaining their support and confirming government legitimacy.

Said another way, UW seeks to avoid the following:
- Alienating the general population sufficiently to generate recruits for al Qaeda and the Taliban
- Undermining the occupation
- Losing control of the countryside
- Being forced to extend the length of the occupation beyond which is acceptable to the U.S. population

A strong argument can be made that current U.S. strategy is creating the opposite effect.

The former chairman of the U.S. Joint Chiefs of Staff, Air Force General Richard B. Myers, believes that this current war against global terrorism resembles that of World War II in at least one significant way. He has told Congress:

During World War II, the services showed a remarkable capacity to learn from the experience. At the beginning of the war, they faced conditions they had not prepared for, but managed to adapt themselves in the midst of the fight, and within a short time had established an extraordinary degree of teamwork and combat efficiency. We face a similar task today—to defeat multiple enemies who are capable of striking us with asymmetric means from locations around the world. Winning this new global war will require us to exhibit the same flexibility in adapting to changing conditions.[6]

General Myers is right with regard to the need "to adapt" in handling the mismatches presented by the enemy and creating our own mismatches over the enemy. We might even use the term "transformation." We cannot afford a one-dimensional or two-dimensional fighting force. Transformation must not be restricted to a single event where some tinkering is done with organizations or policy. Transformation and adaptation must be the hallmark of any capability to provide for the national defense, and particularly to fight an unorthodox opponent, and it begins with thinking organizations. Our military forces must be able to adapt to the environment in order to win. That also means transforming how we think about fighting and how we fight. Conventional warfare is quite different from unconventional warfare. Al Qaeda can elect to attack the United States using "different" means, but the challenge confronting the U.S. military is to be able to fight and win in all forms of warfare.

Our military forces have had mixed results in trying to cope with unconventional or insurgent threats. We have the tools but lack the blueprints for executing forms of warfare that do not conform to standard warfare conventions. There is much to be learned from segment two and the successful employment of special operation forces against a conventional opponent. There are also severe limitations in using SOF in a conventional role. More important, the U.S. military risks undermining national policy objectives if it insists on responding with conventional forces where they are inappropriate.

Can we fight an unconventional enemy and win? The jury is still out. We had great success on the ground early in Afghanistan against a conventional opponent. The subsequent employment of conventional forces has done little to stabilize the country or bring key Taliban and al Qaeda leaders to justice. The current "American Way of War" is inadequate to combat an elusive, determined, and deadly enemy that operates outside the framework of the nation-state and in the unconventional milieu.

What Works

Low-level independent action by semiautonomous forces is one part of the answer to how to defeat al Qaeda (and other terrorist organizations) on their home turf. We must constantly generate our own mismatches over the enemy. Rather than micromanagement from above, the answer seems to be a bottoms-up approach. The fact that CENTCOM headquarters remains in Tampa, out of the theater, tends to reinforce a concept of small trusted units that have the capability and authority to act quickly and decisively. Still, the more important part of the answer is in how our leaders think, and we are far from any acceptance of true unconventional warfare as a distinct warfighting concept within the U.S. military hierarchy, including the special operations forces.

CONTINGENCY THEORY AND PROCESSES OF INNOVATION

The case of Afghanistan validates the propositions posited by both contingency theory and the literature on military innovation. Modifications to the propositions are not necessary, though their "grammar" requires modification to suit the unique logic of war. Afghanistan clearly shows that inertia is affecting organizational change and innovation. The study also reveals the inability of the current DoD structure to adapt to the requirements of unconventional warfare. The following modified propositions reflect the logic contained in the literature on contingency theory and processes of innovation but are expressed in the context of, and unique "grammar" for, unconventional warfare:

- UW needs its structure, leadership style, and control systems to be adaptive to the prevailing situation.
- Maintaining the capability to conduct UW requires an incentive structure that promotes UW.
- UW requires a focus on and thorough knowledge of the external enviroment (area of operations).
- UW requires a simple chain of command and freedom of action extended to the smallest forward-based units.
- UW needs an enemy with exploitable vulnerabilities.
- UW needs a separate and different organizational culture.
- UW capability must not be dependent on conventional sponsorship.
- UW can benefit from advanced technologies.
- Waging unconventional warfare requires political and military patrons who understand its potential and limitations.
- Waging UW requires civilian and military leadership that possess a strategic mentality.

The study also reveals the inability of the current DoD structure to conform to these modified propositions.

What does the study of organizational theory in general and contingency theory, in particular, tell us about how to organize military power? Organizational scholars have concluded that Weberian-type bureaucracy found in many large, modern organizations is ineffective in coping with the demands of a dynamic and uncertain environment. Additionally, standardized procedures, a fundamental tenet of bureaucracy, inhibit innovation and the flexibility necessary to effectively operate under conditions of uncertainty. Contingency theory is the alternative organizational model for environments where Weberian bureaucracy falls short.

SOF AND THE WAR ON TERROR

What we really need is probably a special forces—not commandos, but rather people who are thinking through the kind of environment they are going to fight in and who have enough intelligence information to do the proper things. We have enormous problems knowing the areas in which we are going to fight.[7]

Those leading the war on terrorism have emphasized from the beginning that this war would be unlike other wars. Yet, the comments about how different the war on terrorism would be have become less frequent as the war has progressed. The cause of this, perhaps, is that the most visible part of the war, the fighting in Afghanistan, turned out to look similar to many past wars. Even our methods of fighting have been familiar to students of conventional conflicts. As a result, the Taliban and al Qaeda are making a comeback and are again controlling sectors of Afghanistan.

Still, we should not be misled by these more familiar methods into thinking that the defense secretary and others were wrong in claiming that the war on terrorism would be different. In Afghanistan, we first had to get through the Taliban to get at al Qaeda. But to suppress al Qaeda requires an altogether different set of tactics, techniques, and procedures. Even more important, it demands a different approach and strategy, one that differs from the current one because al Qaeda differs from the Taliban. Al Qaeda employs terrorism. Terrorism is more directly a political and psychological struggle than war, because terrorists maneuver around a country's military shield and strike directly at the political process by targeting noncombatants. As terrorism is a political and psychological struggle, so must countering it be. Destroying the Taliban or even the leaders of al Qaeda will not necessarily mean the defeat of the terrorism they support, inspire, and organize. To defeat or suppress such terrorism requires us to deal with more than just the terrorists. In the same way they maneuver around our military shield to strike us, we must maneuver around them to counter their political, psychological, and material support. This is where the war on terror is different from other wars. And this is where the current Pentagon bureaucracy cannot organize to engage the threat effectively.

The idea that to succeed against terrorism we must do more than just catch terrorists should not be interpreted to mean that we must appeal to or even appease terrorists' potential supporters. On the contrary, intimidation and fear can be highly effective tools. A way to conceptualize this strategic struggle is to think in terms of an onion: at the innermost core is the terrorist organization itself, composed of strategists and operatives firmly committed to the cause. In the layer immediately surrounding the terrorists are their supporters, who provide them logistical assistance and intelligence. They, in turn, are protected by a layer of sympathizers, who help fund and resource them. Next are the neutrals, the uncommitted population. Finally, in the outer rings of the onion are individuals who oppose the terrorists, their methods, and their aims. If they are to operate, the terrorists must stay hidden and protected, for which they need their layers of supporters and sympathizers. But they must also convert the neutrals into sympathizers and supporters if they are to grow in strength. To counter them thus requires stripping away their sympathizers and supporters, and keeping neutrals from being intimidated or seduced. An imprecise use of force can ultimately prove counterproductive. Said another way, we cannot risk driving people toward the center of the onion.[8]

INTELLIGENCE

Intelligence is decisive, because in struggles such as the one the United States is engaged in with al Qaeda, the enemy operates clandestinely in small groups, without the infrastructure of established military organizations, and can easily blend in with ordinary populations. Yet, while our technical means of collection are unparalleled, impressive, and useful, they are also limited. Our best sources of intelligence are likely to be the layers of people among whom the terrorists hide. Gaining their cooperation and eliciting the intelligence they hold is another reason to work on the terrorists' supporters and sympathizers. Peeling them away will not only get us closer to the terrorists themselves, but will also limit terrorists' operational effectiveness. It is here that special operations forces, operating in a true unconventional warfare mode, can make a decisive contribution.

WHAT SHOULD SOF DO IN THE TWENTY-FIRST CENTURY?

If the conflict of the twenty-first century really requires a "special force," one that can function in a wide variety of ambiguous situations where violence is always possible, there is little thinking in the SOF senior ranks that points the way for such a force. In fact, doctrine for the conduct of unconventional warfare did not advance markedly during the 1990s, and most special operation views remained firmly fixed on hyperconventional missions.[9] USSOCOM illustrated this when it released its first formal doctrinal publication in 1996. Titled Special Operations in Peace and War, it offers the following definition: "Special operations encompass the use of small units in direct or indirect military actions that are focused on strategic or operational objectives. They require units with combinations of specialized personnel, equipment, training or tactics that exceed the routine capabilities of conventional military forces."[10]

The publication then offers three historical examples of special operations, all from World War II and all largely conventional: the Doolittle bomber raid on Tokyo in 1942, the 1940 German glider assault on a Belgian fortress, and the reconnaissance missions conducted by the Sixth U.S. Army Special Reconnaissance Unit (Alamo Scouts).[11] The last two were conventional missions. The first, although using conventional means, was conducted for psychological purposes. This uneasy mixture of conventional and unconventional reflects the general approach to SOF roles that have been detailed in chapter 2 of this study.

Unconventional Warfare and Direct Action

At some risk of distortion, we may say that the SOF engage in two distinctly different, but complementary kinds of combat mission: those involving direct action and unconventional warfare. Direct action missions are short-duration operations directed at specific targets, usually of high strategic or operational value. Speed and accuracy on the ground are critical to success. There are a number of ways to think about unconventional warfare, and numerous different definitions have been offered over the years. Members of the special forces often boil UW down to any effort in which they work by, through, and with indigenous forces. From a special forces perspective, the goal of UW is to help win a war by working with, as opposed to neutralizing or fighting around, local populations. UW represents a classically indirect, and ultimately local, approach to waging warfare. To work with indigenous forces, the SOF must win their trust. To do this, they live with them, eat with them, and share the same living conditions. They also take the opportunity to study local practices and learn social preferences. Building trust invariably takes time, but the payoff comes in a better understanding of the operational environment and the ability to solicit the kind of solid intelligence that enables operations.

The Conventional-Unconventional Rub

It becomes all too easy to confuse unorthodox methods with unconventional warfare. We see this most vividly, perhaps, in reactions to what has been hailed as the most unconventional aspect of the war in Afghanistan, the triple marriage among special forces and combat controllers on the ground, Northern Alliance forces, and air assets. This represents only a fraction of what the SOF are capable of and what full-fledged unconventional warfare should involve. Yet, fascination with such efforts and thoughts that they could herald a paradigmatic shift in warfare merely reinforce the Pentagon's long-standing preoccupation with rapidly achieved, measurable effects. That this happens to be the antithesis of the attitude necessary for supporting the slow, indirect methods of unconventional warfare should also give us pause, but is not surprising. Unfortunately, the failure of UW to mesh with the Pentagon's (and SOCOM's) preferences is a recurring phenomenon.

For instance, the idea to join the SOF to the Northern Alliance in Afghanistan came from the CIA, not from the military. Then, following the Taliban's defeat, the military failed to capitalize on the UW skills that helped topple the government and that then could have been directed at building support among other segments of the Afghan population in order to acquire intelligence and limit the resources going to Taliban and al Qaeda remnants. As soon as conventional army forces arrived in country, and the army gained control over the SOF, hunting down Taliban and al Qaeda became the priority, despite the fact that intelligence was so scarce that these operations turned up little. Conventionalization also intensified. The SOF were able to operate in an unconventional or, at least, innovative fashion when they worked for the CIA. This arrangement would quickly end, as would the ability to operate innovatively.

The attitudes that mark the SOF's relations with the rest of the military, as well as the SOF's internal relations, reveal a status hierarchy that exists in practice, but not on paper. In the same way conventional forces tend to misunderstand and insufficiently appreciate what the SOF can do, within the SOF, those who practice direct action tend to misunderstand and insufficiently appreciate what UW can do. Identifying the tenaciousness and pervasiveness of this hierarchy is important for understanding the problem the military, including the SOF, will have in conducting the war on terrorism, because what the war on terrorism (as opposed to wars on nation-states) requires is the opposite of what the hierarchy prefers. The hierarchy prefers conventionalization and direct action over UW. The war on terrorism requires the use of special forces teams, and civil affairs and psychological operations units, all tasked to do UW. Success in this war will require an emphasis on winning local cooperation. Conventional and direct action forces are least likely to elicit this, while UW forces are most likely to. Meanwhile, the intelligence they gather will make direct action more effective and ideally, over time, and as we succeed, less necessary.

The prejudices that favor direct action over UW are so entrenched, however, that it will be difficult if not impossible to overcome them in the near term. Consequently, it is unlikely that DoD or USSOCOM will develop something that approximates this range of reactive and preemptive capabilities, even though unconventional threats are guaranteed to persist. In the immediate context of the war on terrorism and beyond, it will likely take outside intervention to shake up the military's attitudinal hierarchy.

Developing an Unconventional Warfare Force

Why does SOF not embrace UW as its principal mission? In part, because it is very hard to define and prepare for UW. But there are cultural reasons as well. Since the Vietnam War, part of the problem is the attractiveness of direct action, combating terrorism and special reconnaissance as missions. Such missions, and the resulting image of deadly resourceful fighters, are the principal reasons soldiers undergo the extraordinary hardships of special operations training and duty. These commando-like activities are close to the conventional model of warfighting and have great appeal, and thus tend to consume a disproportionate amount of attention and training time. They are high-visibility, immediate-gratification missions, well within the comfort zone and easily identified with by both conventional forces and the SOF. But conventional forces can often perform the same missions.[12]

Why Unconventional Warfare Cannot Take Root

The above discussion illustrates many of the propositions of contingency theory and military innovation and helps explain why UW is beyond the capability of the U.S. military, including the special operations forces. Contingency theory tells us that structure and leadership style must be adaptive to the diverse nature of the external settings. Understanding the external environment, in its many forms, is at the center of developing viable action plans and properly organizing to carry out those plans. Furthermore, the diverse nature of the threat calls for a simple, effective control system that allows for differentiated solutions in rapidly changing settings. Next, the organization must establish incentives that reward people who demonstrate success operating within the organizational model. Finally, it is important to remember that there is no single best way to organize for all situations.

How does the literature on innovation help explain the inability of the U.S. military to wage unconventional warfare? First, organizations develop cultures. Organizational culture can be enabling in that it fuels the accomplishment of organizational goals. It can aid in building a solid corporate team. However, it can also inhibit experimentation and marginalize people who have ideas that are at odds with the organizational culture. Next, those who hold power and authority in the organization have a vested interest in holding on to that power and authority and in the doctrine associated with their status. They are reluctant to change, and, therefore, they are even more reluctant to innovate. Last, innovation calls for people who both have the ability to think strategically and understand the potential and limitations of departing from the status quo. As something new, the innovation will be difficult, perhaps impossible, to specify in advance. Orders to innovate are inherently ambiguous and therefore difficult to carry out.

From Special Operations to Unconventional Warfare

Resurrecting a UW capability will require a real change in thinking, at the national policy level, within the Department of Defense and in the SOF community. At the highest levels, it will require a change in strategic thinking and policymaking to accept UW as an important arena that is not peripheral to national interests but that is one that can add significantly to our security.

For the Defense Department, it means a serious, long-range investment in personal training and education at a time when technology and hardware solutions are far more popular. It means restructuring rank and salary scales as well as other incentives to retain trained personnel. Technology can no longer be allowed to drive strategy as it has in the development of "battlefield dominance" concepts and "precision engagement." This means that any changes will likely be made without the support of the major industrial suppliers who stand to profit from high-tech approaches. Furthermore, it means a willingness to allocate scarce intelligence resources to the analysis of UW problems.

Within special forces, it will mean a willingness to place less emphasis on the image and skills of the commando and much more on the ability to apply military, civil, and psychological capabilities at the tactical and operational levels. Not everyone will be capable of this transition.

Most important, for all of these groups and organizations, it means a shift in expectations. For the most part, UW is devoid of clean solutions and clear victories. Nor is it usually rapid. This means a willingness to accept lengthy commitments and incremental progress. None of these adjustments will be easy. But all of them are necessary and important if the United States is to thrive in the complex and dangerous environment of the twenty-first century.

There is much potential work for a UW force, and there will continue to be a wide variety of unconventional challenges. Indeed, arguably, only resources and national policy considerations limit the degree of possible involvement. The reality, however, is much different. Meeting the challenges to conduct those poorly defined forms of engagement termed unconventional warfare will require a different organization and a different organizational culture. This capacity does not come cheaply, and it may mean heavy expense in areas where the Pentagon prefers not to spend its money.

In 1985 the late representative Dan Daniel seemed to understand the incompatible nature of unconventional and conventional thinking when he said:

As I have watched the revitalization of our special operations capability proceed over the last few years, I have become convinced that the readiness enhancements and force structure increases now under way, while essential, are, in reality, treating the symptoms but not the disease. The heart of the matter lays not in the forces themselves, but the way in which they were integrated into the national security structure.[13]

The above statement seems as relevant today as it was in 1985. Daniel's statement was used to support the argument for the revitalization and reorganization of the SOF in order to provide the United States with capable special operations forces. Representative Daniel further argued that, if SOF were not unified as a separate command or service, the result would be abuse and misuse and, ultimately, the forces would not be able to provide the capability they were designed to provide. Daniel further stated:

Special operations run counter to the conventional view of how wars are fought; training and equipment for SOF are distinct from that required for conventional soldiers, sailors, and airmen; secrecy is essential and elitism is unavoidable; and SOF is most often effective during peacetime. Essentially, SOF has never "fit in" with the conventional forces because SOF operations do not square with the core imperatives of the individual Services and are, in fact, so different that there is little basis for understanding. . . . They are viewed as secretive, elitist, and worst of all, a political time bomb.[14]

Because of these problems, Daniel argued that the only way the SOF could provide strategic utility was by being unified and consolidated as a separate service or agency.

Daniel's arguments were viewed by his contemporaries and others as being "too hard to do" and were too radical at the time to be considered or embraced. Eventually, additional legislative changes came in the form of the Cohen-Nunn Bill. In fact, the current organizational structure of the SOF is largely a result of the Cohen-Nunn Amendment to the 1986 Defense Reorganization Act. In 1986 Senators William Cohen and Sam Nunn introduced a bill to force the DoD to reorganize and restructure SOF. In their bill, Cohen and Nunn listed the following reasons why Congress should get involved in SOF reform:

- The threat to the United States and its allies from unconventional warfare, including terrorism, is rising.
- Since the conclusion of the Korean conflict, the use of force by the United States had been primarily in response to guerrilla insurgencies and terrorist attacks. This will continue to be the most likely use of force in the foreseeable future.
- The capabilities needed to respond to unconventional warfare are not those traditionally fostered by the Armed Forces of the United States, and the planning and preparation emphasis within the Defense Department has been overwhelmingly on fighting a large-scale war.

- The Department of Defense has not given sufficient attention to the tactics, doctrines, and strategies associated with those combat missions most likely to be required of the Armed Forces of the United States in the future.
- Problems of command and control repeatedly beset [the] military of the United States engaged in counterterrorist and counterinsurgency operations, as was evident with the Mayaguez incident, the Iranian hostage rescue mission; and the Grenada operation.[15]

CREATING A NEW SERVICE FOR UNCONVENTIONAL WARFARE

Although there were dramatic positive changes with the passage of the Cohen-Nunn and Defense Reorganization legislative acts, the above-mentioned problems are still affecting the DoD and SOF today. The creation of SOCOM has done much to ensure the long-term existence and enhancement of the SOF. At the same time, SOCOM has also obscured the current dilemma of ineffective UW capacity to support national policy. Representative Daniel's claim that SOF "runs counter to the view of how wars are fought" was influential in the passing legislation by Congress to create a separate command to enable the SOF to develop capabilities necessary to provide the president and defense secretary alternative military options to support national policy. Today, the same logic requires extracting the UW capabilities (special forces, psychological operations, civil affairs, and necessary support and intelligence units) from SOCOM and establishing a separate service, with operational responsibilities, whose single mission would be unconventional warfare. Just as history has shown the services were not successful at supporting SOF capabilities, SOCOM has not been successful at enhancing UW capabilities. SOCOM has demonstrated a bias for direct action and other similar missions at the expense of nurturing unconventional warfare.

RECOMMENDATIONS

First, legislation must be passed to create a separate service.[16] This service will provide the nation with unconventional warfare forces. This service will also have global operational responsibilities and will answer to the national command authorities.[17] The creation of this force should be a zero-sum game for the DoD. USSOCOM has sufficient assets to continue with their current operational focus after transferring all UW assets and a proportional support structure. Like the other services, it should be located within the Washington, D.C, area. The new service secretary will also serve as the unconventional warfare adviser to the president. The new service might be called the Department of Strategic Services.

Secondly, because of the nature of UW, this new service will be authorized to coordinate directly with other agencies of government without having to go through the Joint Staff. This will help to ensure that unconventional options get to the desks of the national command authorities and that unconventional solutions are not conventionalized by the Joint Staff.

Third, career progression and promotion incentive structures will have to be built from the ground up. Unlike the "up or out" policy in today's military, the concept behind this personnel system would be to make the best possible fit between the operational requirements associated with a specific job and the individual skills and experience of the service member. The system would allow a person to remain in a position for extended periods of time, assuming his performance is satisfactory.

Fourth, service members will require education and training beyond the current standard. The strength of UW is in its regional and cultural focus, and we must capitalize on this strength. Additional emphasis is needed on language, network analysis, intelligence collection, basic civics, international relations, interagency familiarization, regional studies, and negotiating skills. In-country training, similar to that currently available to foreign area officers, would aid in creating a unique national asset. Furthermore, this service will need its own staff and war colleges to educate officers to think strategically and unconventionally. A parallel education system for noncommissioned officers will also be needed.

Fifth, carefully select UW areas of responsibility based on world dynamics, not on current force structure. Allocate the UW units, then determine the headquarters structure. This may mean that one theater has many units oriented on subregional areas and ethnic groups while another may require only a few. At the same time, move all UW assets, minus the service headquarters, institutional education and training, and required support, into the theaters. It takes a long time, sometimes years, to cultivate an area and to inculcate regional expertise. Consequently, a UW force cannot change its regional and language orientation every few years and be expected to develop a significant degree of expertise or cultural understanding.

A separate military service that emphasizes unconventional warfare cultivates regional experts through on-the-ground experience. Additionally, mutual trust and understanding as a result of personal and sustained contact with regional personalities may be the most important outcome of a permanent forward presence. In most nations, personal relationships are key to trust and understanding. Who you are personally is often more important than what you represent. UW forces can develop these relationships and facilitate the critical interface to enhance U.S. security. Maintaining a forward presence could reassure nervous nations and increase regional stability. Furthermore, in the event of an incident or conflict, these elements would provide a ready source of firsthand regional expertise as well as a timely, though limited military response.

In conclusion, among the most serious potential errors stemming from a misreading of the Afghan campaign would be to overestimate the capacity of the United States to wage unconventional warfare. If Afghanistan were evidence of a new American way of war that could defeat enemies quickly, cheaply, with little U.S. casualty exposure and a limited U.S. political footprint, then a neoimperial foreign policy underwritten by frequent American military intervention would seem attractive to many. Similarly, it would make intervention in any given theater in the ongoing war on terrorism seem more attractive. But defeating an enemy on the battlefield and winning a war are rarely synonymous. Winning a war calls for more than defeating one's enemy in battle. Harry Summers made this discovery in 1975 in Hanoi while negotiating an end to hostilities with the North Vietnamese. Summers told a North Vietnamese colonel that they never defeated the Americans on the battlefield. The North Vietnamese colonel responded, "That may be so, but it is also irrelevant."[18]

⬛ Notes

INTRODUCTION

[1] Deborah D. Avant, *Political Institutions and Military Change—Lessons from Peripheral Wars* (Ithaca, NY: Cornell University Press, 1994), 3.

[2] Ibid., 4.

[3] Jay W. Lorsch and Stephen A. Allen III, *Managing Diversity and Interdependence—An Organizational Study of Multidivisional Firms* (Boston: Harvard Business School Press, 1973), 187.

[4] Craig M. Cameron, "The U.S. Military's Two-Front War, 1963–1988," in *The Sources of Military Change*, ed. Theo Farrell and Terry Terriff (Boulder, CO: Lynne Rienner Publishers, 2002), 119.

[5] Avant, 10–11.

[6] Deborah D. Avant and James H. Lebovic, "U.S. Military Responses to Post–Cold War Missions," in *The Sources of Military Change*, ed. Theo Farrell and Terry Terriff (Boulder, CO: Lynne Rienner Publishers, 2002), 152.

[7] Avant, 13.

[8] Ibid.

CHAPTER 1

[1] Luttwak's conception of attrition warfare is an expanded version of the DoD definition. However, Lutwak's conception of "relational maneuver" is quite different than the DoD definition of maneuver warfare.

[2] Edward Luttwak, "Notes on Low Intensity Conflict," Parameters (December 1983): 333–42.

[3] Ibid.

[4] Ibid.

[5] Harold Kennedy, "Will Special Ops Success Change the Face of War?" National Defense (February 2002): 20-21.

[6] Bob Woodward, Bush at War (New York: Simon & Schuster, 2002), 25.

[7] Ibid., 43.

[8] Ibid.

[9] Ibid., 44.

[10] Senior CIA official from Counterterrorism Center (CTC), interviewed by author, March 11, 2002, Bagram, Afghanistan.

[11] Ibid.

[12] See Dan Baltz, Bob Woodward, and Jeff Himmelman, "Afghan Campaign's Blueprint Emerges," Washington Post, January 29, 2002; Woodward, 51.

[13] See CTC interview; Woodward, 53, 61.

[14] The CIA's proposal also called for an expansion of current authorities in order to conduct a range of operations from routine propaganda to lethal covert action in a timely manner anywhere in Asia, the Middle East, and Africa. The president would sign a Memorandum of Notification on September 17 giving the CIA the broadest and most lethal authority in its history.

[15] See CTC interview; Washington Post, January 29, 2002; Woodward, 72, 75, 78.

[16] See Bob Woodward and Dan Baltz, "At Camp David, Advise and Dissent," Washington Post, January 31, 2002; Woodward, 79, 80, 84.

[17] Ibid.

[18] Ibid.

[19] Stephen Biddle, Afghanistan and the Future of Warfare: Implications for Army and Defense Policy (Carlisle, PA: Strategic Studies Institute, 2002), 1.

[20] See Bob Woodward and Dan Baltz, "We Will Rally the World," Washington Post, January 28, 2002; Woodward, 60, 84.

[21] Woodward, 82–83.

[22] See Washington Post, January 28, 2002; Woodward, 84–85, 98.

[23] See Carl Conetta, *Strange Victory: A Critical Appraisal of Operation Enduring Freedom and the Afghanistan War* (Cambridge, MA: Commonwealth Institute Project on Defense Alternatives, 2002), 3.1, Research Monograph #6; Woodward, 98, 123.

[24] Woodward, 129.

[25] Ibid., 139, 142.

[26] Ibid., 140, 142–43.

[27] Ibid., 157–58, 160.

[28] Ibid., 174–75, 183.

[29] Author's January 13, 2003 Monterey, California, interview with Lt. Col. Mike Kingsley, Commander USAF Special Operations Detachment, South, Jacobabad, Pakistan; Woodward, 185.

[30] Woodward, 185.

[31] Ibid., 188.

[32] See Kingsley; Woodward, 195.

[33] Woodward, 201–2.

[34] Ibid., 209–10.

[35] Ibid., 210.

[36] See Kingsley; Woodward, 213.

[37] Woodward, 222.

[38] See CTC interview; Woodward, 239.

[39] CIA officer interviewed by author, March 22, 2002, Gardez, Afghanistan; Woodward, 249–50.

[40] Woodward, 254.

[41] Ibid., 265.

[42] Current airpower theory ranks support to ground forces as the lowest priority.

[43] Michael E. O'Hanlon, "A Flawed Masterpiece," Foreign Affairs 81 (March/April 2002).

[44] Ibid.

[45] Ibid.

[46] JSOTF commander, interview by author, Bagram, Afghanistan, March 14, 2002.

[47] Maj. Gen. Franklin "Buster" Hagenbeck, Commander, CJTF (combined joint task force) Mountain, interview by author, Bagram, Afghanistan, March 11, 2002.

[48] Dr. Gordon H. McCormick first articulated this phenomenon in March 2002 in Afghanistan after careful observation of the threat and the U.S. military response. Dr. McCormick was actually commenting on the overall nature of the military response to include command and control.

CHAPTER 2

[1] Thomas K. Adams, US Special Operations Forces in Action—The Challenge of Unconventional Warfare (London: Frank Cass, 1998), 1.

[2] Joint Publication 1-02, DOD Dictionary of Military and Associated Terms. (Washington, DC: GPO, 2002)

[3] Joint Pub 3-07, Joint Doctrine for Military Operations Other Than War (Washington, DC: GPO, 1995), ix.

[4] USSOCOM Pub 1, Special Operations in Peace and War (Washington, DC: GPO, 1996), 1–2.

[5] DA FM 100-25, Doctrine for Army Special Operations Forces (Washington, DC: GPO, 1996), 2.

[6] Adams, 7.

[7] Ibid., 8.

[8] See Eliot A. Cohen, Commandos and Politicians (Cambridge, MA: Center for International Affairs, 1978), 53–57; Adams, 10.

[9] Adams, 10.

[10] Dennis Steele, "A Force of Great Utility That Cannot Be Mass-Produced," Army Magazine (April 1992): 24.

[11] Ibid., 32.

[12] Ibid., 11.

[13] Ibid.

[14] Ibid., 12.

[15] Ibid.

[16] Ibid., 13.

[17] Joint Publication 1, *Joint Warfare of the Armed Forces of the United States* (Washington, DC: GPO, 1995).

[18] Adams, 13.

[19] Ibid.

[20] Stability and Support Operations (SASO). online database, available from http://www.globalsecurity.org/military/ops/saso.htm accessed January 29, 2003.

[21] These definitions have been edited from USSOCOM facts sheets and statements.

[22] United States. Dept. of the Army. Operations, Washington, DC: Headquarters, Dept. of the Army, 1993, Glossary-9.

[23] Hans J. Morgenthau, *Politics Among Nations* (New York: Alfred J. Knopf, 1973), 29.

[24] See Seymon Brown, *New Forces in World Politics* (Washington, DC: Brookings Institute, 1974), 186; Adams, 18.

[25] Adams, 19.

[26] Ibid., 20.

[27] Ibid., 21.

[28] USASOC, *To Free from Oppression: A Concise History of US Army Special Forces,* Civil Affairs, Psychological Operations and The John F. Kennedy Special Warfare Center and School (Ft. Bragg, NC: USASOC Directorate of History, 1994), 113.

[29] Adams, 21.

[30] The Marines are perhaps the most progressive of the services in addressing the emerging conflict environment that can include warfighting and peacekeeping simultaneously as well as operating among a highly differentiated civilian population.

[31] Adams, 22.

[32] Ibid., 27.

[33] Notwithstanding Washington's intentions, UW played an important role during the American Revolution and ultimately positioned the Continental Army to win at Yorktown. Nathaniel Greene's and Francis Marion's operations to win the South

proved to be an impressive integration of conventional and unconventional warfare that defeated a more powerful British opponent.

[34] Adams, 26.

[35] Joseph G. Dawson, "American Civil-Military Operations and Military Government: The Service of Colonel Alexander Doniphan in the Mexican War," Armed Forces & Society, 22, 4 (1996): 556–57.

[36] See Adams, 28; Robert M. Utley, *The Contribution of the Frontier to the American Military Tradition* (Colorado Springs, CO: US Air Force Academy, 1977), 4–5.

[37] See Adams, 28; Russell F. Weigley, History of the United States Army (New York: Macmillan, 1967), 307–9, 314, 317.

[38] USASOC, 1994, 18.

[39] See Michael J. King, *Rangers: Selected Combat Operations during World War II* (Washington, DC: GPO, 1985), 5–9; Adams, 30.

[40] Adams, 31.

[41] Ibid.

[42] King, 5–9.

[43] An illustration of misuse was at Cisterna on January 30, 1944 when a three-battalion Ranger force was employed as regular infantry. A German mechanized force counterattacked the Rangers. Of the 767 Rangers who participated in the mission, 761 were killed or captured.

[44] See Adams, 34; William R. Peers and Dean Brelis, *Behind the Burma Road* (Boston: Little Brown, 1963), 129

[45] See Kermit Roosevelt, ed., *War Report of the OSS* (New York: Walker and Co.,1976), I:9; Adams, 34.

[46] Roosevelt, I:5, 99

[47] Adams, 35.

[48] See Adams, 36; Alfred H. Paddock, *US Army Special Warfare: Its Origins* (Washington, DC: NDU Press, 1982), 15.

[49] See Roosevelt, I:223; Adams, 36.

[50] See Roosevelt, I:223; Corey Ford, *Donovan of the OSS* (Boston, MA: Little Brown, 1970), 109, 129, 169; Adams, 36.

[51] Adams, 36.

[52] See Paddock, 31–32; King, 75; Adams, 40.

[53] Paddock, 31.

[54] See Cohen, 55; Adams, 41.

[55] Ford, 303–4.

[56] See Ford, 312; Adams, 42.

[57] See Adams, 42; William Colby, with Peter Forbath, *Honorable Men: My Life in the CIA* (New York: Simon & Schuster, 1978), 61–62.

[58] Adams, 42.

[59] Aaron Bank, From OSS to Green Beret (New York: Pocket Books, 1986), 114–15.

[60] Adams, 44.

[61] Ibid., 45.

[62] Ibid.

[63] Robert Asprey, *War in the Shadows: Guerrillas in History* (Garden City, NJ: Doubleday & Co., 1975), 745, 744.

[64] Adams, 46.

[65] Maxwell D. Taylor, *Swords and Plowshares* (New York: W. W. Norton, 1972), 174.

[66] Edward N. Luttwak, *On the Meaning of Victory* (New York: Simon & Schuster, 1986), 164–65.

[67] Dwight D. Eisenhower, *Mandate for Change* (New York: Doubleday & Co., Inc., 1963), 454.

[68] Amos Jordan, William Taylor Jr., and Michael Mazarr, *American National Security* (Baltimore, MD: The Johns Hopkins University Press, 1999), 71–72.

[69] Ibid., 74; Adams, 61.

[70] See Maxwell D. Taylor, *The Uncertain Trumpet* (New York: Harper and Bros., 1960), 60–64; Adams, 61.

[71] Taylor, *The Uncertain Trumpet,* 60–64, 158–61.

[72] See Adams, 63; Fred Cook, "Struggle for the South," in From Troy to Entebbe, ed. John Arquilla (New York: University Press of America, Inc., 1996), 79–90.

[73] See Douglas Blaufarb, *The Counterinsurgency Era: US Doctrine and Performance, 1950 to the Present* (New York: Free Press, 1977), 52; Adams, 64.

[74] Adams, 65.

[75] See Blaufarb, 135–41; Adams, 66.

[76] The John F. Kennedy Special Warfare Center and School—the army's special operations university—is responsible for special operations training, leader development, doctrine, and personnel advocacy. The school conducts the complete spectrum of special operations training. In addition to its training role, the school also tests new equipment. The Special Warfare Center and School began as the Psychological Warfare Center in 1952. Civil-affairs training became part of the center's responsibilities when the Civil Affairs School moved from Fort Gordon, Georgia, to Fort Bragg in 1971.

[77] Adams, 67.

[78] Ibid., 69.

[79] Ibid., 68–69.

[80] *United States Special Operations Command History* (MacDill AFB, FL: US SOCOM History & Research Office, 2002), 3.

[81] James R. Locher III, *Victory on the Potomac* (College Station: Texas A&M University Press, 2002), 135–36, 154–56.

[82] Susan L. Marquis, *Unconventional Warfare: Rebuilding U.S. Special Operations Forces* (Washington, DC: Brookings Institute Press, 1997), 81–83.

[83] Ibid., 125–27.

[84] Ibid., 125.

[85] Ibid., 134–35.

[86] Ibid., 138, 142.

[87] See Marquis, 143; *United States Special Operations Command History*, 5.

[88] See Marquis, 144–47; *United States Special Operations Command History*, 5.

[89] Marquis, 177.

[90] Ibid., 178.

[91] Ibid., 179.

[92] See Marquis, 151; *United States Special Operations Command History*, 6.

[93] See Marquis, 165; *United States Special Operations Command History*, 6.

[94] Colin S. Gray, *Explorations in Strategy* (London: Praeger, 1998), 163.

[95] Ibid., 165.

[96] Ibid., 166.

[97] Ibid., 168.

[98] Ibid., 168–69.

[99] The Brandenburgers were a special unit that reported directly to Adm. Wilhelm Canaris, head of the Abwehr intelligence unit. They were enlarged to division size in October 1942. They performed several special missions on the Eastern Front until Canaris and the Abwehr fell out of favor with Hitler.

[100] See Gray, 168–70; Paul Carell, "Brandenburgers in Action Behind the Front," in From Troy to Entebbe, ed. John Arquilla (New York: University Press of America, Inc., 1996), 234–38.

[101] Gray, 174.

[102] Ibid., 179.

[103] Ibid., 180.

CHAPTER 3

[1] Herbert A. Simon, *Administrative Behavior*, 3rd ed. (New York: Free Press, 1976), xvi.

[2] James Q. Wilson, *Bureaucracy—What Government Agencies Do and Why They Do It* (New York: Basic Books, 1989), 23–24.

[3] Ibid., 24.

[4] Chester I. Barnard, *The Functions of the Executive* (Cambridge, MA: Harvard University Press, 1968), 72.

[5] Martin van Creveld, *Fighting Power: German and U.S. Army Performance, 1939–1945* (Westport, CT: Greenwood Press, 1982), 165.

[6] John A. English, *A Perspective on Infantry* (New York: Praeger Publishers, 1981), 67-70.

[7] Wilson, 15.

[8] Barry R. Posen, *The Sources of Military Doctrine, France, Britain, and Germany between the World Wars* (Ithaca: Cornell University Press, 1984), 182–88.

[9] Wilson, 16.

[10] Creveld, 36–37.

[11] Ibid., 28–29.

[12] Ibid., 43–45.

[13] Ibid., 163–64.

[14] Wilson, 26.

[15] Ibid., 11.

[16] Ibid., 12.

[17] Ibid., 335.

[18] Ibid.

[19] Max Weber, *Essays in Sociology,* trans. H. H. Gerth and C. Wright Mills (New York: Oxford University Press, 1976), 214–15, 221.

[20] Ibid., 196–98.

[21] Wilson, 164.

[22] Graham Allison, and Philip Zelikow, *Essence of Decision,* 2nd ed. (New York: Longman, 1999), 13–28.

[23] Ibid., 143–49, 153–76.

[24] Ibid.

[25] Ibid., 255–304

[26] Ibid.

[27] Ibid.

[28] Jay R. Galbraith, *Organization Design* (London: Addison-Wesley Publishing Co., 1977), 28.

[29] Paul R. Lawrence and Jay W. Lorsch, *Organization and Environment: Managing Differentiation and Integration* (Boston: Harvard Business School Press, 1967), 187.

[30] Ibid., 188.

[31] Ibid.

[32] Ibid., 189.

[33] Ibid., 190.

[34] Ibid., 30.

[35] See Lorsch and Allen, *Managing Diversity and Interdependence,* 170–90; "Organizational Theory: Determinants of Structure," available from http://www.analytictech.com/mb021/orgtheory.htm, accessed January 22, 2003.

[36] See Lorsch and Allen, 170–90; "Organizational Theory: Determinants of Structure."

[37] Ibid.

[38] Ibid.

[39] Ibid.

[40] Ibid.

[41] Lorsch and Allen, 170–90.

[42] Lawrence and Lorsch, 168, 209.

[43] David Tucker, "Processes of Innovation" (Monterey, CA: unpublished paper, 2002).

[44] Tucker; Posen, 34–40.

[45] Tucker; Posen, 44, 46.

[46] Tucker; Posen , 47–50.

[47] Tucker; Posen , 54–57, 59.

[48] Tucker; Posen, 60, 74–75, 239.

[49] Tucker; Posen, 173–75.

[50] Tucker; Stephen Peter Rosen, *Winning the Next War: Innovation and the Modern Military* (Ithaca, NY: Cornell University Press, 1991), 11–18.

[51] Tucker; Goldman, 251–54.

[52] Emily O. Goldman, "Mission Possible: Organizational Learning in Peacetime," in *The Politics of Strategic Adjustment, Ideas, Institutions, and Interests,* eds. Peter Trubowitz, Emily O. Goldman, and Edward Rhodes (New York: Columbia University Press, 1999), 255, no. 3.

[53] Tucker.

[54] Tucker; Goldman, 236–37.

[55] Tucker.

[56] Tucker; Goldman, 239–51.

[57] Tucker; Kimberly Marten Zisk, *Engaging the Enemy: Organization Theory and Soviet Military Innovation, 1955–1991* (Princeton, NJ: Princeton University Press, 1993), 12–13.

[58] Zisk, 13.

[59] Tucker.

[60] Tucker; Zisk, 26–27, 20, 23–25, 28.

[61] Ibid., 178–184.

[62] Ibid.

[63] Tucker.

[64] Tucker; Rosen, 21, 256.

[65] Tucker; Zisk, 184.

[66] Tucker.

[67] Ibid.

[68] Ibid.

[69] Tucker; Matthew Evangelista, *Innovation and the Arms Race* (Ithaca, NY: Cornell University Press, 1988), 7, 12, 27–28, 271–72.

[70] Ibid., 59–65.

[71] Tucker.

[72] Jack Snyder, *The Ideology of the Offensive, Military Decision Making, and the Disasters of 1914* (Ithaca, NY: Cornell University Press, 1984), 216.

[73] Williamson Murray, "Innovation, Past and Future," in *Innovation in the Interwar Period,* eds. Williamson Murray and Allan R. Millett (Cambridge, UK: Cambridge University Press, 1998), 302–3.

[74] Harold R. Winton and David R. Mets, eds., *The Challenge of Change, Military Institutions, and New Realities, 1918–1941* (Lincoln: University of Nebraska Press, 2000), 220–33.

[75] Tucker; Robert A. Doughty, "Myth of the Blitzkrieg," in *Challenging the United States Symmetrically and Asymmetrically: Can America Be Defeated?* ed. Colonel Lloyd J. Matthews (USA, Retired) (Carlisle Barracks, PA: U.S. Army War College Strategic Studies Institute, 1998), 59–61, 64.

[76] Wilson, 227.

[77] Theo Farrell, "World Culture and the Irish Army, 1922–1942," in *The Sources of Military Change: Culture, Politics, Technology,* eds. Theo Farrell and Terry Terriff (London: Lynne Rienner Publishers, 2002), 70–82.

[78] Zisk, 6, 26, 184.

[79] Avant, *Political Institutions and Military Change,* 6, 7, 15, 17.

[80] Tucker; Avant, 51–53.

[81] See John Waghelstein, "Preparing the US Army for the Wrong War," *Small Wars and Insurgencies* 10, no.1 (Spring 1999): 22; Robert Wooster, *The Military and United States Indian Policy, 1865–1903* (New Haven, CT: Yale University Press, 1988), 50–51, 60–61.

[82] Avant, 35.

[83] Ibid., 84–85.

[84] Ibid., 34, n. 40.

[85] Ibid.

[86] Max G. Manwaring, *The Inescapable Global Security Arena* (Carlisle, PA: Strategic Studies Institute, 2002), 1.

[87] In 2002 the Strategic Studies Institute of the U.S. Army War College identified 26 ongoing high-intensity wars, 78 low-intensity conflicts, and 178 small-scale internal wars overlapping with the others.

[88] Manwaring, 3.

[89] Ibid., 6.

CHAPTER 4

[1] "Special Operations Forces: The Way Ahead" Statement presented by Gen. Peter J. Schoomaker, commander, U.S. Special Operations Command, to the members of the command. Available at http://www.defenselink.mil/speeches/1998/s19880201-schoomaker.html

[2] See *United States Special Operations Command History,* 4–5; Locher, 312.

[3] David C. Jones, "Past Organizational Problems," Joint Forces Quarterly (Autumn 1996): 26–28.

[4] See Jones, 24–26; John M. Collins, Elizabeth Ann Severns, and Thomas P. Glakas, *U.S. Defense Planning: A Critique* (Boulder, CO: Westview Press, 1982), 61; David Isenberg, *Missing the Point: Why the Reforms of the Joint Chiefs of Staff Won't Improve U.S. Defense Policy* (Washington, DC: Cato Institute, 1988).

[5] Col. Pete Gustaitus, chief J-3, Special Operations Division, JCS, interviewed by author, June 23, 2002, Monterey, California.

[6] JSOTF commander, interview by author, Bagram, Afghanistan, March 14, 2002.

[7] Isenberg.

[8] The secretary of defense has recently reversed USSOCOM's traditional role of being the "supporting" commander to that of being the "supported" commander. This means that under certain circumstances, yet to be specified, USSOCOM will plan and execute combat operations anywhere in the world to find, and capture or kill terrorists. Geographic combatant commanders will support USSOCOM for these missions.

[9] Isenberg.

[10] John M. Collins, *Special Operations Forces: An Assessment* (Washington, DC: National Defense University Press, 1996), 123.

[11] Rear Adm. Albert Calland, COMSOCCENT, interviewed by author, March 26, 2002, Doha, Qatar.

[12] Luttwak, "Notes on Low Intensity Conflict."

[13] Ibid.

[14] Ibid.

[15] Russell F. Weigley, *The American Way of War: A History of United States Military Strategy and Policy* (New York: Macmillan Publishing Co., Inc., 1973), xiv.

[16] It is also logical to assume that when militaries of equal competence and resources fight one another, the closer they are to the maneuver end of the continuum, the greater will be their effectiveness.

[17] Luttwak, "Notes on Low Intensity Conflict," 337.

[18] Many argue that the recent wars in Afghanistan and Iraq constitute a departure from the attrition model. They also highlight the key role of the SOF. The efficiency of the attrition model has certainly improved through better intelligence, surveillance and reconnaissance (ISR). While a degree of "maneuver" is noticeable at the tactical level, the operational and strategic levels have not changed and remain locked in the attrition model using standard organizational arrangements and operational methods.

[19] Andrew F. Krepinevich, *The Army and Vietnam* (Baltimore, MD: The John Hopkins University Press, 1986), 165.

[20] The purpose of the PRTs is to extend the influence of the Afghan government outside Kabul, to encourage international and nongovernmental organizations to operate in rural areas outside of Kabul, and to facilitate reconstruction. The PRT focus is on the coordination of the reconstruction process, identification of reconstruction projects, conducting village assessments, and liaising with regional commanders. PRT interactions with local leaders and elders also aims to establish and maintain positive relations with the population and enable a more stable and secure environment.

[21] M. Evans, "Marines to Face Guerrilla War as Taliban Fighters Change Tactics," Times Online, March 21, 2002. Retrieved on October 30, 2003 from http://www.timesonline.co.uk/article/0,,1164-242636,00.html

[22] Donald Rumsfeld, "Major Combat over in Afghanistan," May 1, 2003, http://www.cnn.com/2003/WORLD/asiapcf/central/05/01/afghan.combat/index.html, accessed August 11, 2003.

[23] As cited in Robert Taber, *The War of the Flea* (New York: Lyle Stuart, 1965), 157.

[24] David Galula, *Counterinsurgency Warfare—Theory and Practice* (New York: Praeger Publishers, 1964), 72.

[25] C. Gall, "In Afghanistan, Violence Stalls Renewal Effort" New York Times, April 26, 2003, A1.

[26] Capt. Bob Harwood, the commander of TF K–Bar, was the first to use the term "SOF-centric."

[27] TF 11, JSOC, remained under the operational control USCENTCOM.

[28] This conception was used by an Naval Postgraduate School team conducting a study for the director of net assessment, Office of the Secretary of Defense, in February 2003. The study was called, SOLARIUM II—Mobilization for National Survival. Study participants included, Patrick Parker, Raymond Franck, Robert

Harney, Michael Melich, Glenn Robinson, Hy Rothstein, David Tucker, and Anna Simons.

[29] If the "non-Western" elements exist in otherwise Western countries besides the United States, then the CIA will have to develop greater sensitivity and skill in penetrating that world in otherwise "Western" countries.

[30] Martin van Creveld, *Command in War* (Cambridge, MA: Harvard University Press, 1985), 269.

[31] Ibid., 35.

[32] See discussion in chapter 3 on Weberian bureaucracy.

[33] Norbert Wiener, *Cybernetics, or, Control and Communications in the Animal and the Machine,* (Cambridge, MA: MIT Press, 1962), 95–114.

[34] Creveld, Command in War, 264–68.

[35] Ibid., 269–72.

[36] See Gregory D. Foster, "Contemporary C^2 Theory and Research: The Failed Quest for a Philosophy of Command," Defense Analysis 4, no. 3 (September 1988): 211; Thomas J. Czerwinski, "Command and Control at the Crossroads," Marine Corps Gazette (October 1995).

[37] The German army, from the time of Prussian field marshal Helmuth von Moltke on, referred to this concept as Auftragstaktik.

[38] Foster, 211.

[39] Thomas J. Czerwinski, "Command and Control at the Crossroads," Parameters (Autumn 1996): 212–32.

[40] See discussion in chapter 3 on contingency theory.

[41] Thomas P. Coakley, *Command and Control for War and Peace* (Washington, DC: National Defense University Press, 1992), chapters 3 and 4.

[42] See Trevor N. Dupuy, *Understanding War* (New York: Paragon House Publishers, 1987), chapters 12 and 15; Trevor N. Dupuy, interviewed by author, Monterey, California, March 1995.

[43] William T. Sherman, *Memoirs of General William T. Sherman* (New York: Da Capo Press, 1984), 402.

[44] CJTF-Mountain was the combined joint task force headquarters whose nucleus was the 10th Mountain Division. CJTF-180 was the combined joint task force headquarters whose nucleus was the 18th Airborne Corps. CJTF-180 replaced CJTF-Mountain as the military headquarters in charge of prosecuting the war in Afghanistan.

[45] Interviews by author, Bagram, March 2002.

[46] Interview by author, Deh Rawod, Afghanistan, May 26, 2003

[47] Interview by author, Kandahar, May 25, 2003

[48] This also happened to the U.S. Army in Vietnam.

[49] JSOTF-North was TF Dagger and JSOTF-South was TF K-Bar both located in Afghanistan. A crisis reaction element was established in Qatar and JSOTF-West was established in the Horn of Africa.

[50] Although SOF aviation assets existed in theater, they were generally not available to most SOF units.

[51] A conventional general officer had commented that the army's insistence on at least a "two star" headquarters to command operations in Afghanistan was to preempt COMSOCCENT, a "one star," from establishing a viable headquarters in Afghanistan capable of controlling all operations.

[52] It is also possible that the defense secretary himself, based on his own very attrition-oriented concept of militarily defeating an opponent, discounted the SOCCENT's unconventional plan.

[53] One senior military officer commented that Rumsfeld constantly demanded that SOCOM identify targets to strike.

[54] *DOD Dictionary of Military and Associated Terms.* As amended through June 5, 2003.

[55] The lifespan of good intelligence as well as the time frame necessary to get approval to react was made clear in an interview by the author with a specially trained special forces soldier who was responsible for developing low-level human intelligence (HUMINT) sources in Kandahar Province.

[56] Interview by author, Deh Rawod, Afghanistan, May 26, 2003.

[57] J. Wagner, "Gardez Office Opening Signals Shift in Afghanistan Mission," posted on http://www.defendamerica.mil/articles/feb2003/a020403b.html, accessed November 1, 2003.

[58] Ibid.

[59] M. Brown and L. Thompson, "Security on the Cheap: PRTs in Afghanistan," July 7, 2003. Posted on http://www.reliefweb.int/w/rwb.nsf/s1EA67E0645C1816F49 256D5D000016F3, accessed November 1, 2003.

[60] Robert M. Perito, *The U.S. Experience with Provincial Reconstruction Teams in Afghanistan* (Washington: United States Institute of Peace, 2005), Special Report 152.

[61] Wagner.

[62] R. Synovitz, "Afghanistan: U.S.-Led Coalition Expands 'Provincial Recon-struction Teams,'" August 14, 2003, posted on http://www.rferl.org/features/2003/08/ 14082003161741.asp. Accessed November 1, 2003.

[63] A. Maykuth, "An Afghan Rebuilding Takes Shape," Philadelphia Inquirer, October 6, 2003, 1.

[64] Flag rank officer, interview by author, Bagram, Afghanistan, March 12, 2002.

[65] Erik Jansen, "Towards a Strategic Rewards Systems Perspective" PhD diss., University of Southern California, 1986, 20.

[66] Ibid., 1.

[67] K. R. Andrews, *The Concept of Corporate Strategy,* (New York: Jones-Irwin, 1980), 12.

[68] Rear Adm. Albert Calland, interviewed by author via telephone, Coronado, California, March 20, 2003.

[69] SOCOM and its satellite units around the world can now plan and execute their own missions. Previously, SOCOM played a lesser role by providing warriors to regional combatant commands that planned and supervised operations. Now the regional combatant commands can be in a position to support SOCOM-directed operations.

[70] Rowan Scarborough, "Special Ops Gets OK to Initiate Its Own Missions," Washington Times, January 8, 2003.

[71] During the Afghanistan campaign, most of the attack aircraft were flown off the carrier *USS Kitty Hawk,* which was used as a floating base in the Arabian Sea for special operators.

[72] See Tom Bowman, "Special Forces' Role May Expand—Additional Troops, Equipment Sought by Military Leaders; SEALs, Green Berets Included," Baltimore Sun, August 3, 2002; Hunter Keeter, "SOCOM Outlines Acquisition Priorities," Defense Daily, February 13, 2003.

[73] In November 2002, Secretary Rumsfeld directed an independent study to identify better ways for SOCUM to fight the war on terror. The operational concept developed during the study was a true unconventional warfare approach. Gen. (Ret) Larry D. Welch, the study director, did not brief the UW concept that was developed to Secretary Rumsfeld. When questioned, he responded that UW was too esoteric and the defense secretary would not accept it. General Welsh, is a former USAF chief of staff.

[74] Edward E. Lawler III, *Rewarding Excellence* (San Francisco: Jossey-Bass Publishers, 2000), 249.

[75] Edward E. Lawler III, *Strategic Pay-Aligning Organizational Strategies and Pay Systems* (San Francisco: Jossey-Bass Publishers, 1990), 38.

[76] Ibid.

[77] Edward E. Lawler III, *From the Ground Up* (San Francisco: Jossey-Bass Publishers, 1996), 210.

[78] Colin S. Gray, "Handfuls of Heroes on Desperate Ventures: When Do Special Operations Succeed?" Parameters (Spring 1999): 2–24.

[79] Chris Kraul, "In Afghanistan, Militants Stepping Up Their Attacks," Los Angeles Times, April 1, 2003.

CHAPTER 5

[1] Stephen Peter Rosen, "New Ways of War: Understanding Military Innovation," International Security (Summer 1988): 134.

[2] Pete Gustaitus, former chief, J-3 SOD, JCS, interviewed by author, Monterey, California, December 2002.

[3] Maj. Gen. Frank Hagenbeck, interviewed by author, Bagram, Afghanistan, March 11, 2002.

[4] TF 11 (JSOC) remained under the operational control of USCENTCOM.

[5] John Hendren, "High-Tech Strategy Guides Pentagon Plan," Los Angeles Times, July 13, 2002.

[6] Ibid.

[7] Ibid.

[8] Gray, Explorations in Strategy, 174.

[9] Gray, "Handfuls of Heroes," 16.

[10] There has been a reduction in fully funded graduate education programs for military officers. Graduate education is mostly focused on technical degrees. Also, OSD is considering reducing senior service college education from its current ten-month program to a three-month program.

[11] Michael Howard, "The Forgotten Dimensions of Strategy," Foreign Affairs (Summer): 1979; reprinted in Military Strategy: Theory and Application, ed. Arthur F. Lykkee, Jr. (Carlisle Barracks, PA: GPO, 1993), 58–63.

[12] Luttwak, "Notes on Low Intensity Conflict," 336.

[13] Carnes Lord, "Leadership and Strategy," Naval War College Review (Winter 2001).

[14] Ibid.

[15] The "revolution in military affairs" (RMA) is a term that became popular in the early 1990s to describe the changes in military tactics, strategies, and doctrine that follow from (and lead to) the development and deployment of radically new technologies. It also includes such concepts as "information warfare."

[16] Ibid.

[17] Trevor N. Dupuy also makes this point in Understanding War: History and Theory of Combat, 149–64.

[18] In traveling by road between Bagram and Kabul, you see the wreckage of tanks, trucks, artillery, and gun positions, the result of the U.S. bombing campaign. You also see decoys that were bombed.

[19] Peter Finn, "Bin Laden Used Ruse to Flee: Moroccans Say Guard Took Phone at Tora Bora," Washington Post, January 21, 2003.

[20] Military investigators later revealed that the location of the wedding was, in fact, an area occupied by hostile forces that had previously fired on U.S. forces. The

appropriate rules of engagement were followed, but unfortunately the outcome was tragic.

21 Stephen J. Hedges, "Friendly Fire Still Haunts U.S. Military," Chicago Tribune, July 22, 2002.

22 Ibid.

23 Ibid.

24 Ibid.

25 Thomas E. Ricks, "Beaming the Battlefield Home Live Video of Afghan Fighting Had Questionable Effect," Washington Post, March 26, 2002.

26 Interview by author with several members of CJTF-Mountain between March 10 and 20, 2002, in Bagram, Afghanistan.

27 I personally observed this on at least two occasions. General officers would be called into the operations center when Predator would lock onto a target. The generals would watch the video until aircraft engaged the target or the target could no longer be tracked. The generals would then depart the operations center.

28 Interview by author with Maj. Gen. Hagenbeck.

29 During a special forces raid in Deh Rawod in May 2003, Predator's late arrival was cited as a key factor in not capturing a "key" Taliban leader, because he successfully fled the target area during the operation.

30 The author observed CJTF-Mountain command center operations for almost three weeks and interviewed numerous division staff officers in Bagram in March 2002.

31 Thomas E. Ricks, "Un-Central Command Criticized Marine Corps Report Calls Fla. Headquarters Too Far from Action," Washington Post, June 3, 2002.

32 Ibid.

33 Author interview with John Mulholland in Bagram, Afghanistan , March, 2002.

34 At presentations by the author at the Naval Postgraduate School Center for Executive Education to flag-rank officers on UW, the officers understood the different requirements for UW but uniformly questioned whether UW was an appropriate DoD mission. They suggested that the UW role belonged exclusively to the CIA. This suggests an incompatibility between existing military organizational culture and the requirements for UW.

35 Colin S. Gray, Modern Strategy (New York: Oxford University Press, 1999), 277.

36 See Donald M. Snow, Uncivil Wars (Boulder, CO: Lynne Rienner Publishers, 1996), ix; Ralph Peters, "Constant Conflict," Parameters (Summer 1997): 9.

37 Col. C. E. Callwell, Small Wars: Their Principles & Practice (Lincoln: University of Nebraska Press, 1996), 23.

38 Carl von Clausewitz, On War, edited and translated by Michael Howard and Peter Paret (Princeton, NJ: Princeton University Press, 1984), 178.

[39] Gray, *Modern Strategy*, 279.

[40] This is one of the paradoxes in the logic of war that can be added to Edward Luttwak's fine book: Strategy-The Logic of War and Peace.

[41] Gray, *Modern Strategy*, 288, 290.

[42] Kennedy, "Will Special Ops Success Change the Face of War?"

[43] Ibid.

[44] Ibid.

[45] Sean D. Naylor, "Soldiers in Afghanistan Value Safety over Fashion," Army Times, February 19, 2002.

[46] Ibid.

[47] Colin Soloway, "I Yelled at Them to Stop," Newsweek, October 7, 2002.

[48] Ibid.

[49] Ibid.

[50] Ibid.

[51] Luttwak, "Notes on Low Intensity Conflict."

[52] I interviewed the commander of Special Operations Command, Central Command, at his headquarters in Qatar in March 2002. When asked about the C^2 arrangement, he stated clearly that he liked special forces working for 10th Mountain Division, because it demonstrated that the SOF were team players. This C^2 arrangement was obviously satisfactory to the commander, USSOCOM.

[53] J. S. Newton, "McNeill Says Military Force to Eliminate Scourge," Fayetteville Observer (North Carolina), May 30, 2002.

[54] Soloway.

[55] Gray, *Explorations in Strategy*, 151.

[56] Ibid., 152.

[57] James Brooke, "Pentagon Tells Troops In Afghanistan: Shape Up And Dress Right," New York Times, September 12, 2002.

[58] Michael R. Gordon, "A New Kind of War Plan," New York Times, 7 October 2001, 1.

[59] Glenn Collins, "Historians Weigh Attack's Impact on New York City," New York Times, 6 October 2001, 13.

[60] Conetta, Strange Victory, 5.

[61] Ibid., 6.

[62] Tyler Marshall, "Limited, Low Profile Strategy Called Key; Afghanistan: Neither a Massive U.S. Attack nor Token Reprisals Can Achieve America's Objectives, Experts Say," Los Angeles Times, September 25, 2001, 5.

[63] Tom Bowman, Mark Matthews, and Gail Gibson, "Taliban Face Ultimatum; Warning: Give Up Bin Laden or feel Full Wrath of U.S.," Baltimore Sun, September 17, 2001, 1.

[64] Kenneth R. Bazinet, "Bush Urges Afghans to Dump Taliban; Backs Revolt but Says U.S. Not Targeting Gov't," NY Daily News, September 26, 2001, 21.

[65] See Pamela Constable, "U.S. Hopes to Attract Moderates in Taliban; Powell Sees Them in New Afghanistan," Washington Post, October 17, 2001, 24; Doyle Mcmanus and John Daniszewski, "U.S. Seeks Signs of Split in Taliban," Los Angeles Times, October 3, 2001, 1.

[66] Conetta, 9.

[67] Richard Boudreaux and Tyler Marshall, "Great Game II Has a Wealth of Players," Los Angeles Times, November 2, 2001, 1.

[68] Edward Gargan, "Taliban Hang On; U.S. Finds They Are Not so Easy to Defeat," Newsday, October 26, 2001, 30.

[69] On March 24, 1999, NATO initiated a bombing campaign, Operation Allied Force, as a means to compel Slobodan Milosevic to cease ethnic cleansing in Kosovo and to pull Serbian forces out of the disputed province. Although initially expected to last a few days, the operation did not conclude until June 10, 1999, seventy-eight days later. Many military analysts believe that it was not until the Kosovo Liberation Army (KLA), a potent ground force, eventually was able to exploit the bombing campaign that Milosevic finally agreed to NATO's terms.

[70] Conetta, 11.

[71] See Patrick Cockburn, "Opposition Force Demands Stepping Up of Air Strikes," The Independent, October 26, 2001, p. 4; David Rohde, "Rebel Alliance Is Frustrated by U.S. Raids," New York Times, October 29, 2001, p. 1

[72] Conetta, 12.

[73] Christian Caryl and John Barry, "Facing a Long, Cold War; The White House Is Casting Its Lot with the Northern Alliance," Newsweek, November 12, 2001.

[74] Conetta, 12.

[75] Tom Bowman and Ellen Gamerman, "Aid Distribution in Afghanistan Deteriorates; General Lawlessness Makes Task Harder than It Was under Taliban," Baltimore Sun, December 5, 2001, 6.

[76] Conetta, 13.

[77] Ibid., 15.

[78] International Herald Tribune, November 28, 2001; Conetta, 17.

[79] Conetta, 17.

[80] Ibid., 18.

[81] Ibid.

[82] See Mamoun Fandy, "Perils of Muslim Rage," Los Angeles Times, January 6, 2002, 3; Warren P. Strobel and Jonathan S. Landay, "PR Firm Hired to Help US Image with Muslims," Knight Ridder Newspapers, October 19, 2001.

[83] Bryan Bender, "Terror War Remaps US Troop Deployments," Boston Globe, 17 Jan. 2002, 1.

[84] Conetta, 20.

[85] Gray, Modern Strategy, 290.

[86] Ibid.

[87] Joint doctrine defines UW as a "broad spectrum of military and paramilitary operations, normally of long duration, predominantly conducted by indigenous or surrogate forces who are organized, trained, equipped, supported and directed in varying degrees by an external source. UW encompasses guerrilla warfare and other direct offensive, low visibility, covert or clandestine operations, as well as the indirect activities of subversion, sabotage, intelligence activities and evasion and escape."

[88] Gray, Explorations in Strategy, 165.

[89] Ibid., 167.

[90] Clausewitz, On War, 75.

[91] Gray, Explorations in Strategy, 168–74.

[92] Ibid., 179.

[93] The competencies necessary for UW are also key in defeating insurgencies. In contrast with UW, counterinsurgency operations aim to reinforce the legitimacy of the incumbent regime and eliminate any legitimacy held by the insurgents.

[94] Gray, Explorations in Strategy, 181.

[95] Maj. Gen. Karl Eikenberry, chief, Office of Military Coordination, interview by author, Kabul, Afghanistan, June 1, 2003.

[96] Ibid.

[97] Reviewing documents from USCENTCOM, CJTF-180, and CJSOTF confirmed this focus. Additionally, interviews by the author with the commander of CJTF-180, chief of staff 10th Mountain Division, CJSOTF commander, and an SF battalion commander also confirmed this mission focus.

[98] This was confirmed through interviews with senior SOF leaders. Junior leaders do routinely meet with local leaders but are not in positions to fundamentally change the focus of the military effort.

[99] Edward Geary Lansdale, In the Midst of Wars: An American's Mission to Southeast Asia (New York: Fordham University Press, 1991), 70.

[100] The story of Master Sergeant M's private UW campaign is the result of multiple interviews with M, followed up by an interview of his battalion commander, who stated that M was the best team sergeant in the battalion.

[101] The CIA would stop supporting militia units as soon as those units exhausted their usefulness to the Agency. This was done regardless of ongoing DoD efforts with these militias.

[102] The phrase "force in being" is an adaptation of the phrase "fleet in being" first used by British admiral Lord Torrington in 1690. The phrase expresses the concept of deterrence that a credible military force has on potential aggressors.

[103] When discussing Master Sergeant M's efforts with his chain of command, they acknowledged his success. However, they were quick to point out that his team did not record any direct "kills" during their operations in Urgun.

[104] Delta Force is considered the "elite of the elite" within the special operations community. Its mission focus is hostage rescue and direct action. Its priority and resource allocation is several orders of magnitude higher than all five special forces groups combined, while its personnel strength is relatively low. The term "Delta Envy" was first used by Dr. Gordon H. McCormick after talking with senior special forces officers in Afghanistan and observing operations.

CHAPTER 6

[1] James Risen and Dexter Filkins, "Al Qaeda Fighters Are Said to Return to Afghanistan," New York Times, September 10, 2002, 1.

[2] Ibid.

[3] Harold Kennedy. "Will Special Op Success Change the Face of War?" National Defense (February 2002).

[4] Gary I. Wilson and Greg Wilcox, *Military Response to Fourth Generation Warfare in Afghanistan* (Menlow Park, CA: SRI International, 2002).

[5] Ibid.

[6] Paul Mann, "Modern Military Threats: Not All They Might Seem?" Aviation Week & Space Technology (April 22, 2002).

[7] Rowan Scarborough, "Pentagon Eyes Cuts," Washington Times, December 13, 1996, 1.

[8] This conception was used by an Naval Postgraduate School team conducting a study for The director of net assessment, Office of the Secretary of Defense in February 2003. The study was called, SOLARIUM II—Mobilization for National Survival. Study participants included: Patrick Parker, Raymond Franck, Robert Harney, Michael Melich, Glenn Robinson, Hy Rothstein, David Tucker, and Anna Simons.

[9] Adams, US Special Operations Forces in Action, (London: Frank Cass, 1998), 287.

[10] Special Operations in Peace and War (United States Special Operations Command Pub 1, 1996), 1–2.

[11] Ibid., 1–3, 1–4.

[12] Adams, 307.

[13] Dan Daniel, "US Special Operations: The Case for a Sixth Service," Armed Forces Journal (August 1985): 70.

[14] Ibid., 72.

[15] Marquis, Unconventional Warfare, 134–35.

[16] Discussions about this recommendation should focus on the strategic impact of the organization and not on whether a relatively small organization warrants a separate service. Strategic effectiveness is more important than administrative efficiency.

[17] The national command authorities consist of the president and the secretary of defense.

[17] Harry G. Summers, Jr., *On Strategy: The Vietnam War in Context* (Carlisle, PA: Strategic Studies Institute, 1983), 1.

▤ Bibliography

Adams, Thomas K. *US Special Operations Forces in Action—The Challenge of Unconventional Warfare*. London: Frank Cass, 1998.

Allison, Graham, and Philip Zelikow. *Essence of Decision*, 2nd ed. New York: Longman, 1999.

Andrews, K. R. *The Concept of Corporate Strategy*. New York: Jones-Irwin, 1980.

Asprey, Robert. *War in the Shadows: Guerrillas in History*. Garden City, NJ: Doubleday & Co., 1975.

Avant, Deborah D. *Political Institutions and Military Change, Lessons from Peripheral Wars*. Ithaca, NY: Cornell University Press, 1994.

Avant, Deborah D., and James H. Lehovic. "U.S. Military Responses to Post–Cold War Missions." In *The Sources of Military Change*, edited by Theo Farrell and Terry Terriff, 139–60. Boulder, CO: Lynne Rienner Publishers, 2002.

Baltz, Dan, Bob Woodward, and Jeff Himmelman. "Afghan Campaign's Blueprint Emerges." *Washington Post*, January 29, 2002.

Bank, Aaron. *From OSS to Green Beret*. New York: Pocket Books, 1986.

Barnard, Chester I. *The Functions of the Executive*. Cambridge, MA: Harvard University Press, 1968.

Bazinet, Kenneth R. "Bush Urges Afghans to Dump Taliban; Backs Revolt but Says U.S. Not Targeting Gov't." *NY Daily News*, September 26, 2001.

Bender, Bryan. "Terror War Remaps US Troop Deployments." *Boston Globe*, January 17, 2002.

Biddle, Stephen. *Afghanistan and the Future of Warfare: Implications for Army and Defense Policy*. Carlisle, PA: Strategic Studies Institute, 2002.

Blaufarb, Douglas. *The Counterinsurgency Era: US Doctrine and Performance, 1950 to the Present*. New York: Free Press, 1977.

Boudreaux, Richard, and Tyler Marshall. "Great Game II Has a Wealth of Players." *Los Angeles Times*, November 2, 2001.

Bowman, Tom. "'Special Forces' Role May Expand—Additional Troops, Equipment Sought by military leaders; SEALs, Green Berets included." *Baltimore Sun,* August 3, 2002.

Bowman, Tom, and Ellen Gamerman. "Aid Distribution in Afghanistan Deteriorates; General Lawlessness Makes Task Harder Than It Was under Taliban." *Baltimore Sun,* December 5, 2001.

Bowman, Tom, Mark Matthews, and Gail Gibson. "Taliban Face Ultimatum; Warning: Give Up Bin Laden or Feel Full Wrath of U.S." *Baltimore Sun,* September 17, 2001, 1.

Brooke, James. "Pentagon Tells Troops in Afghanistan: Shape Up and Dress Right." *New York Times,* September 12, 2002.

Brown, M., and L. Thompson. "Security on the Cheap: PRTs in Afghanistan." July 7, 2003. Posted on http://www.reliefweb.int/w/rwb.nsf/s1EA67E0645C1816F49256D5 D000016F3, accessed November 1, 2003.

Brown, Seymon. *New Forces in World Politics.* Washington, DC: Brookings Institute, 1974.

Calland, Rear Adm. Albert. Interviewed by author via telephone, March 20, 2003, Coronado, California.

———. COMSOCCENT. Interviewed by author, March 26, 2002, Doha, Qatar.

Callwell, Col. C. E. *Small Wars: Their Principles & Practice.* Lincoln: University of Nebraska Press, 1996.

Cameron, Craig M. "The U.S. Military's Two-Front War, 1963–1988." In *The Sources of Military Change,* edited by Theo Farrell and Terry Terriff, 119–38. Boulder, CO: Lynne Rienner Publishers, 2002.

Carell, Paul. "Brandenburgers in Action behind the Front." In *From Troy to Entebbe,* edited by John Arquilla, 234–38. New York: University Press of America, Inc., 1996.

Caryl, Christian, and John Barry. "Facing a Long, Cold War; The White House Is Casting Its Lot with the Northern Alliance." *Newsweek,* November 12, 2001.

CIA officer. Interviewed by author, March 22, 2002, Gardez, Afghanistan.

CIA senior official from Counterterrorism Center. Interviewed by author, March 11, 2002, Bagram, Afghanistan.

Clausewitz, Carl von. *On War,* edited and translated by Michael Howard and Peter Paret. Princeton, NJ: Princeton University Press, 1984.

Coakley, Thomas P. *Command and Control for War and Peace.* Washington, DC: National Defense University Press, 1992.

Cockburn, Patrick. "Opposition Force Demands Stepping Up of Air Strikes." *The Independent,* October 26, 2001.

Cohen, Eliot A. *Commandos and Politicians.* Cambridge, MA: Center for International Affairs, 1978.

Colby, William, with Peter Forbath. *Honorable Men: My Life in the CIA.* New York: Simon & Schuster, 1978.

Collins, Glenn. "Historians Weigh Attack's Impact on New York City." *New York Times,* October 6, 2001.

Collins, John M. *Special Operations Forces: An Assessment.* Washington, DC: National Defense University Press, 1996.

Collins, John M., Elizabeth Ann Severns, and Thomas P. Glakas. *U.S. Defense Planning: A Critique.* Boulder, CO: Westview Press, 1982.

Conetta, Carl. *Strange Victory: A Critical Appraisal of Operation Enduring Freedom and the Afghanistan War.* Cambridge, MA: Commonwealth Institute Project on Defense Alternatives, 2002.

Constable, Pamela. "U.S. Hopes to Attract Moderates in Taliban; Powell Sees Them in New Afghanistan." *Washington Post,* October 17, 2001.

Cook, Fred. "Struggle for the South." In *From Troy to Entebbe,* edited by John Arquilla, 79–90. New York: University Press of America, Inc., 1996.

Creveld, Martin van. *Fighting Power: German and U.S. Army Performance, 1939–1945.* Westport, CT: Greenwood Press, 1982.

———. *Command in War.* Cambridge, MA: Harvard University Press, 1985.

Czerwinski, Thomas J. "Command and Control at the Crossroads." *Marine Corps Gazette* (October 1995), 13.

———. "Command and Control at the Crossroads." *Parameters* (Autumn 1996): 121–32.

DA FM 100-25. *Doctrine for Army Special Operations Forces.* Washington, DC: GPO, 1996.

Daniel, Dan. "US Special Operations: The Case for a Sixth Service." *Armed Forces Journal* (August 1985): 70–74.

Dawson, Joseph G. "American Civil-Military Operations and Military Government: The Service of Colonel Alexander Doniphan in the Mexican War." *Armed Forces & Society* 22, no. 4 (1996): 555–72.

Doughty, Robert A. "Myth of the Blitzkrieg." In *Challenging the United States Symmetrically and Asymmetrically: Can America Be Defeated?* edited by Colonel Lloyd J. Matthews (USA, Retired), 59–79. Carlisle Barracks, PA: U.S. Army War College Strategic Studies Institute, 1998.

Dupuy, Trevor N. *Understanding War: History and Theory of Combat.* New York: Paragon House Publishers, 1987.

Eikenberry, Maj. Gen. Karl, chief, Office of Military Coordination. Interview by author, June 1, 2003, Kabul, Afghanistan.

Eisenhower, Dwight D. *Mandate for Change.* New York: Doubleday & Co., Inc., 1963.

English, John A. *A Perspective on Infantry.* New York: Praeger Publishers, 1981.

Evangelista, Matthew. *Innovation and the Arms Race.* Ithaca, NY: Cornell University Press, 1988.

Evans, M. "Marines to Face Guerrilla War as Taliban Fighters Change Tactics." *Times Online,* March 21, 2002. Retrieved on October 30, 2003 from http://www.timesonline. co.uk/article/0,,1164-242636,00.html

Fandy, Mamoun. "Perils of Muslim Rage." *Los Angeles Times,* January 6, 2002.

Farrell, Theo. "World Culture and the Irish Army, 1922–1942." In *The Sources of Military Change: Culture, Politics, Technology,* edited by Theo Farrell and Terry Terriff, 69–90. London: Lynne Rienner Publishers, 2002.

Finn, Peter. "Bin Laden Used Ruse to Flee: Moroccans Say Guard Took Phone at Tora Bora." *Washington Post,* January 21, 2003.

Ford, Corey. *Donovan of the OSS.* Boston, MA: Little Brown, 1970.

Foster, Gregory D. "Contemporary C² Theory and Research: the Failed Quest for a Philosophy of Command." *Defense Analysis* 4, no. 3 (September 1988): 201–28.

Galbraith, Jay R. *Organization Design.* London: Addison-Wesley Publishing Co., 1977.

Gall, C. "In Afghanistan, Violence Stalls Renewal Effort" *New York Times,* April 26, 2003.

Galula, David. *Counterinsurgency Warfare—Theory and Practice.* New York: Praeger Publishers, 1964.

Gargan, Edward. "Taliban Hang On; U.S. Finds they Are Not so Easy to Defeat." *Newsday,* October 26, 2001.

Goldman, Emily O. "Mission Possible: Organizational Learning in Peacetime." In *The Politics of Strategic Adjustment, Ideas, Institutions, and Interests,* edited by Peter Trubowitz, Emily O. Goldman, and Edward Rhodes, 233–66. New York: Columbia University Press, 1999.

Gordon, Michael R. "A New Kind of War Plan." *New York Times,* October 7, 2001.

Gray, Colin S. "Handfuls of Heroes on Desperate Ventures: When Do Special Operations Succeed?" *Parameters* (Spring 1999): 2–24.

———. *Explorations in Strategy.* London: Praeger, 1998.

———. *Modern Strategy.* New York: Oxford University Press, 1999.

Gustaitus, Col. Pete, chief J-3, Special Operations Division, JCS. Interviewed by author, June 23, 2002, Monterey, California.

———. Interviewed by author, December 2002, Monterey, California.

Hagenbeck, Franklin (Buster), commander, CJTF Mountain. Interview by author, March 11, 2002, Bagram, Afghanistan.

Hedges, Stephen J. "Friendly Fire Still Haunts U.S. Military." *Chicago Tribune,* July 22, 2002.

Hendren, John. "High-Tech Strategy Guides Pentagon Plan." *Los Angeles Times,* July 13, 2002.

Howard, Michael. "The Forgotten Dimensions of Strategy." *Foreign Affairs* (Summer 1979), 46–51; reprinted in *Military Strategy: Theory and Application,* ed. Arthur F. Lykkee Jr. Carlisle Barracks, PA: GPO, 1993.

Isenberg, David. *Missing the Point: Why the Reforms of the Joint Chiefs of Staff Won't Improve U.S. Defense Policy.* Washington, DC: Cato Institute, 1988.

Jansen, Erik. "Towards a Strategic Rewards Systems Perspective." PhD diss., University of Southern California, 1986.

Joint Publication 1-02, *DOD Dictionary of Military and Associated Terms.* Washington, DC: GPO, 2002.

Joint Publication. 3-07, *Joint Doctrine for Military Operations Other Than War.* Washington, DC: GPO, 1995.

Jones, David C. "Past Organizational Problems." *Joint Forces Quarterly* (Autumn 1996): 23–28.

Jordan, Amos, William Taylor Jr., and Michael Mazarr. *American National Security.* Baltimore, MD: The Johns Hopkins University Press, 1999.

JSOTF commander. Interview by author, March 14, 2002, Bagram, Afghanistan.

Keeter, Hunter. "SOCOM Outlines Acquisition Priorities." *Defense Daily,* February 13, 2003.

Kennedy, Harold. "Will Special Ops Success Change the Face of war?" *National Defense* (February 2002): 20–21.

King, Michael J. *Rangers: Selected Combat Operations during World War II.* Washington, DC: GPO, 1985.

Kingsley, Lt. Col. Mike, commander, USAF Special Operations Detachment, South, Jacobabad, Pakistan. Interviewed by author, January 13, 2003, Monterey, California.

Knowlton, Brian. "U.S. Military Narrows Focus in Afghanistan." *International Herald Tribune,* November 28, 2001.

Kraul, Chris. "In Afghanistan, Militants Stepping Up Their Attacks." *Los Angeles Times,* April 1, 2003.

Krepinevich, Andrew F. *The Army and Vietnam.* Baltimore, MD: The John Hopkins University Press, 1986.

Lansdale, Edward Geary. *In the Midst of Wars: An American's Mission to Southeast Asia.* New York: Fordham University Press, 1991.

Lawler, Edward E. III. *From the Ground Up.* San Francisco: Jossey-Bass Publishers, 1996.

———. *Rewarding Excellence.* San Francisco: Jossey-Bass Publishers, 2000.

———. *Strategic Pay-Aligning Organizational Strategies and Pay Systems.* San Francisco: Jossey-Bass Publishers, 1990.

Lawrence, Paul R, and Jay W. Lorsch. *Organization and Environment: Managing Differentiation and Integration.* Boston: Harvard Business School Press, 1967.

Locher, James R. III. *Victory on the Potomac.* College Station: Texas A&M University Press, 2002.

Lord, Carnes. "Leadership and Strategy." *Naval War College Review* (Winter 2001): 139–44.

Lorsch, Jay W., and Stephen A. Allen III. *Managing Diversity and Interdependence—An Organizational Study of Multidivisional Firms.* Boston: Harvard Business School Press, 1973.

Luttwak, Edward N. *On the Meaning of Victory.* New York: Simon & Schuster, 1986.

———. "Note on Low Intensity Conflict." *Parameters* (December 1983): 333–42.

Man, Paul. "Modern Military Threats: Not All They Might Seem?" *Aviation Week & Space Technology* (April 22, 2002).

Manwaring, Max G. *The Inescapable Global Security Arena.* Carlisle, PA: Strategic Studies Institute, 2002.

Marquis, Susan L. *Unconventional Warfare: Rebuilding U.S. Special Operations Forces.* Washington, DC: Brookings Institute, 1997.

Marshall, Tyler. "Limited, Low Profile Strategy Called Key; Afghanistan: Neither a Massive U.S. Attack nor Token Reprisals Can Achieve America's Objectives, Experts Say." *Los Angeles Times,* September 25, 2001.

Maykuth, A. "An Afghan Rebuilding Takes Shape." *Philadelphia Inquirer,* October 6, 2003.

Mcmanus, Doyle, and John Daniszewski. "U.S. Seeks Signs of Split in Taliban." *Los Angeles Times,* October 3, 2001.

Morgenthau, Hans J. *Politics Among Nations.* New York: Alfred J. Knopf, 1973.

Murray, Williamson. "Innovation, Past and Future." In *Innovation in the Interwar Period,* edited by Williamson Murray and Allan R. Millett, 300–328. Cambridge, UK: Cambridge University Press, 1998.

Naylor, Sean D. "Soldiers in Afghanistan Value Safety over Fashion." *Army Times,* February 18, 2002.

Newton, J. S. "McNeill Says Military Force to Eliminate Scourge." *Fayetteville Observer,* May 30, 2002.

O'Hanlon, Michael E. "A Flawed Masterpiece," *Foreign Affairs* 81 (May/June 2002): 47–63.

"Organizational Theory: Determinants of Structure," available from http://www.analytictech.com/mb021/orgtheory.htm, accessed January 22, 2003.

Paddock, Alfred H. *US Army Special Warfare: Its Origins.* Washington, DC: NDU Press, 1982.

Peers, William R. and Dean Brelis, *Behind the Burma Road.* Boston: Little Brown, 1963.

Peters, Ralph. "Constant Conflict." *Parameters* (Summer 1997): 4–14.

Posen, Barry R. *The Sources of Military Doctrine—France, Britain, and Germany between the World Wars.* Ithaca, NY: Cornell University Press, 1984.

Ricks, Thomas E. "Beaming the Battlefield Home Live Video of Afghan Fighting Had Questionable Effect." *Washington Post,* March 26, 2002.

———. "Un-Central Command Criticized Marine Corps Report Calls Fla. Headquarters Too Far from Action." *Washington Post,* June 3, 2002.

Risen, James, and Dexter Filkins. "Al Qaeda Fighters Are Said to Return to Afghanistan." *New York Times,* September 10, 2002.

Rohde, David. "Rebel Alliance Is Frustrated by U.S. Raids." *New York Times,* October 29, 2001.

Roosevelt, Kermit, ed. *War Report of the OSS.* New York: Walker and Co., 1976.

Rosen, Stephen Peter. "New Ways of War: Understanding Military Innovation," *International Security* (Summer 1988): 134.

———. *Winning the Next War: Innovation and the Modern Military.* Ithaca, NY: Cornell University Press, 1991.

Rumsfeld, Donald. "Major Combat over in Afghanistan," May 1, 2003, http://www. cnn.com/2003/WORLD/asiapcf/central/05/01/afghan.combat/index.html, accessed August 11, 2003.

Scarborough, Rowan. "Pentagon Eyes Cuts." *Washington Times,* December 13, 1996, 1.

———. "Special Ops Gets OK to Initiate Its Own Missions." *Washington Times,* January 8, 2003.

Sherman, William T. *Memoirs of General William T. Sherman.* New York: Da Capo Press, 1984.

Simon, Herbert A. *Administrative Behavior,* 3rd ed. New York: Free Press, 1976.

Snow, Donald M. *Uncivil Wars.* Boulder, CO: Lynne Rienner Publishers, 1996.

Snyder, Jack. *The Ideology of the Offensive, Military Decision Making, and the Disasters of 1914.* Ithaca, NY: Cornell University Press, 1984.

Soloway, Colin. "I Yelled at Them to Stop," *Newsweek,* October 7, 2002.

"Special Operations Forces: The Way Ahead." Statement presented by Gen. Peter J. Schoomaker, commander, U.S. Special Operations Command, to the members of the command. Retrieved from http://www.defenselink.mil/speeches/1998/s19980201-schoomaker.html

Special Operations in Peace and War. United States Special Operations Command Pub 1, 1996.

Stability and Support Operations (SASO). Retrieved from http://www.globalsecurity. org/military/ops/saso.htm, accessed January 29, 2003.

Steele, Dennis. "A Force of Great Utility That Cannot Be Mass-Produced." *Army Magazine* (April 1992): 24–33.

Strobel, Warren P., and Jonathan S. Landay. "PR Firm Hired to Help US Image with Muslims." *Knight Ridder Newspapers,* October 19, 2001.

Summers, Harry G. Jr. *On Strategy: The Vietnam War in Context.* Carlisle, PA: Strategic Studies Institute, 1983.

Synovitz, R. "Afghanistan: U.S.-Led Coalition Expands 'Provincial Recon- struction Teams.'" August 14, 2003. Retrieved from http://www.rferl.org/ features/2003/08/14082003161741.asp, accessed November 1, 2003.

Taber, Robert. *The War of the Flea.* New York: Lyle Stuart, 1965.

Taylor, Maxwell D. *Swords and Plowshares.* New York: W. W. Norton, 1972.

———. *The Uncertain Trumpet.* New York: Harper and Bros., 1960.

Tucker, David. "Processes of Innovation." Unpublished paper, Naval Postgraduate School, Monterey, California, 2003.

United States Special Operations Command History. MacDill AFB, FL: US SOCOM History & Research Office, 2002.

United States. Dept. of the Army. *Operations,* Washington, DC: Headquarters, Dept. of the Army, 1993.

USASOC, *To Free from Oppression: A Concise History of US Army Special Forces, Civil Affairs, Psychological Operations and The John F. Kennedy Special Warfare Center and School.* Ft. Bragg, NC: USASOC Directorate of History, 1994.

USSOCOM Pub 1. *Special Operations in Peace and War.* Washington, DC: GPO, 1996.

Utley, Robert M. *The Contribution of the Frontier to the American Military Tradition.* Colorado Springs, CO: US Air Force Academy, 1977.

Waghelstein, John. "Preparing the US Army for the Wrong War," *Small Wars and Insurgencies* 10, no.1 (Spring 1999): 22.

Wagner, J. "Gardez Office Opening Signals Shift in Afghanistan Mission." Retrieved from http://www.defendamerica.mil/articles/feb2003/a020403b.html, accessed November 1, 2003.

Weber, Max. *Essays in Sociology,* translated by H. H. Gerth and C. Wright Mills. New York: Oxford University Press, 1976.

Weigley, Russell F. *History of the United States Army.* New York: Macmillan, 1967.

———. *The American Way of War: A History of United States Military Strategy and Policy.* New York: Macmillan Publishing Co., Inc., 1973.

Wiener, Norbert. *Cybernetics, or Control and Communications in the Animal and the Machine.* Cambridge, MA: MIT Press, 1962.

Winton, Harold R., and David R. Mets, eds. *The Challenge of Change, Military Institutions, and New Realities, 1918–1941.* Lincoln: University of Nebraska Press, 2000.

Wilson, Gary I., and Greg Wilcox, *Military Response to Fourth Generation Warfare in Afghanistan.* Menlow Park, CA: SRI International, 2002.

Wilson, James Q. *Bureaucracy—What Government Agencies Do and Why They Do It.* New York: Basic Books, 1989.

Woodward, Bob. *Bush at War.* New York: Simon & Schuster, 2002.

Woodward, Bob, and Dan Baltz. "At Camp David, Advise and Dissent," *Washington Post,* January 31, 2002.

———. "We Will Rally the World," *Washington Post,* January 28, 2002.

Wooster, Robert. *The Military and United States Indian Policy, 1865–1903.* New Haven, CT: Yale University Press, 1988.

Zisk, Kimberly Marten. *Engaging the Enemy: Organization Theory and Soviet Military Innovation, 1955–1991.* Princeton, NJ: Princeton University Press, 1993.

⠿ Index

CA (civil affairs), 18, 20, 22, 26–27, 29, 38, 92, 115
Camp David, 5, 7
Carter, Jimmy, 39
CD (counterdrug activities), 23
CENTCOM (U.S. Central Command), 4, 91, 93, 109, 112, 113, 121, 128, 129, 134, 135, 167, 171
Central Intelligence Agency (CIA), xvi, 1, 4–10, 12, 32–33, 37–38, 91, 93, 97, 111, 121, 127, 134, 160–61, 176, 184n14, 195n29, 199n34, 203n101
Central Intelligence Group (CIG), 3º3
Cheney, Dick, 6, 91
CIA (Central Intelligence Agency), xvi, 1, 4–10, 12, 32–33, 37–38, 91, 93, 97, 111, 121, 127, 134, 160–61, 176, 184n14, 195n29, 199n34, 203n101
CIG (Central Intelligence Group), 33
civic action, 98, 160
civil affairs (CA), 18, 20, 22, 26–27, 29, 38, 92, 115
civil military operations (CMO), 115, 117
CJSOTF, 111, 162, 202n97
CJTF-180, 108–14, 162, 195n44, 202n97
CJTF Mountain Division (10th Mountain Division), 13–14, 99–100, 108, 110, 114, 128–29, 134–35, 142, 195n44, 200n52, 202n97
Clausewitz, Carl von, 25, 137–38, 155, 168–69
CM (countermine activities), 23
CMO (civil military operations), 115, 117
Colby, William, 32
Cole, 93
combating terrorism (CT), 22, 177
combat search and rescue (CSAR), 5, 8–9, 23
command and control (C²), 103–14, 117, 118–19
COMSOCCENT (special operations component of USCENTCOM), 93, 112–13, 196n51, 196n52
contingency theory, 49, 53–59
counterdrug activities (CD), 23

countermine activities (CM), 23
counterproliferation (CP), 22
Counterterrorist Joint Task Force, 39
CP (counterproliferation), 22
Crowe, William J. Jr., Adm., 40, 42
CSAR (combat search and rescue), 5, 8–9, 23
CT (combating terrorism), 22, 177

DA (direct action), 22, 92–94, 102, 162, 175–77, 180, 203n104
Dalili, Muhammed, 116
Daniel, Dan, 40, 179–80
DCI (director of central intelligence), 4, 93
Deh Rawod (place), 115, 199n29
Delta envy, 163, 203n104
Delta forces, ix, 17, 203n104
Department of Defense (DoD), xiv, xvi, xvii, 6, 10, 11, 16, 17, 25, 37, 38, 39, 40, 41, 42, 73, 88, 91, 93, 100, 101, 102, 111, 114, 121, 127, 128, 143, 166, 172, 176, 178, 179, 180, 183chap1n1, 199n34, 203n101
Desert One (operation), 39
Desert Storm (operation), 19, 129
direct action (DA), 22, 92–94, 102, 162, 175–77, 180, 203n104
DoD (Department of Defense), xiv, xvi, xvii, 6, 10, 11, 16, 17, 25, 37, 38, 39, 40, 41, 42, 73, 88, 91, 93, 100, 101, 102, 111, 114, 121, 127, 128, 143, 166, 172, 176, 178, 179, 180, 183chap1n1, 199n34, 203n101
Donovan, William O., 30–32
Downing, Wayne J., Lt. Gen., 19, 25
DPG (defense planning guidance), 129

Egyptian Islamic Jihad, 164
Eisenhower, Dwight D., 35–36
Enduring Freedom (operation) (OEF), xiii, 2, 144–45, 149, 150–53

F-16, 133
Fahim, Mohammed, 11
FID (foreign internal defense), 22

☰About the Author

HY ROTHSTEIN earned a BS degree in general engineering from the United States Military Academy, an MA in military art and science from the U.S. Army Command and General Staff College, and an MA in law and diplomacy and a Ph.D. in international relations from the Fletcher School, Tufts University. He was a career special forces officer and retired in 1999 after thirty years of active-duty service. He currently teaches in the Department of Defense Analysis at the Naval Postgraduate School, Monterey, California.

THE NAVAL INSTITUTE PRESS is the book-publishing arm of the U.S. Naval Institute, a private, nonprofit, membership society for sea service professionals and others who share an interest in naval and maritime affairs. Established in 1873 at the U.S. Naval Academy in Annapolis, Maryland, where its offices remain today, the Naval Institute has members worldwide.

Members of the Naval Institute support the education programs of the society and receive the influential monthly magazine Proceedings and discounts on fine nautical prints and on ship and aircraft photos. They also have access to the transcripts of the Institute's Oral History Program and get discounted admission to any of the Institute-sponsored seminars offered around the country. Discounts are also available to the colorful bimonthly magazine *Naval History*.

The Naval Institute's book-publishing program, begun in 1898 with basic guides to naval practices, has broadened its scope to include books of more general interest. Now the Naval Institute Press publishes about one hundred titles each year, ranging from how-to books on boating and navigation to battle histories, biographies, ship and aircraft guides, and novels. Institute members receive significant discounts on the Press's more than eight hundred books in print.

Full-time students are eligible for special half-price membership rates. Life memberships are also available.

For a free catalog describing Naval Institute Press books currently available, and for further information about joining the U.S. Naval Institute, please write to:

Customer Service
U.S. Naval Institute
291 Wood Road
Annapolis, MD 21402-5034
Telephone: (800) 233-8764
Fax: (410) 269-7940
Web address: www.navalinstitute.org